GOD & MORALITY

IN CHRISTIAN TRADITIONS

New Essays on Christian

Moral Philosophy

J. CALEB CLANTON
KRAIG MARTIN

editors

Abilene Christian University Press

GOD AND MORALITY IN CHRISTIAN TRADITIONS
New Essays on Christian Moral Philosophy

Library of Congress Cataloging-in-Publication Data

Names: Clanton, J. Caleb, 1978– editor. | Martin, Kraig, Ph.D. editor.
Title: God and morality in Christian traditions : new essays on Christian moral
    philosophy / J. Caleb Clanton, Kraig Martin.
Description: Abilene : ACU Press, 2022. | Includes bibliographical references.
Identifiers: LCCN 2021053750 (print) | LCCN 2021053751 (ebook) |
    ISBN 9781684261529 (paperback) | ISBN 9781684268887 (epub)
Subjects: LCSH: Christian ethics.
Classification: LCC BJ1251 .G575 2022 (print) | LCC BJ1251 (ebook) | DDC 241—dc23/
    eng/20220126
LC record available at https://lccn.loc.gov/2021053750
LC ebook record available at https://lccn.loc.gov/2021053751

Cover design by ThinkPen Design
Interior text design by Scribe Inc.

For information contact:
Abilene Christian University Press
ACU Box 29138
Abilene, Texas 79699
1-877-816-4455
www.acupressbooks.com

22 23 24 25 26 27 28 / 7 6 5 4 3 2 1

Contents

Acknowledgments

A number of people have been helpful in bringing this volume to fruition, and we owe them a debt of gratitude. Foremost, a word of thanks to the authors who accepted the initial invitation to contribute to the special issue on "God, Ethics, and Christian Traditions" in the journal *Religions*. Thanks go also to the editors, assistant editors, copyeditors, and the dozens of anonymous peer reviewers of *Religions* for their input on the various stages of the manuscripts that culminated in that special issue, several essays of which make up the lion's share of this present volume. We are grateful for the opportunity to reuse much of that material here.

Thanks go also to the provost of Lipscomb University, W. Craig Bledsoe, as well as to David G. Holmes, dean of the College of Liberal Arts and Sciences at Lipscomb, for supporting Caleb Clanton's research agenda. And thanks go to the provost of Harding University, Marty Spears, as well as to the dean of the College of Bible and Ministry at Harding, Monte Cox, for supporting Kraig Martin's pursuit of this project.

Lastly, we would like to thank Gloria Qi, Chris Metress, Aaron Simmons, Josh Strahan, and Jason Fikes for their support and advice on various matters in putting this volume together.

Introduction

J. Caleb Clanton and Kraig Martin

This new collection of essays contemplates the philosophic relationship between God and morality within historic Christian traditions. This is not to say that the views presented here are all directed toward some unified, singular thesis about, say, the necessity of God (or the lack thereof) for the objectivity of moral values and duties or about, say, some specific way in which Christian theism yields (or does not yield) a particular verdict concerning some concrete issue in applied ethics. The scope of this volume is broader than that, in no small part because the questions of morality in relation to God span more widely than that.

Consider a few of the questions in the general vicinity: Assuming that morality is connected in some important way to the creator and sustainer of the universe, what is the proper way of conceiving of that relationship? Is it the divine *intellect* or the divine *will*—or *both*—that serves as the fundamental ground of morality? How does the existence of God, or faith in God, affect how we might discern our moral obligations or otherwise perceive moral value? What are the implications of the Fall for moral knowledge? How should we understand, and in turn deal with, the deep moral disagreements that exist between Christians and non-Christians—or even important moral disagreements *among* Christians themselves? How does God's existence, or faith in God's existence, affect our sense of moral motivation? How should it affect not just the doxastic dimensions of religious life but the *practice* of being in the world? How do the virtues and the vices factor in? What can be learned by taking seriously specific subtraditions and denominational heritages within the broader Christian tradition? What can be learned by engaging different figures in the Christian tradition—ranging from Augustine of Hippo, Evagrius of Pontus, Thomas Aquinas, John Duns Scotus, Andrew of Neufchateau, Pierre d'Ailly, Jean Gerson, and John Calvin to Soren Kierkegaard, G. K. Chesterton, Dietrich Bonhoeffer, Simone Weil, and C. S. Lewis?

Those are a few of the questions that surface when doing Christian moral philosophy. And the essays contained in this volume take them up with insight and pluck. These essays were originally drafted in response to a formal call for papers for a special issue of the journal *Religions* entitled "God, Ethics, and Christian Traditions." As the guest coeditors of that special issue, we invited a range of moral philosophers to do their work by thinking *out of*, or engaging *with*, our common Christian heritage. Importantly, we also welcomed them to engage not only with the *shared* heritage of the Christian faith but also with the particularized and distinctive lineages from which, and within which, they work and live—or, alternatively, as inspired by some specific figure within the various Christian traditions.

Happily, the project proved fruitful in multiple ways, and two ways in particular. First, our invitation was met by philosophers from a *variety* of different Christian backgrounds. The authors represented in this volume hail from Roman Catholic, Reformed (Calvinist), Anglican, Pentecostal, Baptist, evangelical, and Stone-Campbell traditions. We take this denominational diversity to be a vital feature of this volume, in part because it offers at least a small glimpse into the panoply of intellectual resources for thinking about God and morality—together with some of their limitations—contained within the various Christian traditions. In our view, Christian scholars can do their best work when they take a look over one another's shoulders, so to speak. We hope this volume can serve that end. Second, the response to our invitation was met by an impressive array of accomplished Christian philosophers, each of whom is a forceful and fecund thinker in his or her own right. Theological diversity would wilt on the vine without the intellectual rigor these philosophers can bring to the table. This volume offers both.

And so it seems fitting to us that the project undertaken here found its initial launching point in connection to the Stone-Campbell

Restoration tradition with which we, the coeditors, and the publisher of this volume are affiliated. One of the salient, albeit imperfectly actualized, features of this particular Christian lineage is its ecumenical aspiration—to be neither Catholic nor Protestant, nor this or that flavor of Christian, as it were, but *simply Christian*. There is an oft-repeated phrase that of course predates the Stone-Campbell movement of the nineteenth century and whose precise origins are unclear but that nonetheless enjoys something of a pride of place as a statement of the ethos of the Stone-Campbell heritage: "Unity in essentials; liberty in nonessentials; charity in all things." It is in that spirit that the following pages are presented as a unified effort to think about God and morality—an effort undertaken by philosophers hailing from sundry streams but still very much within a common Christian vintage.

On Christian Moral Philosophy

Since this volume is intended as a contribution to Christian moral philosophy, we should speak not only to the origins of this project but also to what we take the general landscape of Christian moral philosophy to be. One way to do that is by taking stock of the prevalent positions taken up by Christian thinkers.

One especially prominent position within the history of Christian moral reflection is what commonly falls under the heading of natural law theory. On this view, our moral obligations arise in connection to facts about the sort of creatures we are by nature—facts that we can discover and reason about for ourselves, facts that God is responsible for. Accordingly, there is something like a divinely imprinted grain to the universe, and so the better part of wisdom is to discern the direction of that grain and act *with* it and not against it. Within the Christian tradition at least, this view is commonly, though not exclusively, associated with Roman Catholicism, thanks in no small part to the influence of Thomas Aquinas. Of course, natural law theory has an ancient pedigree that predates the Christian tradition,

9

and—what's more—its resonance has been wide and deep among philosophers both in and outside of Catholicism, and even among decidedly secular or nontheist thinkers. In fact, it has been described, for example, as being effectively equivalent to *traditional morality itself*—as what at least used to be "*the* mainstream western tradition of thought about morality."[1]

A second fairly standard position among Christian moral philosophers is that of theological voluntarism, or what is perhaps better known as divine command theory. On this view, moral obligations are explained not by pointing to facts about the sorts of creatures we are by nature, but rather by appealing directly to God's commands or some other prescriptive act of the divine will. Historically speaking, this framework has been associated with Protestant reformers and is, to one degree or another, traceable to several late medieval figures who preceded and influenced Reformation theology and philosophy—from Scotus and Ockham to Gabriel Biel. Eventually, the divine command theorist's position hardened in the work of Reformation figures such as Martin Luther and John Calvin, who held not just that divine commands *can* on some occasions give rise to moral obligations but rather that *only* God's commands can give rise to moral obligations.[2] Perhaps unsurprisingly, divine command theories of ethics are often associated with (typically Protestant) traditions that emphasize the supremacy of God's will and the special importance of divine revelation.

Virtue ethics is a third general orientation commonly seen among Christian thinkers. While virtue theory predates Christianity, it has been enthusiastically appropriated throughout the broader Christian tradition, tracing back at least as far as the early church fathers. Some biblical scholars go further and hold that virtue theory even influenced the thinking and teaching of Jesus himself, via the influence of the ancient Greeks on Israel.[3] In any case, many Christian moral philosophers think out of this general framework, with only a secondary interest in natural law theory or divine command theory. Of course, it remains an open question as to how virtue ethics meshes with natural law theory or divine command theory. But in at least some respects, virtue ethics need not even be seen as a competitor. Generally speaking, moral philosophy done in the mode of virtue ethics is simply less concerned with questions about the origins of moral obligations, or even of moral value, and is more focused on questions about what traits or dispositions lead to human flourishing, which flourishing is contemplated in a way that is informed by, or at least consistent with, scripture and traditional Christian teachings.

Of course, Christian moral philosophy is sometimes done in a way that doesn't fall neatly into any of the three categories mentioned above. For example, some philosophers follow Augustine in contemplating sin—and wrongdoing, more generally—as *disordered love*. This idea has been tremendously influential throughout the Christian tradition, even up to recent years, and it clearly represents an ethical framework of sorts. But it remains unclear exactly how such an Augustinian outlook should be subsumed under the banner of, say, natural law theory or divine command theory or virtue theory. Along similar lines, other Christian thinkers approach specific issues in applied ethics (by contending that Christians should or should not endorse this or that action, public policy, or social cause) in a way that does not appear to rely on any of the above mentioned positions. So the point remains the same: even though there are some fairly standard positions among Christian moral philosophers, things get messier when we try to map out the full landscape of what might reasonably count as *Christian* moral philosophy.

At least one of the reasons why this can be challenging is that it is hard to give a neat account of what constitutes moral philosophy to begin with. And this is at least partly because the study of moral philosophy is the study of several different questions and several related but nonetheless distinct concepts. Take the distinction between the *right* and the *good*, for example. Talking about the good and the right is a quick and dirty way of talking about the distinction between deontic concepts (obligatory, permissible, wrong) and axiological or value concepts (good, neutral, bad). To see how this distinction in turn complicates the sketch of the landscape of moral philosophy, and Christian moral philosophy in particular, consider how it factors into the analysis and evaluation of a divine command theory of ethics, for example.

Divine command theorists hold that moral obligations arise from (or *only* from) God's commands. Accordingly, the metaphysical ground of moral obligation is the divine command itself. But what does this account entail about the *good*? Since most philosophers are willing to accept that at least some acts have positive moral value without necessarily being morally obligatory, most clearly accept a distinction between the good and the right. With that distinction in mind, then, we might ask: Should the proponent of divine command theory claim that divine commands are the source not only for moral obligation but of moral value (i.e., the good) too? This is perhaps unsurprisingly a contested point, as well as the source of some confusion in evaluating the theory—or so it appears.

But even if we restrict the scope of divine command theory in such a way that makes it only a theory about moral obligation, and even if we just ignore the question of moral value altogether, there are still further complications that arise when thinking about what should count as moral philosophy. Some positions in moral philosophy are focused on explaining the *foundations* or *causes* of our obligations, which falls within the domain of metaethics. Other positions fall more squarely in the domain of normative ethics, where one considers the data of moral experience (e.g., that this or that set of actions seem morally praiseworthy or blameworthy) and seeks to articulate a theory that fits those data. And sometimes that sort of theorizing is done with no concern for answering questions of causation or metaphysical foundations. For example, a virtue ethicist might claim that we ought to do what the virtuous person would do, but need not be committed to any claim about the cause or origin of that obligation.

Despite these complexities, philosophers can make, and have made, progress in moral theorizing. One does moral philosophy when one attempts to answer questions about the nature or origins of moral obligations or moral value, or when one attempts to answer specific questions about what is morally obligated or valuable in specific contexts, among others. And one does Christian moral philosophy when one takes up those questions in a way that engages with Christian presuppositions, perspectives, affirmations, and traditions. The essays in this volume are excellent examples of just that sort of philosophizing.

What Lies Ahead

It remains for us to briefly introduce the chapters ahead. The first three chapters in the volume deal squarely with natural law theory. Natural law theory has been criticized in a variety of ways, by thinkers both inside *and* outside of Christian circles. For example, some have said that natural law theory makes divine revelation unnecessary, since it links our moral obligations to facts about the kinds of creatures we are—facts we can discover by means of unaided human reason. Others have contended that, if natural law theory were true, then there should be a universally shared set of moral beliefs, which we don't seem to observe. Other critics complain that natural law theory ignores the effects of the Fall in corrupting our ability to reason morally. Finally, others follow David Hume and accuse natural law theory of illegitimately deducing a prescriptive *ought*-claim from a descriptive *is*-claim. In the first chapter, Francis J. Beckwith explains these four objections and responds to them in defense of natural law theory in the Catholic tradition.

The fourth objection to natural law mentioned above—that natural law theory commits the is-ought fallacy—is leveled both by critics of natural law theory in general and also by many proponents of the so-called *new* natural law theory, who contend for a theory that has much in common with traditional natural law theory, but with important differences, particularly with respect to moral epistemology. In the second chapter, Christopher Tollefsen articulates this new natural law theory, particularly in connection to its account of human rights. One of the objections to this view is that it allegedly leaves God out of the picture, so to speak. Tollefsen argues that the new natural law account of human rights cannot be sustained without some vital role for God's creative activity.

J. Caleb Clanton and Kraig Martin also take up issues related to natural law theory in chapter 3, though not by way of offering either a critique or defense. Rather, they chart out some of the intellectual history surrounding the debate about the metaphysical foundation of morality and whether, most fundamentally, it is the divine *reason* (intellect) or the divine *will*. In their view, Thomas Aquinas offers a model according to which the divine will always follows the order of the divine intellect, while John Duns Scotus presents a model according to which the divine will has greater freedom such that, on at least some occasions, the divine will can be rationally *under*determined by the divine intellect. According to Clanton and Martin, Scotus's view makes room for what we might think of as a *two-source theory* for explaining the metaphysical foundations of morality, which marks a clear break from Aquinas's one-source natural law theory—and a significant step in the direction of divine command theory.

In chapter 4, Janine Marie Idziak picks up on the tradition of moral theorizing that is at least partly inspired by Scotus (among others), a tradition that places greater emphasis on the divine will. In her view, divine command theories of ethics can be nuanced according to how one contemplates the relationship between the divine will and the divine intellect (reason). Idziak shows how three key figures who followed in the voluntarist-leaning trajectory of Scotus—namely, Andrew of Neufchateau, Pierre d'Ailly, and Jean Gerson—differently approached the relationship between God's will and God's intellect. Accordingly, each thinker presents a different formulation of theological voluntarism. Idziak concludes by showing the relevance of this historical survey to contemporary debates in moral philosophy.

According to one widely influential contemporary philosopher, Stephen Darwall, morality in no way pivots on an accountability to God, but rather on an accountability to other humans, who are the root source of moral obligations. As Darwall sees it, moral obligations stem from the justified demands made by other humans, or the justified demands that *would* be made by other humans in *an idealized moral community*. C. Stephen Evans argues in chapter 5 that this metaethical position, ironically, falls prey to some of the very same objections commonly leveled against divine command theories of ethics. However, unlike the divine command theorist, Darwall's constructivist position lacks the resources to respond with any punch. One such objection is that hypothetical demands that are never actually made cannot possibly ground real obligations, and Evans suggests that Darwall's view would be improved by recognizing God as a member of the moral community.

The next three chapters deal with considerations related to our epistemic limitations. In chapter 6, Daniel Bonevac discusses the implications of John Calvin's *multiplicity thesis*, according to which any answer to a philosophical question requires at least two different answers: one set that answers the question in the context of humanity and creation *prior* to the Fall; another set that answers it in the context of humanity and creation *after* the Fall. Bonevac argues that, prior to the Fall, knowledge of God, moral obligations, and moral value is direct and noninferential in Calvin's view. After the Fall, our knowledge of these things is indirect, fallible, and requires divine revelation.

In chapter 7, Blake McAllister considers the fact of deep moral disagreement between Christians and non-Christians. He contends that deep and substantial moral disagreement can exist between two parties without it being the case that one of the parties is irrational. McAllister develops an epistemological framework according to which both parties can be rational, assuming they approach different sets of evidence from different perspectives. He concludes by arguing that his perspectivalism does not entail relativism or skepticism, but instead opens new opportunities for resolving moral disagreements.

Of course, moral disagreements exist not only between Christians and non-Christians; there are also deep moral disagreements between Christians and *other* Christians—and sometimes disagreements even with the same denomination or congregation. In chapter 8, Michael Beaty considers an especially salient case of deep disagreement currently dividing many denominations, and he considers it in connection to the free church tradition to which Baptists, Churches of Christ, and many other denominations and congregations belong. With attention to Baptist heritage in particular, Beaty argues that the free church tradition faces an epistemological crisis with respect to how to adjudicate the debate surrounding the moral permissibility of homosexual unions. Beaty explains how this crisis both highlights and is animated by key theological and ecclesial commitments and how they are variously prioritized within different Baptist circles and congregations.

In chapter 9, Mac S. Sandlin argues that Augustine's famous maxim "love and do what you want" is defensible only in light of certain theological commitments, especially since postlapsarian humans love so very poorly. For example, he contends that, especially given Augustine's position on the fallenness of humanity, the only way such a maxim could be reasonably justified is by cojoining it with certain views of the Holy Spirit, among other views. These include (1) a distinction between what should be enjoyed for its own sake, and what should be used instrumentally, (2) a view of the proper ordering of the loves, and (3) a doctrine of the Holy Spirit as the inner-Trinitarian love of the Father and the Son. Assuming these three positions, Augustine's maxim is sensible enough, even in light of Augustine's views about the fallenness of humanity.

In chapter 10, J. Aaron Simmons argues that church *practice*, and not merely church belief or doctrine, stands in need of philosophical attention. Specifically, he argues that a certain kind of liturgy, which he calls a *militant liturgy*, offers critical and constructive resources for philosophy of religion. In explaining this militant liturgy, Simmons first makes use of the notion of the Church Militant (vs. the Church Triumphant) as found in the work of Kierkegaard. In light of that notion, Simmons develops Bonhoeffer's idea of "costly grace" and Weil's idea of "afflicted love" and speaks to the resources these notions provide.

In the final chapter of this volume, Brandon Dahm discusses the often neglected but no less relevant capital vice of acedia—the restless boredom with, and lack of care for, higher spiritual goods—and he offers two practical remedies: wonder and gratitude. First, Dahm explains how virtues and vices can affect how we see things and how acedia in particular can damage this vision. The person who is stricken by acedia is bored and restless because the higher demands placed on her life are empty, devoid of beauty or value. Dahm entertains ways that wonder and gratitude can repair this damaged perspective, and he offers concrete interventions for growing in gratitude and wonder. One such practice, following Chesterton, is that we look for the blessings in the ordinary circumstances of life. When our eyes are opened to the wondrous meaning in the demands of our workaday lives, when we learn to be grateful for those goods, we can correct our vision and can be freed from the noonday demon of acedia.

This book, we hope, is something like the exercise in fighting acedia that Dahm wisely recommends, where we practice a recognition of the wonderful intellectual resources that God has given us in the history of the Church Universal, and within the varied Christian traditions in particular, and where we give thanks for those good gifts. Ultimately, our hope is that, out of that recognition and gratitude for those goods, we can better work to develop, nurture, and apply those intellectual gifts—and to put their various fruits into practice in our lives.

Notes

1 See, respectively, David S. Oderberg's and Robert P. George's comments on NLT in their blurbs on the back cover of Gomez-Lobo (2001).
2 We trace this intellectual history in chapter 4 of our *Nature and Command: On the Metaphysical Foundations of Morality* (forthcoming).
3 See, for example, Pennington (2017, 29–38).

References

Clanton, J. Caleb, and Kraig Martin. 2022. *Nature and Command: On the Metaphysical Foundations of Morality*. Knoxville: University of Tennessee Press.

Gomez-Lobo, Alfonso. 2001. *Morality and the Human Goods: An Introduction to Natural Law Ethics*. Washington, DC: Georgetown University Press.

Pennington, Jonathan T. 2017. *The Sermon on the Mount and Human Flourishing: A Theological Commentary*. Grand Rapids, MI: Baker Academic.

 CHAPTER 1

Catholicism and the Natural Law

A Response to Four Misunderstandings

Francis J. Beckwith

ABSTRACT: This [essay] responds to four criticisms of the Catholic view of natural law: (1) it commits the naturalistic fallacy, (2) it makes divine revelation unnecessary, (3) it implausibly claims to establish a shared universal set of moral beliefs, and (4) it disregards the noetic effects of sin. Relying largely on the Church's most important theologian on the natural law, St. Thomas Aquinas, the author argues that each criticism rests on a misunderstanding of the Catholic view. To accomplish this end, the author first introduces the reader to the natural law by way of an illustration he calls "the ten (bogus) rules." He then presents Aquinas's primary precepts of the natural law and shows how our rejection of the ten bogus rules ultimately relies on these precepts (and inferences from them). In the second half of the [essay], he responds directly to each of the four criticisms.

The purpose of this [essay] is to respond to several misunder-standings of the Catholic view of the natural law. I begin with a brief account of the natural law, relying primarily on the work of St. Thomas Aquinas, the Church's most important theologian on this subject. I then move on and offer replies to four criticisms of the natural law that I argue rest on misunderstandings: (1) the natural law commits the so-called naturalistic fallacy, (2) the natural law makes scripture superfluous, (3) the natural law mistakenly claims that there is a universally shared body of moral beliefs, and (4) the natural law ignores the noetic effects of sin. My replies are not intended to be exhaustive, but merely suggestive of how a Catholic natural law advocate can respond to these criticisms. Moreover, I do not explore the differing schools of thought embraced by those who identify as natural law theorists. However, attentive readers will quickly recognize the view I am presenting as aligning most closely with what is sometimes called the "old natural law," a view whose advocates defend the idea that, for natural law to work, it requires something like an Aristotelean–Thomistic metaphysics.

The Natural Law

According to the *Catechism of the Catholic Church* (2000, 1956), "The natural law, present in the heart of each man and established by reason, is universal in its precepts and its authority extends to all men. It expresses the dignity of the person and determines the basis for his fundamental rights and duties." This means that morality is real, that it is natural and not a mere human artifice or construction, that all human beings can know it when we exercise our reason, and that it is the measure by which we judge how we should treat others as well as ourselves. This is the moral law to which Martin Luther King Jr. was referring in his famous *Letter from a Birmingham Jail* (1963): "A just law is a man-made code that squares with the moral law or the law of God. An unjust law is a code that is out of harmony with the moral law." For King, we can assess the goodness or badness of ordinary human law—whether criminal or civil—by testing it against a natural moral law that we did not invent. Although this way of conceptualizing our understanding of law is rarely verbalized in common conversation, our moral reflexes almost always indicate that we presuppose it. Think, for example, of how you would react if any one of the following rules were embedded in the laws of your own government:[1]

1. Parents may abandon their minor children without any justification and without any requirement to provide financial support.

2. It is permissible for a city or state to pass *post facto* laws.

3. The maximum punishment for first-degree murder is an all-expense-paid vacation to Las Vegas.

4. Any city or state may pass secret laws that the public cannot know.

5. Anyone may be convicted of a crime based on the results of a coin toss.

6. All citizens are forbidden from believing, propagating, or publicly defending the view that there is a moral law against which nations and individuals are measured.

7. Your guilt or innocence in a criminal trial depends entirely on your race and not on a judge or jury's deliberation on legitimately obtained evidence.

8. Government contracts are to be distributed based on family connections and bribes and not on the quality of the bids.

9. Original parenthood is to be decided by a special board of experts appointed by the governor and not on whether one sires or begets the child.

10. No citizen may believe, propagate, or publicly defend the view that there is a transcendent source of being that has underived existence.

When you reject these ten (bogus) rules (as you should), you do so on the basis of something you already know. You reject rules 1 and 9 because you know that parents have a natural obligation to care for their offspring and that original parenthood is determined by siring and begetting. This is why adoptive parenthood without the explicit permission of the child's natural parents is just a species of kidnapping.[2] You reject rules 2 and 5 because you know that law should be based on reason. It is unreasonable to prosecute someone for a crime that was not a crime when she committed it, and it is unjust for a court to determine a verdict by an arbitrary and capricious method. Along similar lines, you reject rules 4 and 7. An unknowable law is like a *post facto* law, and one's race is as relevant to one's criminal guilt or innocence as is a coin flip. You reject 8 because you know that it is unjust for a government to award someone a contract based on their genealogy and willingness to bribe, for neither has any bearing on whether one deserves the contract. You reject rule 3 because you know that human life is sacred and that a just society must reflect that in its laws. To reward someone for intentionally killing the innocent is an abomination. Because you know that the human mind has a natural inclination to know not only particular and mundane truths but universal and transcendent truths as well, you reject rule 10. For rule 10 essentially prohibits the full exercise of a power that is distinctly human, what Aquinas called "speculative reason."[3] And finally, you reject rule 6 because you know that societies and individuals can be properly judged by a moral law external to their own practices and beliefs. You know on a personal level that you sometimes fall short of the moral law's requirements.[4] Like all of us, you make excuses, rationalize, or ignore your own moral indiscretions, though on occasion you are moved by conscience to confess your wrongdoing. But what is true of individuals is also true of civilizations, for it seems perfectly permissible for one to issue judgments about the conduct of nations that have perpetuated atrocities and injustices, even when those nations' apologists rattle off a litany of excuses and rationalizations or feign ignorance.

According to the Catholic Church, your rejection of the ten bogus rules is the result of your acquaintance with the natural law, even if you are not conspicuously aware of it. This is possible because human beings are ordered toward certain goods, and as rational animals, we have the capacity to recognize and make judgments about those goods and realize that we ought to choose them. As Aquinas notes, "Since . . . good has the nature of an end, and evil, the nature of a contrary, hence it is that all those things to which man has a natural inclination, are naturally apprehended by reason as being good, and consequently as objects of pursuit, and their contraries as evil, and objects of avoidance" (1920, I.II, q. 94, art. 2, *respondeo*). What Aquinas is saying here is that we are, in a sense, hardwired to acquire knowledge of the precepts of the natural moral law, just as we are hardwired to learn mathematics and speak a language and discover rules about them.[5] To understand what Aquinas means, we will review his brief account of what are sometimes called the primary precepts of the natural law. It is from these primary precepts, Aquinas argues, that we can derive other precepts, which he calls the secondary precepts of the natural law (I.II, q. 94, art. 5, 6).

(1) "Good is to be done and pursued, and evil is to be avoided" (Aquinas 1920, I.II, q. 94, art. 2, *respondeo*). Calling this the first precept of the natural law, Aquinas grounds it in the commonsense observation that every human being knows at some level that she ought to seek after what she believes is good for her, even if it is *not really* good for her. The alcoholic, for example, pursues the bottle because he desires the good of being at rest, to attain some sense of internal peace and contentment. When he conquers his addiction and changes his ways, he does so because he more fully understands how best to fulfill this first precept. He realizes that by his excessive drinking he had unwittingly been violating the precept, that he in fact was not really doing good or avoiding evil. Although you reject each of the ten bogus rules for specific reasons—for example, the precept that one ought not to intentionally kill the innocent—your duty to act in accordance with those reasons depends on this more general precept: good should be done and evil avoided.

(2) "Whatever is a means of preserving human life, and of warding off its obstacles, belongs to the natural law" (Aquinas 1920, I.II, q. 94, art. 2, *respondeo*). Like all living things, human beings have an inclination to continue in existence. But unlike those other living

things—which are directed by mere instinct or learned behavior, and not by intellect and will—human beings can apprehend the sort of existence appropriate to the kind of being we are. So when Aquinas talks about "preserving human life," he does not mean *mere* biological existence. We do, of course, apprehend the evil of killing, since we apprehend what is good for us. But we also know that the preservation of human life consists in far more than mere survival, but must include the sorts of relationships, institutions, and communal goods that make life worth living and allow us to flourish consistent with the ends of our nature.[6]

Although we rightly conclude from this precept that we ought to avoid death and not kill, we also come to recognize, by the exercise of our reason, that preserving the life appropriate to our species entails that killing may sometimes be justified and death should not be avoided at all costs. Thus, we come to believe that there are cases of permissible killing (e.g., just war, self-defense) as well as cases in which not avoiding death is not a violation of the natural law (e.g., martyrdom, certain supererogatory acts).[7] The justification of those apparent exceptions is the result of a further elaboration of the natural law. Take, for example, self-defense. Because I have an inclination to preserve my life, I have a right to protect it, which means that there may be occasions in which my exercise of that right results in the death of the assailant trying to unjustly take my life. As we shall see in the fourth primary precept, because we are rational and social beings that are ordered toward the shunning of ignorance, knowing the truth about God, and living with others in peace, we can infer from the natural law's primary precepts more precise precepts about the extent to which we are permitted to kill ("You may kill in self-defense so that your life may not be unjustly taken by someone who does not want to live at peace with others") or not avoid death ("Your duty to God, which is your highest duty, may require that you die for your faith if denying it is the only way to avoid death"). Hence your rejection of bogus rule 3 is based on a secondary precept of the natural law: one should not intentionally kill the innocent.

(3) "There is in man an inclination to things that pertain to him more specially, according to that nature which he has in common with other animals: and in virtue of this inclination, those things are said to belong to the natural law, 'which nature has taught to all animals' . . . , such as sexual intercourse, education of offspring and so forth" (Aquinas 1920, I.II, q. 94, art. 2, *respondeo*). Here, Aquinas is telling us that our sexual powers are ordered toward reproduction and that we have a solemn responsibility to our offspring that are brought into being from the exercise of those powers. Like all animals, we have a natural inclination to reproduce and care for our young. But unlike other animals, we possess intellect and will, which means that we can choose to resist our natural inclinations while still apprehending why it is sometimes evil to do so. For this reason, we infer from this primary precept of the natural law that child abandonment and state denial of parental rights are both prima facie evil. As should be obvious, your knowledge of this secondary precept of the natural law is the reason why you reject bogus rules 1 and 9.

(4) "There is in man an inclination to good, according to the nature of his reason, which nature is proper to him: thus man has a natural inclination to know the truth about God, and to live in society: and in this respect, whatever pertains to this inclination belongs to the natural law; for instance, to shun ignorance, to avoid offending those among whom one has to live, and other such things regarding the above inclination" (Aquinas 1920, I.II, q. 94, art. 2, *respondeo*). Here, Aquinas is saying that we have an inclination to reason well and eschew ignorance (because we are beings with intellect), live peaceably with others (because we are socially dependent beings), and know the highest truth (because we are beings with intellect that may exercise speculative reason). That is, we are naturally ordered toward these ends and to intentionally act contrary to them is to engage in evil. It is clear from your rejection of bogus rules 2, 4, 5, 6, 7, 8, and 10 that you already know this. Bogus rules 2 and 4 intentionally make citizens ignorant of the law, bogus rules 5, 7, and 8 enshrine irrationality in the law, and bogus rules 6 and 10 prohibit citizens from

pursuing and expressing the highest truths about morality and God.[8] Also, all the bogus rules in one way or another make it extraordinarily difficult to avoid "offending those among whom one has to live."

For Aquinas and the Catholic Church, natural law is not the only kind of law. There is eternal law, divine law, and human law, all of which are essential to understanding the natural law. Eternal law is the order of the universe in the mind of God. Divine law is Sacred Scripture. And human law is the civil law and law of nations instituted by human governments. I will have more to say about each in section 2, since some of the misunderstandings to which I will respond are often the result of natural law's critics ignoring one or more of these other types of law.

Four Misunderstandings

In this section, I am going to assess four misunderstandings of the natural law. I intend nothing more than to offer corrections to how some critics of the natural law conceptualize it. Thus, my comments are not meant as a defense of the truth of the natural law (though I believe it is true) but, rather, as a clarification of what the Catholic Church (and Aquinas) actually believes about the natural law. Because the second, third, and fourth misunderstandings are clustered together in a famous article by the Evangelical theologian, Carl F. H. Henry (1995), I address them together under one heading.

THE NATURAL LAW COMMITS THE
SO-CALLED NATURALISTIC FALLACY

Some critics of the natural law argue that it commits what is sometimes called the "naturalistic fallacy," that its advocates mistakenly try to derive an "ought" from an "is," a normative conclusion from a factual premise. So for example, it would be fallacious for one to argue from the fact that peyote is a naturally growing substance to the conclusion that one ought to consume peyote. In the same way, points out the critic, the natural law theorist fallaciously argues from the facts of human inclinations to the conclusion that one ought not to intentionally act contrary to them.

Although it is certainly true that it is sometimes fallacious to attempt to derive a normative conclusion from a factual premise—for example, pot smoking is legal; therefore you ought to smoke pot—this is not always the case. For one thing, the "facts" with which the natural law theorist is working are embedded in a teleological worldview, one in which all living creatures have natures that tell us what is good for them as well as inclinations that move these creatures to those good ends. The sapling in your backyard, for example, is ordered toward becoming an oak tree and thus it has inclinations to perform photosynthesis and absorb minerals from the soil for that end. Because we know the sapling's nature, we know that it becoming an oak tree is a perfection of its nature and thus good for it do so. But as I have already noted, human beings are not like other creatures, for we have intellect and will and are thus able to make real choices that may be contrary to or consistent with the good to which our inclinations are ordered. So for example, if one is purposely ignorant, abandons one's children, or intentionally kills an innocent bystander, then one has made an immoral choice contrary to the goods to which one is ordered, which includes the acquisition of knowledge, the caring for one's offspring, the preserving of human life, and living at peace with others.

To be sure, some philosophers reject natural teleology altogether, along with the Aristotelean–Thomistic metaphysics on which its advocates typically rely, while others, the so-called "new natural law theorists," believe that the truth of natural law does not depend on natural teleology (see Lee 2019; Crowe 2017). But given the modesty of our task—to merely offer conceptual clarification on how the Catholic Church, and how Aquinas (as conventionally interpreted),[9] understands the natural law[10]—there is no need to wade into those extra- and intramural disputes in this venue.

Second, outside of explicit discussions of natural law, we often make legitimate judgments that seem to rely on natural facts that imply good ends that one ought to pursue. Consider first the comments made by Richard Dawkins about Kurt Wise, a Harvard-trained paleontologist. Wise was brought up in a Fundamentalist Christian home in which he was taught that the Bible teaches that the earth is no more than ten thousand years old. Not only did Wise not abandon this belief after earning his Harvard PhD, but he came to the conclusion that if he were to do so, he would be abandoning his faith in Scripture, the Word of God.[11] So by sticking with his young earth views, Wise recognized that he had given up any chance of landing a professorship at a major research university. In an autobiographical essay quoted by Dawkins, Wise laments, "With that, in great sorrow, I tossed into the fire all my dreams and hopes in science" (Ashton 2000; quoted in Dawkins 2006, 285). In his assessment of Wise's decision, Dawkins writes,

> As a scientist, I am hostile to fundamentalist religion because it actively debauches the scientific enterprise. It teaches us not to change our minds, and not to want to know exciting things that are available to be known. It subverts science and saps the intellect. The saddest example I know is that of the American geologist Kurt Wise. . . . The wound, to his career and his life's happiness, was self-inflicted, so unnecessary, so easy to escape. All he had to do was toss out the Bible. Or interpret it symbolically, or allegorically, as the theologians do. Instead, he did the fundamentalist thing and tossed out science, evidence and reason, along with all his dreams and hopes. (2006, 284, 285)

Note the teleological reasoning undergirding Dawkins's assessment of Wise. He is saying that Wise—an intelligent, gifted, and well-credentialed scientist—ought to have used his talents in a way that would have led to his happiness, and that his fundamentalist beliefs were an impediment to that end. Because of the sort of being Wise is—a being with intellect and will whose end is happiness—he has an obligation to make choices consistent with that end. Aquinas, unsurprisingly, concurs: "Man's last end is happiness; which all men desire, as Augustine says (De Trin. xiii, 3,4)" (1920, I.II, q. 1, art. 8, *sed contra*).[12]

Now consider the fanciful case of David and his optometrist, Thomas. Suppose David is examined by Thomas, who tells him, "It looks like you are nearsighted and you *ought to* use corrective lenses."[13] David replies, "But doc, you just made an illicit inference, for you can't get an ought from an is. Just because I am nearsighted doesn't mean that I ought to use corrective lenses. At least that's what Hume taught me."[14] Thomas, having read Aquinas, responds with a series of questions, to which David offers a series of replies: "Should you do good and avoid evil?" "Yes." "Is improved eyesight good for you?" "Yes." "Would corrective lenses improve your eyesight?" "Yes." "So if you should do good and avoid evil, and if using corrective lenses is good for you, should you use corrective lenses?" "Yes." "Sounds like a valid inference to me. Read Aquinas's *On Being and Essence* and call me in the morning" (Aquinas 1968).

Third, the natural law critic seems to rely on the very sort of reasoning she claims is fallacious when employed by the natural law theorist. For she is arguing that, because the natural law theorist mistakenly attempts to derive an ought from an is, you ought not to follow the natural law theorist's example. The critic seems to be assuming that our mental faculties—the powers we employ when we exercise our reason—are ordered toward a good end, knowledge, and that believing in natural law theory is counter to that end. But that is equivalent to assuming the truth taught by the fourth primary precept of the natural law: shun ignorance because your mind is ordered to the good of knowledge!

NATURAL LAW MAKES SCRIPTURE SUPERFLUOUS, MISTAKENLY AFFIRMS UNIVERSAL MORAL BELIEFS, AND IGNORES THE NOETIC EFFECTS OF SIN

Christian critics of the natural law sometimes depict it as a theory that marginalizes scripture, overrates the universality of common moral beliefs, and ignores our fallen human nature. One such critic,

Carl F. H. Henry, writes, "The three contentions of the Thomist doctrine of natural law that evoke evangelical criticism are: (1) that independently of divine revelation, (2) there exists a universally shared body or system of moral beliefs, (3) that human reasoning articulates despite the noetic consequences of the Adamic fall" (1995, 55). Henry is mistaken on all three points. (1) There are two senses in which the natural law is not independent of divine revelation (which Aquinas calls the divine law). First, the natural law and the divine law (the Old and New Testaments) are both derived from the same eternal law, which is the order of the created universe in the mind of God. Because God is the creator of human nature, and because knowing the natural law requires the exercise of human reason, Aquinas says that "by the natural law the eternal law is participated proportionately to the capacity of human nature" (1920, I.II, q. 94, art. 4, a.1). In a sense, then, the natural law, because it depends on the deep structure of our nature, is a reflection of the eternal law in the mind of God. Second, the natural law is not independent of divine law insofar as the natural law is deficient for securing our supernatural end. Writes Aquinas, "If man were ordained to no other end than that which is proportionate to his natural ability, there would be no need for man to have any further direction, on the part of his reason, in addition to the natural law and humanly devised law which is derived from it" (II.I, q. 91, art. 4, *respondeo*). Here, Aquinas mentions both natural law and human law as being inadequate for the end to which we are ordained: beatitude, eternal happiness in union with God. (Human law, as noted above, refers to the civil law and the law of nations, which are derived from the natural law. They are, in a sense, applications of the natural law to the conditions of particular peoples.) For this reason, we need the divine law, a special communication from God to human beings that could not be derived from human reason.

Aquinas also tells us that we need the divine law "because, on account of the uncertainty of human judgement, especially on contingent and particular matters, different people form different judgments on human acts; whence also different and contrary laws result" (Aquinas 1920, II.I, q. 91, art. 4, *respondeo*). In other words, because the natural law by itself, without the help of the divine law, cannot quell many doubts about what a human being "ought to do and what he ought to avoid, it was necessary for man to be directed in his proper acts by a law given by God, for it is certain that such a law cannot err" (Aquinas 1920, II.I, q. 91, art. 4, *respondeo*). As the *Catechism* states, "The precepts of natural law are not perceived by everyone clearly and immediately. In the present situation sinful man needs grace and revelation so moral and religious truths may be known 'by everyone with facility, with firm certainty and with no admixture of error'" (2000, 1960, quoting Pius XII 1950, 3).[15] The natural law, for example, can tell us that the union of one man and one woman is good, but without the divine law, one cannot know that marriage is a sacrament or that it is indissoluble. In the same way, the natural law can tell us that there are four cardinal virtues, but it cannot tell us that there are theological virtues called faith, hope, and charity.

(2) The Church does not claim that "there exists a universally shared body or system of moral beliefs." Henry seems to be saying that the Church believes that all human beings have an infallible and complete access to the correct set of moral rules: "Natural law theory promises uniformity of truth claims and of moral conviction and behavior" (1995, 58). To be sure, the Church does teach that everyone knows the primary precepts of the natural law, but given differing cultural conditions in a diversity of societies and the role that human passions play in obstructing the natural law in particular cases, the Church recognizes that there is no one "universally shared body or system of moral beliefs" as Henry claims. As the *Catechism* (2000, 1957) states, "Application of the natural law varies greatly; it can demand reflection that takes account of various conditions of life according to places, times, and circumstances. Nevertheless, in the diversity of cultures, the natural law remains as a rule that binds men among themselves and imposes on them, beyond the inevitable differences, common principles."

Consider first the various forms of government as well as the wide range of civil and criminal laws throughout the world. In most cases, the differences arise as a consequence of a nation's history and traditions. Some nations, like the United States, have constitutions. Others are nonconstitutional monarchies. Germany outlaws "extremist symbols," while the United States does not. In some societies, the death penalty is permitted. Most of the world drives on the right side of the road, while citizens of the United Kingdom (and a few others) drive on the left. In all societies, homicide, theft, rape, and insurrection are violations of the criminal law, though there are disagreements on precise definitions and degrees as well as what would constitute appropriate punishments. The point is that all legitimate human law[16]—even in its wide diversity—reflects the natural law insofar as it is an attempt to recognize and protect those goods to which we are ordered.

Consider now the contested issue of abortion.[17] We often think that the differing sides in this debate hold radically different moral views.[18] They most certainly do on the question of the moral permissibility of abortion, but is it disagreement all the way down? Not at all. Take, for example, one of the secondary precepts of the natural law: it is wrong to intentionally kill innocent persons. Both pro-lifers and pro-choicers agree with this precept. Where they disagree is on the question of what constitutes an innocent person. Pro-lifers believe that all unborn human beings are innocent persons, whereas pro-choicers don't. Some pro-choicers argue that the unborn are not persons (see Warren 1973), whereas others argue that, even if they are persons, they are not technically "innocent" since those that are unwanted are unwelcome intruders on the woman's bodily integrity (see Thomson 1971; Boonin 2019). The point here is that even on an issue like abortion, one over which there is deep disagreement, each side defends its view under the assumption that a precept of the natural law is true.

(3) As should be obvious from my responses to Henry's first and second points, the Church does in fact take seriously the noetic effects of sin. Aquinas, for instance, explains that when it comes to the natural law's secondary precepts, "the natural law can be blotted out from the human heart, either by evil persuasions, just as in speculative matters errors occur in respect of necessary conclusions;

or by vicious customs and corrupt habits, as among some men, theft, and even unnatural vices, as the Apostle states (Romans 1), were not esteemed sinful" (1920, II, q. 94, art. 6, *respondeo*). This explains why many human beings, though having knowledge of the primary precepts of the natural law, nevertheless commit great evils. The murderer, for example, knows the good of the preservation of life, for he not only seeks to protect his own life but often kills for the sake of his own interests, the good of his life as he understands it. He is indeed corrupt. But we can only make that judgment if we already know the sort of human being he ought to be—that is, if we already know the natural law.

Conclusions

My intent in this essay was not to argue for the truth of the Catholic view of the natural law (even though I believe it is true) but rather to suggest (by using the ten bogus rules) (1) that the natural law comes more naturally to us than we may ordinarily suspect; (2) that it may very well be, in the words of J. Budziszewski, "what we can't not know" (2011); and (3) that four of the most common criticisms of the natural law rest on misunderstandings of it. This, of course, does not mean that one cannot critique the natural law on other grounds, or that one may not reasonably conclude that there are rival ethical theories that do just as well (if not better) in accounting for the common moral intuitions on which our rejection of the ten (bogus) rules seems to rest.

Notes

1 This list is inspired by Lon Fuller's fictional story of an evil monarch named Rex (Fuller 1969, 33–41).

2 An exception would be cases in which the parents of minor children die without having provided in their will directions for their children's

guardianship. But even here state laws reflect the primacy of original parenthood by allowing guardianship to the closest relatives (e.g., grandparents, aunt, uncle) with the best interests of the child in mind (e.g., an abusive alcoholic grandparent may be bypassed for a close family friend or aunt).

3   "Now, there are some objects of speculation that depend on matter for their being, for they can only exist in matter. And these are sub-divided. Some depend on matter both for their being and for their being understood, as do those things whose definition contains sensible matter and that, as a consequence, cannot be understood without sensible matter. For example, it is necessary to include flesh and bones in the definition of man. It is things of these sort that physics or natural science studies. On the other hand, there are some things that, although dependent upon matter for their being, do not depend on it for their being understood, because sensible matter is not included in their definitions. This is the case with lines and numbers—the kinds of objects with which mathematics deals. There are still other objects of speculative knowledge that do not depend upon matter for their being because they can exist without matter; either they never exist in matter, as in the case of God and the angels, or they exist in matter in some instances and not in others, as in the case of substance, quality, potency, act, one and many, and the like. The science that treats of all these is theology or divine science, which is so called because its principal object is God. By another name it is called metaphysics; that is to say, beyond physics, because it ought to be learned by us after physics, for we have to proceed from sensible things to those that are non-sensible. It is also called first philosophy, inasmuch as all the other sciences, receiving their principles from it, come after it" (Aquinas 1953, q. 5. a. 1; in order to make this quote more accessible, I slighted edited it from how it appears in the original).

4   C. S. Lewis put it more eloquently: "These, then, are the two points I wanted to make. First, that human-beings, all over the earth, have the curious idea that they ought to behave in a certain way, and cannot really get rid of it. Secondly, that they do not in fact behave in that way" ([1952] 1997, 21).

5   Just as some human beings cannot learn mathematics or master a language because of immaturity or disability, some human beings never come to know the natural law for the same reasons. This is why it is wrong to say that Aquinas or the Catholic Church teaches that the natural law is innate in each and every human being.

6   This is a point made by J. Budziszewski: "Preservation of its being means not the preservation of its bare existence, but the preservation of the mode of life that the *fulfillment* of its nature requires—a mode of life that is shaped by all of its natural inclinations, not just the first inclination, but others too" (2014, 249).

7   A supererogatory act is one that is above and beyond the call of duty, as in the case of a soldier jumping on a live grenade to save his buddies. He does not will his own death, but he knowingly sacrifices his own life to save others. (We know he is not willing his own death because he would not be disappointed if the grenade turned out to be a dud.) Perhaps this is the sort of sacrifice Jesus had in mind when he said, "No one has greater love than this, to lay down one's life for one's friends" (John 15:13 NRSV).

8   It is important to note here that Aquinas and the Church are not suggesting that moral relativists and atheists do not exist. What they are saying is that human beings have a natural inclination *to pursue* ultimate truths about morality and God. After all, the moral relativist's rejection of the natural law and the atheist's rejection of God's existence means that each has an inclination to pursue the truth of these questions, even though each arrives at answers antithetical to conclusions drawn by Aquinas and the Church. Nevertheless, the Church maintains that we are ordered toward these ends because they really do exist, and that in the case of God we cannot know him in the fullest sense until we experience him in the beatific vision in the afterlife.

9   I say "as conventionally interpreted," since the new natural law theorists believe that their interpretation of Aquinas—which challenges the conventional interpretation—is the correct one. For more, see Lee (2019).

10 The *Catechism* affirms teleology as integral to its explication of the natural law: "The moral law *presupposes the rational order, established among creatures for their good and to serve their final end*, by the power, wisdom, and goodness of the Creator. All law finds its first and ultimate truth in the eternal law" (US Conference of Catholic Bishops 2000, 1951; emphasis added).

11 It should go without saying that Wise's literalistic interpretation of the Bible—in particular, the first chapters of Genesis—is not the only way to interpret Scripture while maintaining a high view of it. See, for example, Carroll (2002).

12 As I note elsewhere, "Although Aquinas believed that God, the Sovereign Good, 'is the object and cause of Happiness,' one need not believe in God to recognize, as Dawkins does, that human beings by nature are ordered

toward happiness. Aquinas, of course, maintained that nothing short of God could suffice for Perfect Happiness, since everything that gives us imperfect happiness—pleasure, bodily goods, wealth, honor, intellectual accomplishments—is fleeting and temporary. Nevertheless, the point here is that Dawkins, despite his best efforts, cannot rid himself of the common sense reflexes that require the reality of final causality" (Beckwith 2019, 82; quoting Aquinas 1920, I.II, q. 5, art. 5, *respondeo*).

13 This dialogue is inspired by a similar one authored by Budziszewski (2014, 248).

14 Hume writes, "In every system of morality, which I have hitherto met with, I have always remarked, that the author proceeds for some time in the ordinary ways of reasoning, and establishes the being of a God, or makes observations concerning human affairs; when all of a sudden I am surprised to find, that instead of the usual copulations of propositions, *is*, and *is not*, I meet with no proposition that is not connected with an *ought*, or an *ought not*. This change is imperceptible; but is however, of the last consequence. For as this *ought*, or *ought not*, expresses some new relation or affirmation, 'tis necessary that it should be observed and explained; and at the same time that a reason should be given; for what seems altogether inconceivable, how this new relation can be a deduction from others, which are entirely different from it. But as authors do not commonly use this precaution, I shall presume to recommend it to the readers; and am persuaded, that this small attention would subvert all the vulgar systems of morality, and let us see, that the distinction of vice and virtue is not founded merely on the relations of objects, nor is perceived by reason" ([1739] 2000, 302).

15 English translation of *Humani Generis* quote is unique to *Catechism*. The Vatican's official translation of the encyclical differs slightly. It can be found online here: http://www.vatican.va/content/pius-xii/en/encyclicals/documents/hf_p-xii_enc_12081950_humani-generis.html (accessed on 21 May 2021).

16 I say "legitimate human law" because Aquinas holds that some so-called human laws are unjust and thus not real laws. See Aquinas (1920, II.I, q. 96, art. 4, *respondeo*).

17 For two different moral perspectives on the question, see Beckwith (2007) and Boonin (2002).

18 I am aware that there is a spectrum of views on abortion, that there are not just two camps, as popular media often portray it. But for the point I am trying to make here, it is not necessary that I cover all those views.

References

Aquinas, Thomas. 1920. *Summa Theologica*. Translated by Fathers of the English Dominican Province. Available online: http://www.newadvent .org/summa/ (accessed on 21 May 2021).

——. 1953. *Super Boethium De Trinitate*. Translated by Armand Mauer. Toronto. Available online: https://isidore.co/aquinas/english/BoethiusDeTr.htm #51 (accessed on 21 May 2021).

——. 1968. *On Being and Essence (De Ente Et Essentia)*. Translated by Armand Maurer. Toronto: Pontifical Institute Mediaeval Studies.

Ashton, John F. 2000. *In Six Days: Why 50 Scientists Choose to Believe in Creation*. Green Forest, AR: Master Books.

Beckwith, Francis J. 2007. *Defending Life: A Moral and Legal Case against Abortion Choice*. New York: Cambridge University Press.

——. 2019. *Never Doubt Thomas: The Catholic Aquinas as Evangelical and Protestant*. Waco, TX: Baylor University Press.

Boonin, David. 2002. *A Defense of Abortion*. New York: Cambridge University Press.

——. 2019. *Beyond Roe: Why Abortion Should Be Legal—Even If the Fetus Is a Person*. New York: Oxford University Press.

Budziszewski, J. 2011. *What We Can't Not Know: A Guide*. Revised and expanded ed. San Francisco: Ignatius.

——. 2014. *Commentary on Thomas Aquinas' Treatise on Law*. New York: Cambridge University Press.

Carroll, William E. 2002. "Creation, Evolution, and Thomas Aquinas." *Revue des Questions Scientifiques* 171:319–47.

Crowe, Jonathan. 2017. "Metaphysical Foundations of Natural Law Theories." In *The Cambridge Companion to Natural Law Jurisprudence*, edited by George Duke and Robert P. George, 103–29. New York: Cambridge University Press.

Dawkins, Richard. 2006. *The God Delusion*. London: Bantam.

Fuller, Lon L. 1969. *The Morality of Law*. Rev. ed. New Haven, CT: Yale University Press.

Henry, Carl F. H. 1995. "Natural Law and Nihilistic Culture." *First Things* 49:55.

Hume, David. (1739) 2000. *A Treatise on Human Nature*. Edited by David Fate Norton and Mary J. Norton. Oxford: Clarendon.

King, Martin Luther Jr. 1963. *Letter from a Birmingham Jail*. April 16. Available online: https://www.africa.upenn.edu/Articles_Gen/Letter_Birmingham .html (accessed on 21 May 2021).

Lee, Patrick. 2019. "The New Natural Law Theory." In *The Cambridge Companion to Natural Law Ethics*, edited by Tom Angier, 73–91. New York: Cambridge University Press.

Lewis, Clives Staples. (1952) 1997. *Mere Christianity*. London: Collins.

Pius XII. 1950. *Humani Generis*. August 12. Available online: http://www.vatican .va/content/pius-xii/en/encyclicals/documents/hf_pxii_enc_12081950 _humani-generis.html (accessed on 21 May 2021).

Thomson, Judith Jarvis. 1971. "A Defense of Abortion." *Philosophy & Public Affairs* 1:47–66.

United States Conference of Catholic Bishops. 2000. *Catechism of the Catholic Church: Revised in Accordance with the Official Latin Text Promulgated by Pope John Paul II*. 2nd ed. Washington, DC: United States Conference of Catholic Bishops.

Warren, Mary Anne. 1973. "On the Moral and Legal Status of Abortion Rights." *Monist* 57:43–61.

 CHAPTER 2

God, New Natural Law Theory, and Human Rights

Christopher Tollefsen

ABSTRACT: Critics of the "New" Natural Law (NNL) theory have raised questions about the role of the divine in that theory. This paper considers that role in regard to its account of human rights: can the NNL account of human rights be sustained without a more or less explicit advertence to "the question of God's existence or nature or will"? It might seem that Finnis's "elaborate sketch" includes a full theory of human rights even prior to the introduction of his reflections on the divine in the concluding chapter of *Natural Law and Natural Rights*. But in this essay, I argue that an adequate account of human rights cannot, in fact, be sustained without some role for God's creative activity in two dimensions, the ontological and the motivational. These dimensions must be distinguished from the epistemological dimension of human rights—that is, the question of whether epistemological access to truths about human rights is possible without reference to God's existence, nature, or will. The NNL view is that such access is possible. However, I will argue, the epistemological cannot be entirely cabined off from the relevant ontological and motivational issues and the NNL framework can accommodate this fact without difficulty.

The "New" Natural Law (NNL) theory articulated and defended over the past fifty or more years by figures such as Germain Grisez,

Joseph Boyle (2020a, 2020b), John Finnis, and others, represents a significant achievement in the domains of foundational ethics, applied ethics, political and legal philosophy, philosophy of action, and reinterpretation of the thought of St. Thomas Aquinas.[1] It is not, of course, without its critics in each of these areas. "Traditional" natural law theorists in particular object to NNL theory's strong separation of practical from theoretical reason (Veatch 1990), its particular applied conclusions on matters such as capital punishment (Feser and Bessette 2017) and vital conflict cases in bioethics (Furton 2014), its denial of the "transcendence of the common good" (Goyette 2013), its rejection of the relevance of "closeness" as a criterion of what is intended (Jensen 2014), and its Thomistic bona fides (Pakaluk 2020).[2]

Many such critics also believe that the NNL theory understates or ignores the role that God plays in ethics. Fulvio Di Blasi, for example, declares flatly, "There is no role for God in the new natural law theory" (Di Blasi 2013, 35); and Stephen Long writes of the NNL theory that it involves a "negation of the essentially theonomic character of the natural law" (Long 2013, 107). Such critics are often triggered by the stark claim of John Finnis in *Natural Law and Natural Rights* that his intention in that book is to offer "a rather elaborate sketch of a theory of natural law without needing to advert to the question of God's existence or nature or will" ([1980] 2011, 49). Yet Finnis does go on to offer philosophical reflections on precisely those topics, and he believes those reflections are far from redundant. In particular, worries about ultimate meaning and the further point of morality require investigation into the existence of an uncaused cause whose character as such is distinctly personal, and who might therefore have communicated with human persons an invitation to enter into a personal relationship with that being (chap. 13).[3] Any worries that the NNL theory ignores or has "no role for" God are certainly unwarranted.

Nevertheless, questions can reasonably be asked about the role of the divine in the NNL theory, and this paper considers that role as regards one particular aspect of the theory: its account of human rights. The question at issue is this: can the NNL account of human rights be sustained *without* a more or less explicit advertence to "the question

40

of God's existence or nature or will"? The question arises because it might indeed seem like Finnis's "elaborate sketch" includes a full theory of human rights even prior to the introduction of his reflections on the divine in the concluding chapter of *Natural Law and Natural Rights*.

This essay will present a nuanced answer to that question. I will argue that an adequate account of human rights cannot, in fact, be sustained without some role for God's creative activity in two dimensions, the ontological and the motivational. These dimensions must be distinguished from the epistemological dimension of human rights—that is, the question of whether epistemological access to truths about human rights is possible in the absence of reference to God's existence, nature, or will. The NNL view, as articulated by Finnis above, is that such access is possible. But as I will argue, the epistemological cannot be entirely cabined off from the relevant ontological and motivational issues and, as I will show, the NNL framework acknowledges and accommodates this fact without difficulty.

The New Natural Law Theory's Account of Human Rights

Following the early twentieth-century jurist Wesley Hohfeld, NNL theorists hold that a "right" in the strict sense always has as its correlative a "duty": I have a right in relation to you that you ϕ if and only if you have a duty to ϕ in regard to me, where ϕ-ing can encompass both acting and refraining from acting ([1919] 2001).[4] The negation of a right is "no-right": I have a no-right that you ϕ if and only if you have no duty to me to ϕ. And the correlative of that no-right is a liberty: you have a liberty not to ϕ if and only if I have no-right that you ϕ. In other words, you have no duty to me to ϕ.

Clearly, then, an assertion of a right will gain in both clarity and action-guiding-ness to the extent that the right is fully presented as a *three-term* right, in which a relationship is identified between some person(s), some interest, and the person(s) with a "duty of respect or

41

promotion of [that] interest and the kind of choice (to act or forbear) that is required of them to fulfill that duty" (Finnis 2011, 2). But as a historical matter the canonical articulation of *human* rights does not adhere to this logical form. In both the *Declaration of Independence* and the *Universal Declaration of Human Rights*, for example, rights held to be natural or human are identified by the claim that "everyone (or: 'all men') has (have) a right to x": a right to life, liberty, property, and so on, without reference to the bearer of the relevant duty. Thus article 3 of the *Universal Declaration* states that "everyone has the right to life, liberty, and security of person"; yet it does not explicitly identify the duty bearer(s) the Hohfeldian formulation requires.

In addition to the lack of reference to a duty bearer, these statements of right are also quite abstract. What is included within the right to life? One would expect that it involves immunity against certain forms of violence or force, but which, and under what circumstances? Are any entitlements to aid included, and if so, under what circumstances? Are preventative measures demanded by the right to life in order to protect life? In a political community, such questions ultimately require concrete legal answers in order for a right to be realized and secured.

But *human* rights are standardly considered to be prepolitical, so vindication of assertions that such rights obtain cannot require the specification provided by a polity's laws. Accordingly, New Natural Law theorists have given close attention to those human rights that both most fully approximate to full three-term specification in their traditional formulations and arguably are paradigmatically prepolitical—namely, those rights, if there are any, that could be considered both universal and absolute.

Finnis notes in *Natural Law and Natural Rights* ([1980] 2011, 211–13) that the *Universal Declaration* identifies certain rights with a different framing than the "Everyone has a right to . . ." of article 3. Article 4, for example, states, "No one shall be held in slavery or servitude; slavery and the slave trade shall be prohibited in all their forms." Finnis argues that the "No one shall be . . ." formulation is used to identify rights that in important respects need no further specification: both their content and the correlative duty bearers are adequately identified. On the one hand, the duty bearer that is correlative to "No one shall be . . ." is "everyone": for each person, it is the case that s/he has a duty *not to do* the act picked out. On the other hand, the act is picked out with adequate precision such that it can be identified by an agent considering practically what to do: of all the options available, any that involve the holding or selling of another into slavery are simply not to be done. The right is thus adequately specified, universal, and absolute: there is no logical space for exception to be made.

Of course, the assertion of such rights requires justification, and in several places NNL theorists have attempted to justify the existence of the morally absolute negative responsibilities that are correlative to morally absolute rights.[5] At its foundations, the theory holds that practical reason, prescribing without error, identifies certain goods as providing noninstrumental reasons for human action. Such goods, which include life, health, knowledge, play, aesthetic experience, friendship, integrity, religion, and marriage, offer distinct and, even in their individual instantiations, incommensurable aspects of a flourishing that, for human beings, is indefinitely and perhaps infinitely variegated. Practical reason further issues a very general norm, the first principle of morality, that in all forms of willing, agents should be open to the integral human fulfillment of all persons including themselves (Finnis, Boyle, and Grisez 1987b).

That norm is then further specified in a general principle that one should never intend damage or destruction of a basic human good. The argument depends first upon the incommensurability of goodness of the options involved. Properly understood, that claim is a denial only of commensurability in terms of the goodness of the options: where options are real, no one option offers all the goodness of the others, plus more.[6] But if options are incommensurable in this way, then a clear justification for damaging an instance of a good—namely, that it would bring about a greater good—is blocked. Second, the status of basic goods as aspects of human flourishing just as such, and hence as providers of reasons for action just as such, generates the claim that in the absence of a greater good, an act in

43

which the agent intends damage to an instance of basic good cannot be an act fully open to the integral directiveness of practical reason; indeed, in itself, it is contrary to that directiveness.

If this norm is to be fully action-guiding, it remains to identify act kinds in which damage to an instance of a basic good is intended. For example: to intend the death of another human being is to intend damage to the basic good of human life; therefore, intending the death of another human being is always and everywhere wrong. NNL theorists have made similar cases for the absolute wrong of lying, torture, rape, and enslavement. In each case, if it is absolutely wrong that the act in question be done to another, then the other has an absolute right that the act not be done to him. Such absolute rights, notably, do not extend to claims against any and all forms of harm brought about as a side effect, for it can be permissible to bring about as a side effect what it is always impermissible to intend. Finnis has been particularly critical of the tendency of European courts to extend the reach of absolute rights beyond what is intended to encompass what is foreseen as a side effect or even merely risked as a side effect (2016).

Human Rights, Human Dignity, and God

What is the relationship, according to the NNL theory, between the triad of human rights, human dignity, and the divine? The question must be investigated along two axes. The first concerns the relationship between human dignity and the scope of human rights; the second concerns the motivational efficacy of human rights.

THE ONTOLOGICAL DIMENSION

Human persons possess, as Robert P. George has noted, a "God-like" power for free choice, the ability to choose between fully deliberated options without anything other than the choosing sufficing for its being *this* option that the agent chooses (2017, 63).[7] This "God-like" power of free choice, a power incapable of existing without also being accompanied by the power of reason, is, as George and others have argued, the source of our dignity, or excellence, and thus radically marks *us*—say, the readers and author of this essay—off from all known nonhuman animals (Lee and George 2008). But NNL theorists defend the further claim that this power or set of powers is essential to the nature of the human being as such and that it is sufficient for possessing this ability in at least radical or root form that one *be* a human being.

If this is correct, then human dignity is possessed equally by *all* human beings, regardless of age, stage of development, disability, or moral state. A human being's dignity cannot be lost by his or her performing horrific acts, or by his or her cognitive incapacitation or disability, and a human being's dignity is present throughout his or her immaturity of developmental stage. So for example, an unborn human being, even at its one-celled zygotic stage, is a human person with full human dignity, provided that, as contemporary embryology holds, that one-celled entity is indeed a human being.[8]

This dignity is the ground for the possession of human rights. Human goods are to be protected and promoted, and not intentionally damaged, in the person of all beings who are perfected by those goods, and entities fall within the scope of that perfection precisely insofar as they possess the dignity of *human persons*. "Human" in "human persons" is essential because the goods are human goods; "persons" is essential because it is as having the special excellence of a free and rational being—again, at least in root capacity—that all human beings are radically equal in status and thus entitled in justice, and as a matter of right, to have the goods in their person respected, promoted, and not intentionally damaged.

Many philosophers dispute this claim that all human beings are human persons with dignity and rights. Personhood, dignity, and rights are held by such philosophers to belong only to some human beings, typically those who have achieved and maintain some physical or psychological marker, such as the development of a rudimentary nervous system or brain, consciousness, or self-consciousness. On such views, a human embryo or fetus has less dignity, or worth, than, say, an adult dog or chimp, whose achieved level of consciousness far exceeds that of the unthinking because immature human being.

Yet no dog or chimp will ever do what it is *natural* for a human embryo to do if it is not prevented by death or debility—namely, be the executor of its own growth and development to the point of being able to exercise the root capacities for consciousness and self-consciousness that were obviously present from its beginning as an organism, since from that beginning, it was destined to develop as a human being and not as a dog or chimp. Human embryos do not become new kinds of organisms when they have developed the active or occurrent ability to, say, think or choose freely; rather, they have developed that ability because of the kind of organism they are, because, that is to say, of their nature. It is, thus, the nature of human beings that grounds their status as human persons, with dignity, and fundamental rights, and since all human beings have this nature, all human beings are persons with dignity and fundamental rights.

Clearly, NNL theorists are committed to two claims about human nature: that there is such a thing as human nature, and that human nature includes the radical capacity for reason and free choice, the powers described by George as "God-like." Can these duplex claims about the nature of the human being be sustained in the absence of something actually God-like, or indeed, actually divine in nature playing the role of creator and sustainer of the beings whose abilities are so profound? Let us call this the *ontological* question of human dignity. Are the NNL theorists' claims about human nature, on which they rest their case for the universal scope of human dignity and thus human rights, dependent upon claims about the divine source of the beings possessed of that nature?

The Department of State's Commission on Unalienable Human Rights, of which I was a member, suggested that questions of dignity and rights could stand clear of questions of natural theology and the ontology of human nature: "However philosophical debates about reason, nature, and God might be resolved, the Declaration's affirmation of rights inherent in all human beings everywhere has, over the centuries, become deeply woven into American beliefs, practices, and institutions, and undergirds the nation's moral and political inheritance" (2020, 11). The idea here is that affirmation of inherent human rights can be sustained even if the "philosophical debates" about God and nature are resolved as an atheist would resolve them, in virtue of the entrenched role of human rights in the fabric of our common life and history.

But we should distinguish between the epistemological and the ontological possibilities. It is the standard natural law view that some and perhaps many moral truths may be *known* by unaided human reason, without adverting to knowledge of God's existence, or activity, or will. So the unique nature of the human person, and the unique moral status that attends that nature, may be recognized "naturally"; such knowledge is epistemically possible.[9]

But is such a *nature* possible—ontologically possible—in a world such as that described by secular naturalism? It seems not: secular naturalism is, to begin with, deeply skeptical of claims that there are natures at all (Silver 2006). But even more importantly, naturalism, or materialism, must hold that no merely material being could possess the radical capacity of free choice; such a being would be determined by the laws of material nature. Hence the common and correct recognition of most such worldviews that libertarian freedom is incompatible with the naturalistic worldview (Coyne 2012).

The picture of the human person that emerges from that worldview is likewise, and for that very reason, not compatible with the idea of equal dignity and equal rights for all human beings. For in the absence of the radical equality that follows from a radically equal endowment of a capacity for rational freedom—even when that capacity is in fact blocked by disease or developmental failure or injury—it seems *obvious* that human beings are not in fact equal in any deep or important sense. What is seen as valuable is not what human beings are but what they can more or less occurrently do. Secular naturalism seems in fact generally to acknowledge this, holding, as we have seen, that not that every human being possesses human rights, but rather that only those human beings developed to the point of some sort of occurrent use of reason, or occurrent ability to choose autonomously, are subjects of rights. Indeed, on the account of one of the most prominent recent defenders of human rights, even young children do not possess such rights (Griffin 2008).

But what is noteworthy is that just here, the boundaries between the ontological and the epistemological begin to break down. For although any natural law view is committed to a claim about the capacity of natural reason, no such view should deny that false theories about nature and human nature can impede reason's endeavors to come to the truth about morality and human rights. In consequence, although the light of reason is not intrinsically darkened as regards the possibility of truly human rights, it can nevertheless be extrinsically blocked by false theory. So the NNL theory can hold that, ontologically, human rights without God are an impossibility, and that, epistemically, the full scope of human rights is less likely to be acknowledged within a naturalist frame than otherwise. Accordingly, one finds in the work of John Finnis, Germain Grisez, and Robert George, among others, a continual concern for the effects of secularism, a concern not at all inconsistent with their natural law *bona fides*.[10]

THE MOTIVATIONAL DIMENSION

This brings us to the second axis on which the relationship between dignity, rights, and God must be investigated—namely, the issue of the motivational force of human rights. Grant that there are rights pertaining to all human beings as such; it is a further distinctive feature of the NNL account of human rights that the paradigmatic forms of such rights are not merely universal in scope but, as noted above, genuinely absolute: the right not to be enslaved, tortured, killed at will, raped, and the like, are correlative, on the NNL account, to absolute duties never to enslave, torture, kill at will, and so on. Such acts are simply never to be done, regardless of the consequences.

Here, I believe there is a gap between what can be known epistemically and what is possible motivationally. Once again, the traditional natural law view, also held by NNL theorists, is that human reason, tracking the argument given above, can recognize that certain acts are never to be done. That recognition is grounded in an awareness of reasons for action that, while cognitions, are nevertheless also motivations for rational agents. Making good on this claim is central to the NNL theorists' ongoing polemic against noncognitivism and subjectivism.[11]

Moreover, NNL holds that the norms of the natural law arc in themselves protective of the possibility of human fulfillment, and that for agents faced with practical dilemmas, traversing the norms of the natural law is damaging to their own prospects for fulfillment. For action contrary to the norms of the natural law is constitutive of a character that, in its now settled (until repentance of one's choice) opposition to reason and human good, is in various ways alienated not only from reason and human good in oneself but thereby also from other human persons and from God, whose desire for us is that we be fulfilled by human goods in community with others. So there is a reasonable answer to the question "Why be moral?" even when framed in terms of human rights: "Why respect the human rights of others?" The answer: we should respect the rights of others because in fulfilling the norms of justice, which are constitutive of right relationships with other human persons, we are thereby also fulfilling our own selves.

Yet the motivational appeal of any absolute norm is, under the most adverse circumstances, understandably weak, requiring as it does that an agent be willing to sacrifice the prospect of some great good, or suffer some significant evil, as the cost of refusing to act in a way judged always and everywhere impermissible. Such losses and suffering are real, even if they are the reasonably accepted alternative to immoral action.

The record of history suggests both that human beings rarely have the fortitude to resist such temptations and that, as with the relationship between the ontological and the epistemological, failure in the motivational domain works backward to impede what would otherwise be epistemically possible. That is, having given in to the temptation to intend damage and destruction to human goods, human agents proceed down the path of rationalizing such destruction. Even among Christians, justification for lying, for intentional targeting of civilian populations, for torture, and for other violations of absolute norms, and hence absolute human rights, are far from unknown.

As a philosophical ethics, NNL theory acknowledges this fact: reason's claims are unlikely to fully motivate those faced with the most tragic choices. But as it moves closer to natural, and then revealed, theology, the NNL theory offers a further nuanced motivational response that resists a standing temptation toward legalism. On this account, legalism should be understood as the view that moral norms are a form of divine positive law that exists only in an extrinsic or instrumental relationship to the heavenly fulfillment that is available to human persons: "pie in the sky when you die." For the legalist, one must follow the law in the face of temptation, but only in order to achieve some extrinsic benefit; in an eschatological frame, the relevant benefit is some form of fulfillment with God.

The ways in which legalism actually undermines absolutism are clear: if the relationship between natural law and eternal reward is extrinsic, then God can lift the relevant norms, or create exceptions to them; and forgiveness for their violation can be a path to reward even without interior repentance. Legalism in Catholic moral theology has arguably both reinforced and been reinforced by the emerging dominance of universalism, the doctrine that hell is empty.[12]

On the NNL account, by contrast, upright action on earth finds its fulfillment and continuation in the Kingdom of Heaven, an eternally ongoing communion of persons both divine and human, in which human goods are still pursued and realized. Eternal life in the Kingdom is not an extrinsic reward for a morally upright life, but an ongoing realization of the goods around which an upright life is structured. Thus, Grisez has argued, following a well-known passage of the Second Vatican Council, the fruits of good acts will be discovered again in the Kingdom, and, rather than an extrinsic relationship between those ends and heavenly flourishing, the latter will be in part constituted by the properly human choices, actions, and fulfillments of mortal life.[13]

What this means concretely is, of course, necessarily obscure: how the costs of upright action on earth will be set right in the Kingdom cannot be known. But those who with faith seek the Kingdom can be empowered to suffer rather than do injustice in a way witnessed to by many martyrs, with confidence that their suffering will ultimately be redeemed.

God is clearly central to this story of how fully upright action for the Kingdom is possible in the face of human evil and personal suffering. In the motivational, as in the ontological dimension, the NNL theory thus does justice both to the epistemic possibilities traditional to natural law accounts and to the limits of those possibilities, limits that require reference to the divine if they are to be overcome.

Notes

1 The foundations of the theory are summarized in Finnis, Boyle, and Grisez (1987b).

2 The citations are representative but not exhaustive.

3 I discuss Finnis's further reflections in Tollefsen (2020).

4 For a more extensive account of the NNL treatment of human rights, see Tollefsen (forthcoming).

5 See, for example, Lee (2006); and Finnis, Boyle, and Grisez (1987a).

6 The claim does not deny commensurability tout court: the first principle of morality and all other moral principles commensurate, that is, measure against a standard, options for action. The NNL claim is that this commensuration is not accomplished on the basis of the overall goodness but of the reasonableness of the options for action. For further discussion see Boyle (2020b).

7 This libertarian form of free choice is defended in Boyle, Grisez, and Tollefsen (1976).

8 For a review of the biological evidence in regard to zygotes and embryos, see George and Tollefsen (2008).

9 Indeed, such recognition might well, by the sorts of considerations introduced in the text, lead to recognition of the more than natural conditions necessary for such a being to come into existence.

10 See, for example, the concerns raised in Finnis (1998); and George (2017).

11 See, in this regard, Boyle (2020b).

12 I have discussed legalism in Catholic moral thought at greater length in Tollefsen (2018).

13 For a more extensive account of the Kingdom, including an explanation of the way in which Jesus is the Kingdom, in whom all the faithful will be united in communion, see Grisez (2014).

References

Boyle, Joseph. 2020a. "Free Choice, Incomparably Valuable Options, and Incommensurable Categories of Good." In *Natural Law Ethics in Theory and Practice: A Joseph Boyle Reader*, edited by John Liptay and Christopher Tollefsen. Washington, DC: Catholic University of America Press.

———. 2020b. "Reasons for Action: Evaluative Cognitions that Underlie Motivation." In *Natural Law Ethics in Theory and Practice: A Joseph Boyle Reader*, edited by John Liptay and Christopher Tollefsen. Washington, DC: Catholic University of America Press.

Boyle, Joseph, Germain Grisez, and Olaf Tollefsen. 1976. *Free Choice: A Self-Referential Argument*. Notre Dame, IN: University of Notre Dame Press.

Commission on Unalienable Human Rights. 2020. *Report of the Department of State's Commission on Unalienable Human Rights*. Washington, DC: United States Department of State.

Coyne, Jerry. 2012. "You Don't Have a Free Will." *Chronicle of Higher Education*. March 18. Available online: https://www.chronicle.com/article/you-dont-have-free-will/?cid2=gen_login_refresh&cid=gen_sign_in (accessed on 22 July 2021).

Di Blasi, Fulvio. 2013. "The Role of God in the New Natural Law Theory." *National Catholic Bioethics Quarterly* 13:35–45.

Feser, Edward, and Joseph Bessette. 2017. *By Man Shall His Blood Be Shed: A Catholic Defense of Capital Punishment*. San Francisco: Ignatius.

Finnis, John. (1980) 2011. *Natural Law and Natural Rights*. Oxford: Oxford University Press.

———. 1998. "On the Practical Meaning of Secularism." *Notre Dame Law Review* 73:491–516.

———. 2011. Introduction to *Human Rights and Common Good, Collected Essays.* Vol. 3, 1–16. Oxford: Oxford University Press.

———. 2016. "Absolute Rights: Some Problems Illustrated." *American Journal of Jurisprudence* 61:195–215.

Finnis, John, Joseph Boyle, and Germain Grisez. 1987a. *Nuclear Deterrence, Morality and Realism.* Oxford: Oxford University Press.

———. 1987b. "Practical Principles, Moral Truth, and Ultimate Ends." *American Journal of Jurisprudence* 32:99–151.

Furton, Edward. 2014. "Tollefsen on the Phoenix Case." *Ethics and Medics* 39:3–4.

George, Robert P. 2017. "Natural Law, Human Dignity, and God." In *Natural Law Jurisprudence*, edited by George Duke and Robert P. George, 57–75. New York: Cambridge University Press.

George, Robert P., and Christopher Tollefsen. 2008. *Embryo: A Defense of Human Life.* New York: Doubleday.

Goyette, John. 2013. "On the Transcendence of the Political Common Good: Aquinas vs. the New Natural Law Theory." *National Catholic Bioethics Quarterly* 13:133–55.

Griffin, James. 2008. *On Human Rights.* Oxford: Oxford University Press.

Grisez, Germain. 2014. "Human Persons' True Ultimate End: The Continuity between the Natural End and the Spiritual End." Paper presented at the 37th Annual Conference of the Fellowship of Catholic Scholars, Pittsburgh, September 26–27. Vol. 37, 91–122.

Hohfeld, Wesley N. (1919) 2001. *Fundamental Legal Conceptions.* Abingdon: Ashgate.

Jensen, Steven. 2014. "Causal Constraints on Intention." *National Catholic Bioethics Quarterly* 14:273–93.

Lee, Patrick. 2006. "Interrogational Torture." *American Journal of Jurisprudence* 51:131–47.

Lee, Patrick, and Robert P. George. 2008. "The Nature and Basis of Human Dignity." *Ratio Juris* 21:173–93.

Long, Steven. 2013. "Fundamental Errors of the New Natural Law Theory." *National Catholic Bioethics Quarterly* 13:105–31.

Pakaluk, Michael. 2020. "On What a Theory of Natural Law Is Supposed to Be." *Persona y Derecho* 82:167–200.

Silver, Lee. 2006. *Challenging Nature: The Clash of Science and Spirituality at the New Frontiers of Life.* New York: HarperCollins.

Tollefsen, Christopher. 2018. "The Future of Roman Catholic Bioethics." *Journal of Medicine and Philosophy* 43:667–85.

———. 2020. "The Good of Play in John Finnis's *Natural Law and Natural Rights*." *Persona y Derecho* 83:571–90.

———. Forthcoming. "New Natural Law Foundations of Human Rights." In *The Cambridge Handbook of Natural Law and Human Rights*, edited by Tom Angier, Iain Benson, and Mark Retter. Cambridge: Cambridge University Press.

Veatch, Henry. 1990. *Swimming against the Current in Contemporary Philosophy: Occasional Essays and Papers*. Washington, DC: Catholic University of America Press.

CHAPTER 3

Aquinas and Scotus on the Metaphysical Foundations of Morality

J. Caleb Clanton and Kraig Martin

ABSTRACT: This essay retraces some of the contrast between Aquinas and Scotus with respect to the metaphysical foundations of morality in order to highlight how subtle differences pertaining to the relationship between the divine will and the divine intellect can tip a thinker toward either an unalloyed natural law theory (NLT) or something that at least starts to move in the direction of divine command theory (DCT). The essay opens with a brief consideration of three distinct elements in Aquinas's work that might tempt one to view him in a DCT light, namely: his discussion of the divine law in addition to the natural law; his position on the so-called immoralities of the patriarchs; and some of his assertions about the divine will in relation to justice. We then respond to each of those considerations. In the second and third of these cases, following Craig Boyd, we illustrate how Aquinas's conviction that the divine will follows the ordering of the divine intellect can help inform the interpretive disputes in question. We then turn our attention to Scotus's concern about the freedom of the divine will, before turning to his discussion of the natural law in relation to the Decalogue as a way of stressing how his two-source theory of the metaphysical foundations of morality represents a clear departure from Aquinas in the direction of DCT.

Introduction

Within the Christian tradition at least, Thomas Aquinas is clearly the thinker most closely associated with natural law theory (NLT), according to which moral obligations arise in connection to facts about the sort of creatures we are by nature—facts that God is responsible for, facts that we can discover and reason about for ourselves. Yet this familiar depiction of Aquinas can start to seem less straightforward in light of two considerations. One is simply that, admittedly, it is at least somewhat anachronistic to talk about Aquinas as a proponent of NLT in the first place: It is not as though he was, for example, a participant in the crisply defined debates between contemporary advocates of NLT, on the one hand, and, on the other hand, contemporary advocates of divine command theory (DCT), according to which moral obligations arise more directly in connection to God's commands or some other prescriptive act of the divine will. Obviously, Aquinas precedes such precise categories, which we readily acknowledge. Of course, anachronistic classification can sometimes be a helpful heuristic nonetheless. At any rate, the familiar depiction of Aquinas as a proponent of NLT can seem less straightforward in light of yet a second consideration: In recent years, some scholars have either classified him among the proponents of DCT or appropriated his work in making a case for DCT (see, for example, Idziak 1989, 49, 56; Quinn 1990, 357–59; Rooney 1995; Dougherty 2002). Although we think that the interpretive evidence suggests that Aquinas probably fits most comfortably in the unalloyed NLT camp—and, hence, that he is *not* properly classified as a proponent (or even a protoproponent) of DCT—our primary aim in this paper is not to settle interpretive disputes about Aquinas. Rather, our goal is to highlight some of the key nuances in his work that surface when addressing those sorts of interpretative disputes—nuances that evolved among some of his medieval successors and that took them in importantly different directions with respect to the metaphysical foundations of morality. An especially illustrative example of this can be seen in the work of John Duns Scotus, whose reflections on the natural law help stake out what Hannes Möhle has christened "a clear break and a new beginning" vis-à-vis Thomistic NLT (2003, 314).

This essay, accordingly, retraces some of the contrast between Aquinas and Scotus with respect to the metaphysical foundations of morality in order to highlight how subtle differences pertaining to the relationship between the divine will and the divine intellect can tip a thinker toward either an unalloyed NLT or something that at least starts to move in the direction of DCT. While we unavoidably wade into interpretive waters here, our aim is narrower than, say, demonstrating that Aquinas's moral theory is or is not consistent with recent articulations of DCT. Rather, we highlight subtleties in the work of Aquinas and Scotus that we think can be cultivated as resources for understanding and advancing contemporary debates in theistic metaethics—particularly those related to the divide between NLT and DCT, for example.

We proceed as follows. The essay opens with a brief consideration of three distinct elements in Aquinas's work that might tempt one to view him in a DCT light, namely: his discussion of the divine law in addition to the natural law; his position on the so-called immoralities of the patriarchs; and some of his assertions about the divine will in relation to justice. We then respond to each of those considerations. In the second and third of these cases, following Craig Boyd, we illustrate how Aquinas's conviction that the divine will follows the ordering of the divine intellect can help inform the interpretive disputes in question. We then turn our attention to Scotus's concern about the freedom of the divine will, before turning to his discussion of the natural law in relation to the Decalogue as a way of stressing how his two-source theory of the metaphysical foundations of morality represents a clear departure from Aquinas in the direction of something more akin to DCT.

Aquinas on the Divine Law and the Natural Law

As a prelude to his famous discussion of the natural law in the *Summa Theologiae*, Aquinas distinguishes four types of law: eternal law, natural law, human law, and divine law (*Summa Theologiae* Ia–IIae, q. 91 in Aquinas 2002, 16–26).[1] Eternal law is the rule and measure of acts dictated by God's perfect practical reason (ST Ia–IIae, q. 91, a. 1 in Aquinas 2002, 16–17). Because God is eternal, so are the dictates of God's practical reason. The natural law is that subset of the eternal law in which humans can participate (ST Ia–IIae, q. 91, a. 2 in Aquinas 2002, 18). That is, the natural law is that portion of the eternal law to which we have epistemic access and according to which we can freely order our lives. In turn, the natural law is valid and binding for us in virtue of its relationship to the dictates of God's practical reason. Human law is composed of dictates of practical reason derived through the process of human reasoning on the indemonstrable first precepts of the natural law (in conjunction with contingent facts) that are then put into place and promulgated by one who has care of a particular community (ST Ia–IIae, q. 91, a. 3 in Aquinas 2002, 19). Lastly, divine law consists of specially revealed dictates from God that, Aquinas says, are "necessary to give direction to human life" (ST Ia–IIae, q. 91, a. 4 in Aquinas 2002, 21).

Now one might be tempted to think that Aquinas is committed to at least something akin to DCT (in addition to NLT) precisely because he allows for a subset of the law that flows directly from God's commands—that is, the divine law. Suppose, for example, that God commands us to ϕ, where ϕ's obligatoriness is in principle indiscernible through the use of supernaturally unaided human reasoning. We might be tempted to think, then, that the obligation to ϕ in this case arises *solely* in virtue of the divine command itself—and not as a result of its connection to the natural or eternal law. Accordingly, there would appear to be *two* fundamental sources of moral obligation at play here: The natural law, which are the dictates of God's eternal practical reason to which we have epistemic access, and the divine law, which are the special revelations of God's will. And if so, then it would be inaccurate to depict Aquinas as *merely* a proponent of NLT.

Notice, though, that there are at least two ways one might construe Aquinas's depiction of the divine law. On the one hand, consistent with the view just presented, one might read him as saying that the divine law is a set of special determinations of the divine will that causes or constitutes (or otherwise provides the ontological ground of) moral obligations. Call this the *ontological* interpretation for short. On the other hand, one might read Aquinas as saying that the divine law is a set of specially revealed epistemic aids for humans with respect to some set of moral obligations: Without these specially revealed precepts, we would have no way, or at least no easy way, of discerning the relevant obligations. Call this the *epistemic* interpretation of the divine law.

There are at least two considerations that point in favor of the epistemic interpretation. First, Aquinas explains that the divine law—which one might imagine would be unnecessary *in addition* to the natural law—is actually needed in order to direct us toward ends that extend beyond our natural ability to ascertain (viz., *eternal blessedness*) and because of the "uncertainty of human judgment," among other such reasons (ST Ia–IIae, q. 91, a. 4 in Aquinas 2002, 21). In other words, Aquinas seems to depict the function of the divine law in decidedly epistemic terms, and not as an ontological supplement to the dictates of God's practical reason.

Second, recall that Aquinas contemplates law as a rule and measure of acts, and he explicitly holds that "it belongs to *reason* to order us to our end" and that ruling and measuring "belongs *only* to reason" (ST Ia–IIae, q. 90, a. 1 in Aquinas 2002, 11; emphasis added). In other words, he gives priority to reason over the will when it comes to the establishment of law. This would seem to suggest that the ontological source of moral obligation is ultimately traceable to the dictates of God's perfect and eternal practical reason, and not to some nonrational source. Accordingly, it seems likely that Aquinas did not think of the divine law as some *additional* primary ontological source of moral obligations, but rather as a set of special epistemic aids for discerning the full scope of our moral obligations. Admittedly, God's commands in the divine law would serve as *infallible* guides to the relevant obligations in question—which is why we should always obey God's command. But claiming that there is a perfect correlation between God's commands and our moral obligations is not enough to qualify one as a proponent of DCT. After all, God's commands might simply perfectly *reiterate* what our moral obligations would be even independent of God's commands. And so to qualify as a proponent of DCT, one needs to claim that moral obligations are caused or constituted by (or are otherwise in a special, tight dependent connection to) divine commands. And insofar as DCT asserts that the relevant connection between the divine commands and moral obligations is more than just correlation—even perfect and infallible correlation—Aquinas's affirmation of the divine law is not enough to qualify him as even a partial proponent of DCT.

Aquinas on the Immoralities of the Patriarchs

The matter gets more complicated, though: One might be tempted to think that Aquinas holds that, at least with respect to some moral obligations, the relevant connection between the divine command and the moral obligation is more than merely epistemic. That is, one might be tempted to think that Aquinas holds that, in some cases, divine commands do more than merely provide needed epistemic aids—they do ontological work, too. After all, Aquinas seems to suggest that certain acts would not have been obligated (and, in fact, would have been morally forbidden) *except that God commanded them*. For this very reason Philip L. Quinn contends that, for Aquinas, "some moral statuses *do* depend on divine commands"—a position that is at least consistent with that of DCT (1990, 359; emphasis added). Quinn points in particular to the following passage in Aquinas's discussion of the Decalogue:

Consequently when the children of Israel, by God's command, took away the spoils of the Egyptians, this was not theft; since it was due to them by the sentence of God.—Likewise when Abraham consented to slay his son, he did not consent to murder, because his son was due to be slain by the command of God, Who is Lord of life and death: for He it is Who inflicts the punishment of death on all men, both godly and ungodly, on account of the sin of our first parent, and if a man be the executor of that sentence by Divine authority, he will be no murderer any more than God would be.— Again Osee [=Hosea], by taking unto himself a wife of fornications, or an adulterous woman, was not guilty either of adultery or of fornication: because he took unto himself one who was his by command of God, Who is the Author of the institution of marriage. (ST Ia–IIae, q. 100, a. 8, ad. 3, as quoted in Quinn 1990, 358)

Now notice that the various acts in question here would normally be regarded as morally impermissible insofar as they seem to involve violations not only of right reason, and hence the natural law, but also of the *divine law* as conveyed in the second table of the Decalogue (at least *anachronistically* so in the case of Abraham and the plundering of Egypt). Nonetheless, in Aquinas's view, the specific acts of these patriarchs were not actually impermissible, as indicated by God's command. So consistent with what Quinn argues, divine commands would appear to make a moral difference for Aquinas.

A curiosity arises here, however. Remember that, for Aquinas, the natural law is composed of a subset of the dictates of God's eternal practical reason, and hence it admits of no exception. So how could right reason at once affirm both (1) that the various classes of acts known as "murder" or "theft" or "adultery" are impermissible *and* (2) that individual instances of these classes are permitted (or even obligated) when commanded by God? Ultimately, on Aquinas's view, the answer is that the precepts conveyed in the second table of the Decalogue—including the relevant injunctions against murder, theft, and adultery—were never actually revoked, despite any appearances to the contrary. He explains, for example, that "the commandments of the second table include the very order of justice to be observed in human society, that nothing improper be done to anyone, and that one should render to others what is their due. For we should so understand the commandments of the Decalogue. *And so the commandments of the Decalogue cannot be dispensed from at all*" (ST Ia–IIae, q. 100, a. 8 in Aquinas 2002, 82; emphasis added). So the specific acts of the patriarchs in question, rather than being dispensations from the law, were permissible simply because they did not ultimately constitute acts of murder or theft or adultery on final analysis, despite any appearances to the contrary. Why is that? In each case, the divine command somehow altered what the act in question was—or at the very least, the divine command alerts us to the fact that, in these special cases, the particular acts were actually different in nature than they may have otherwise appeared to us. Aquinas explains, for example, that "the commandments of the Decalogue, regarding the nature of justice that they include, cannot be changed. But specifications applying the commandments to particular acts, namely specifications whether this or that be murder, theft, or adultery, are indeed variable" (ST Ia–IIae, q. 100, a. 8, ad. 3 in Aquinas 2002, 83).

Think of it this way. Murder is *unjustified* killing. However, Abraham was not unjustified in planning to kill Isaac, precisely insofar as he was directed to do so by God, whose acts are always in accord with reason. And so in this case, Abraham was not actually planning *murder* because he was not planning something unjustified. Similarly, the Israelites did not actually commit an act of theft in despoiling the Egyptians because God's command effectively transferred the relevant property rights as, say, compensation for past injustices. And in marrying Gomer, Hosea did not actually commit adultery, precisely because he carried out God's specially revealed will. Notice the role played by the divine will in Hosea's case, according to Aquinas:

> Fornication is said to be a sin insofar as it is against right reason. Human reason is right when measured by the divine will, which is the first and supreme rule. Consequently, what a man does by

God's will and in obedience to his command is not against right reason, though it may appear to be against its common order: thus a miracle done by God's power is not against nature though against the common natural order. . . . Hosea did not sin by fornicating from a divine command. Yet his intercourse properly speaking was not fornication, though called so in common usage. (ST IIa–IIae, q. 154, a. 2, ad. 2, as quoted in Boyd 1998, 224)

Aquinas makes clear here that a sin is a sin insofar as it is against right *reason*, but that God's *will* is the first and supreme rule of human right reason. So apart from the determination of God's will in the command, Hosea's act would have ordinarily amounted to fornication, and hence as a sin, a point that would seem to speak in favor of Quinn's contention that divine commands make a moral difference for Aquinas.

But does it follow from this that the determinations of God's *will* (as expressed in God's commands) caused or constituted or otherwise ontologically grounded the moral obligation in such a way that accords with the DCT position? Perhaps not. Craig Boyd, for one, concedes that God's commands make some sort of difference in the three cases mentioned above. As Boyd reads Aquinas, however, "it is not simply the case that God's command acts independently of God's reason" (1998, 223). Rather, "it is the divine *reason*, which in some cases exceeds the grasp of human reason, that serves as the standard for morality in Aquinas' moral thought" (223; emphasis added). And that's because, for Aquinas, the divine will follows the ordering of divine reason. So even though God's will, as conveyed in God's commands, indicates the conditions whereby an act (that would have otherwise been murder or theft or fornication) becomes an obligatory act, the divine will is not actually the root source from which the moral obligation arises. Rather, God's will is informed by the dictates of God's eternal practical reason. After all, for Aquinas, a law is simply "a dictate of practical reason by a ruler who governs a perfect community," which is to say that law is simply a dictate of God's eternal practical reason (ST Ia–IIae, q. 91, a. 1 in Aquinas 2002, 16). Hence if

Boyd is correct, while Aquinas might be reasonably understood as conceding that divine commands can make some sort of difference, Aquinas can also be reasonably understood as denying that the divine will (or, command) is the most fundamental ontological ground of the obligation in the way a proponent of DCT would need to claim.

Aquinas on the Divine Will and the Divine Intellect

Still, the dialectic between Quinn and Boyd raises an important question about the relationship between God's reason (or, intellect) and God's will (or, command). How can it be true that the law ultimately belongs to divine *reason*, and yet also true that the divine *will* is the first and supreme rule, as Aquinas explicitly says? To address this question, it will help to pause here and consider Janine Marie Idziak's appropriations of Aquinas in formulating various positive arguments for DCT—appropriations that, again, can leave one with the impression that Aquinas is committed to something akin to DCT.

Idziak attempts to mine Aquinas for helpful historical resources in formulating two positive arguments for DCT—what we might think of as the *argument from first cause for DCT* and the *argument from sovereignty for DCT*. The argument from first cause pivots on the claim that God's will must ultimately be uncaused, and thus dependent on nothing else. Accordingly, morality, like everything else, is traceable back to the uncaused divine will. The argument from sovereignty rests on the claim that the law in the human sphere is that which pleases the sovereign and so the moral law (in general) is that which pleases God, who is sovereign over all.

Now consider the argument from sovereignty first. Obviously enough, such an argument might seem to mesh neatly enough with Aquinas's assertion that the divine will is the "first and supreme rule." After all, if the will of a sovereign is that which rules over a domain, then insofar as God is sovereign over all, God's will is the rule over all—indeed, the first and supreme rule. So we need to ask: is Aquinas's affirmation that the divine will is the first and supreme rule enough to imply that he is thereby committed to DCT?

Not necessarily. Consider how such an inference would be dealt with by Boyd's insistence that, for Aquinas, the divine will "takes its order from the divine intellect" (Boyd 1998, 211). The response here would run much like the response to Quinn: Yes, God's will or command makes a difference, but not in the way needed *for DCT*. And that's because, for proponents of DCT, the divine will or command must be the thing that ultimately grounds the obligation. Yet for Aquinas, the divine intellect is prior to the divine will in grounding the law—after all, the law belongs to *reason*. Boyd notes, for example, "One must be careful, Aquinas warns, to remember that God's will *always* follows the order of divine wisdom in order to avoid the blasphemous perspective of attributing to God a completely arbitrary will" (Boyd 1998, 211; emphasis added).[2] Now admittedly, what Aquinas regards as blasphemy, others later came to see as sound doctrine. At any rate, the point here is just that one strategy for defending Aquinas as a proponent of NLT and *not* DCT—despite the fact that Aquinas allows that divine commands can make some sort of difference—is to respond that, for Aquinas, since the divine will cannot be arbitrary, it must follow the ordering of the divine intellect.

Still, Idziak's appropriation of Aquinas in defense of yet another argument for DCT—namely, the *argument from first cause*—might seem to put pressure back on this very sort of defensive strategy. And that's because the argument from first cause for DCT holds that the divine will must ultimately be altogether *uncaused*.[3] Accordingly, an affirmation of the argument from first cause for DCT would clearly conflict with the defensive strategy underscored by Boyd.

But it is here where we should be careful to note that Aquinas indeed entertains, *but then explicitly rejects*, the line of reasoning animating the argument from first cause for DCT in the first place. So he should not be confused as endorsing Idziak's appropriation of his work in making a positive case DCT. At any rate, Aquinas's consideration of this line of reasoning is instructive, in part because it illustrates how the law belongs to divine reason, while the divine will

65

remains the first and supreme rule. In response to the question "Does justice as found among created things depend simply upon the divine will?" Aquinas entertains the following line of reasoning: "Every will which is just by a principle other than itself is such that its principle should be sought. But 'the cause of God's will is not to be sought,' as Augustine says. The principle of justice therefore depends upon no other than the divine will" (*Questiones Disputatae de Veritate*, q. 23, a. 6, diff. 6 in Aquinas 1954).

Aquinas ultimately replies to that line of reasoning as follows:

> Now the will does not have the character of a first rule, rather, *it is a rule which has a rule, for it is directed by the intellect and reason.* This is true not only in us but also in God, although in us the will is really distinct from the intellect. . . . In God, however, the will is really identical with the intellect. . . . Consequently *the first thing upon which the essential character of all justice depends is the wisdom of the divine intellect*, which constitutes things in their due propor- tion both to one another and to their cause. In this proportion the essential character of created justice consists. But to say that justice depends simply upon the will is to say that the divine will does not proceed according to the order of wisdom, and that is blasphemous. (*Questiones Disputatae de Veritate*, q. 23, a. 6, as quoted in Boyd 1998, 210–11; emphasis added)

Notice here that, on final analysis, the divine intellect—God's perfect and eternal practical reason—appears to stand at the root of all jus- tice.[4] Hence following Boyd's lead, we indeed appear to have good rea- son to contemplate Aquinas among the proponents of an unalloyed NLT after all, despite his affirmation of the primacy and supremacy of the divine will.[5] In a move that keeps his NLT consistently unal- loyed, he contends that the divine will follows the ordering of the divine intellect—the divine will is a rule that has a rule, so to speak. And ultimately, he allows that the divine will and the divine intellect are actually identical in God.

We have no intention of delving into issues related to divine simplicity here.[6] It is enough for us at this juncture to point out that in Aquinas we have a thinker who can be reasonably—albeit anachronistically—classified among the proponents of unalloyed NLT, but within whose work there is enough nuance and difficulty that one might at least get the impression that he also supports something akin to DCT, too. But a vital point for him turns on the relationship between the divine intellect and the divine will: Every divine act proceeds according to the order of wisdom, and to suggest otherwise would be to suggest that the divine act is arbitrary, which would be blasphemous. Accordingly, every decision and act of God must be *determined* by God's reason. Important Christian thinkers who followed Aquinas—such as John Duns Scotus, William of Ockham, and Andrew of Neufchateau in particular—clearly reacted to this sort of position, in part because they thought that it left God *too* constrained. In trying to free God from those constraints, they would eventually move in the direction of placing God's *will*, rather than God's reason, at the center of their explanations of the metaphysical foundations of morality.

Scotus on Contingency and Will

A prime example of this can be seen in Scotus. Aquinas holds that the divine will—and hence God's commands—are ordered according to divine reason, on pain of blasphemy. For Scotus, though, the theological worry seems to cut in the opposite direction: Given Aquinas's position, God's will would be problematically bound. After all, on such a system, God can do or will only what the divine intellect dictates. One worry that can arise here, though, is that such a view would effectively entail that, since God can only ever do or will that which is determined by divine reason, it would be impossible for God to, say, choose *not* to create humanity (or, say, create us in *that* way as opposed to *this* way). Yet many thinkers find it intuitive to suppose that, if it is impossible for S *not* to φ, then, when S φs, S does not φ *freely*. In other words, for many thinkers, it can seem intuitive to think that, without contingency, there could be no freedom—even for God.

This general kind of concern seems to motivate Scotus's emphasis on the will, which he depicts as a kind of power that contrasts with the hardwired inclinations of nature. He writes, for example,

> For a power or potency is related to the object in regard to which it acts only by means of some operation it elicits in one way or another, and there is only a twofold generic way an operation proper to a potency can be elicited. For either [1] the potency of itself is determined to act, so that so far as itself is concerned, it cannot fail to act when not impeded from without; or [2] it is not of itself so determined, but can perform either this act or its opposite, or can either act or not act at all. A potency of the first sort is commonly called "nature," whereas one of the second sort is called "will." (*Questions on the Metaphysics*, IX, q. 15, a. 2.2.a, in Scotus 1997, 139)[7]

The sun's potency is an example of a natural power that cannot fail to act when unimpeded from without. When the sun shines on wet clay, for instance, the clay dries and hardens—in fact, it cannot fail to do so unless something gets in the way. But things are different with the will. When the will chooses to do something, it could have chosen to *not* act at any time prior to having acted. We can lift our hands, *or not*. We can eat the apple, *or not*. So for Scotus, the will is a potency that is contingent, as it is not compelled toward some singular course of action by something else.

Notice what this implies with respect to the divine will. If the divine intellect fully determines the divine will toward one and only one act or command, then, insofar as the divine will and the divine reason are conceptually distinguishable, God's will would lack the character by which Scotus defines the will in the first place. In short, the divine will would cease to be will—precisely because God would be necessitated to a singular course of action and, hence, couldn't choose *not* to act in the way determined by reason.

So there appears to be a problem here in need of a solution. And to articulate a position that preserves God's freedom without thereby entailing that God's acts are utterly unconstrained by reason (and thus problematically arbitrary), Scotus contends that at least some of God's commands are fully determined by reason, and thus they are necessarily commanded by God, while other commands simply are not fully determined but contingent, and thus they could have been different had God chosen otherwise. To explain this solution, and why it matters, we should pause here to consider Scotus's views regarding the relationship between the natural law and the Decalogue.

Scotus on the Natural Law and the Decalogue

For Scotus, a precept can be said to belong to the natural law in one of two ways: either in the *strict* sense or in a loose or *extended* sense. Concerning the first way, he writes, "One way is as first practical principles known from their terms or as conclusions necessarily entailed by them. These are said to belong to the natural law in the strictest sense, and there can be no dispensation in their regard. . . . It is to these that the canon of the *Decrees of Gratian* refers, where it is said that, 'the natural law begins from the very beginning of rational creatures, nor does time change it, but it is immutably permanent'— and this I concede" (*Ordinatio* III, suppl., dist. 37 in Scotus 1997, 202). The idea here is that a precept belongs to the natural law in the strict sense only when its truth is discernable simply by understanding the relevant terms involved—it is *per se notum*, in other words—or when its truth follows necessarily from precepts that are *per se nota*. "Strictly speaking," he writes, "nothing pertains to the law of nature except a principle or a conclusion demonstrated in this fashion" (*Ordinatio* IV, dist. 17 in Scotus 1997, 195).

In some ways, of course, this is a perfectly familiar way of speaking about the natural law. Aquinas, too, holds that the primary precepts of the natural law are *per se nota*, though he depicts them as a subset of the eternal law, and so they are therefore immutable and time-less on his view. While Scotus agrees that the precepts of the natural law in the strictest sense are *per se nota* and even immutable (and hence, he says, they admit of no dispensation), this is not because he depicts them in connection to an eternal law (Möhle 2003, 315), but because he regards them as reflective of, or in possession of, a neces-sary truth—a truth that not even God could make false (*Ordinatio* III, suppl., dist. 37 in Scotus 1997, 199).

For Scotus, though, only the *first* table of the Decalogue—specifically, the first, second, and third commandments—could belong to the natural law in this strictest sense. Why is that? Möhle explains that "since the ultimate end of all action is the attainment of the highest good, and [since] the highest good is identical with God, the only com-mandments that can belong to the natural law in the strict sense are those that have God himself as their object" (2003, 315–16). In other words, only those commandments that have God as their object (viz., the injunction against having other gods or taking the Lord's name in vain or the command to worship God on the Sabbath) are commands that *necessarily* orient humans toward their good, regardless of how God might have otherwise ordered creation. And so the thought is that the truth of these precepts would be knowable simply by properly understanding the relevant terms—"God," "good," and so on. Scotus explains, for example,

> Indeed the first two [commandments], if they be understood in a purely negative sense—i.e., "You shall not have other gods before me" and "You shall not take the name of the Lord, your God, in vain," i.e., "You should show no irreverence to God"— belong to the natural law, taking law of nature strictly, for this follows necessarily: "If God exists, then he alone must be loved as God." It likewise follows that nothing else must be worshipped

as God, nor must any irreverence be shown to him. Consequently, God could not dispense in regard to these so that someone could do the opposite of what this or that prohibits. (*Ordinatio* III, suppl., dist. 37 in Scotus 1997, 202)

If God exists, God is perfectly good. What is good is to be loved, and what is perfectly good is to be loved above all else. So supposing God exists, God is to be loved above all else—*necessarily*. Hence it is necessary that we abstain from showing any irreverence to God. Period.

Scotus offers something of a caveat with respect to the third commandment, however. He recognizes, for example, that "there is some doubt whether this precept of observing the Sabbath pertains to the natural law strictly to the extent that it requires that at some definite time worship be shown to God" (*Ordinatio* III, suppl., dist. 37 in Scotus 1997, 203). The specification that God should be worshipped *on a particular day of the week rather than some other day* does not seem to be a specification known merely by understanding the relevant terms. In fact, that specification seems dispensable enough. So for Scotus, there are clearly cases where, and respects in which, a divine command could simply be *under*determined by divine reason. After all, perhaps it is the case that divine reason does not necessitate the divine will to command a specific, detailed time of worship such that any number of different possible dedicated times of worship would work equally well. If so, the divine intellect might entail that God command that God be worshipped on one of some limited range of possible occasions while remaining, in a sense, indifferent regarding *which* of those specific times God wills. In that case, God's will, as it were, simply picks one. God might well have commanded that the fourth day of the week be set aside, rather than the last, and it is at least possible that reason is antecedently neutral between those two options.

Even if we ignore this particular caveat, though, Scotus still holds that not all of the precepts of the Decalogue possess necessary truths that are *per se nota*—and so not all of them could belong to the natural law in the *strict* sense. Nonetheless, Scotus is careful to say that *all* of the commandments of the Decalogue still belong to the natural law in at least the looser, *extended* sense. He writes, for example,

> The other way in which things belong to the law of nature is because they are *exceedingly in harmony with that law* [=natural law in the strict sense], even though they do not follow necessarily from those first practical principles known from their terms, principles which are necessarily grasped by any intellect understanding those terms. Now, it is certain that all the precepts of the second table also belong to the natural law in this way, since their rightness is very much in harmony with the first practical principles that are known of necessity. (*Ordinatio* III, suppl., dist. 37 in Scotus 1997, 203)

Two points are worth stressing here. First, the second table of the Decalogue—namely, the commandments to honor one's parents and the injunctions against murder, adultery, theft, bearing false witness, and coveting—belong to the natural law in only the *extended* sense, and not in the strict sense. Second, the connection between the second table (and, hence, the natural law in the extended sense) and the natural law in the strict sense is depicted in terms of consonance and not in terms of entailment. That is, the precepts of the second table are *exceedingly harmonious* with what is necessarily true—namely, that God is to be loved—but they are not somehow necessitated by it. John E. Hare explains this point in Scotus by saying that the commands of the second table are *fitting* given the nature of God and of creation, but they are not somehow required by, or deducible from, it (see, e.g., Hare 2009, 97–105; 2015, 102–9). Elsewhere Hare explains, for example,

> God is bound to love the divine essence, and (given that God creates others) to will that those others love it also. So the commandments which tell us to love God have the kind of necessity required for natural law in the strict sense, but the commandments which

tell us how to love our neighbor do not. They are extremely fitting, Scotus says, but still contingent. This is because God is not,
for Scotus, limited in the ways in which we can be ordered to this
final end. We do not know that God is constrained to will that we
reach this end, for example, by following the second table of the
law. (2000, 25)

Simply put, for all we know, God could have commanded differently with respect to the second table. The divine will was not
fully determined by the divine intellect here—it was at most *under-*
determined whether God should issue the commands contained in
the second table, or some other set of commands. Thus, the commands of the second table are not reflective of necessary truths,
precisely because there may be other ways God could have commanded that would also have been harmonious with the necessary
first principles of the natural law (which includes the first table
of the Decalogue).

To illustrate the point at hand, consider the injunction against
theft. The very concept of theft presupposes the concept of private
property. Yet Scotus contends that God could have directed us toward
a good, alternate social order that does not require private property
in the first place. And had God chosen that alternate social order,
rather than the one God decided on, the commandment against
theft would have been unnecessary. Hence the relevant commandment in question does not qualify as a precept of the natural law in
the strict sense precisely because it does not reflect a *necessary* truth.[8]
Scotus explains,

> Given the principle of positive law that life in a community or
> state ought to be peaceful, it does not follow from this necessarily
> that everyone ought to have possessions distinct from those of
> another, for peace could reign in a group or among those living
> together, even if everything was common property. Not even in
> the case of the infirm is private possession an absolute necessity;
> nevertheless, that such persons have their own possessions is

exceedingly consonant with peaceful living. . . . And it is this way, perhaps, with all positive laws [=any precept that is not natural law in the strict sense], for although there is some one principle which serves as the basis for establishing these laws, still positive laws do not follow with the simple [logical] necessity from the principle in question or explicate it as regards certain particular cases. Nevertheless, these explications are greatly in harmony with the first universal principle they clarify. (*Ordinatio* III, suppl., dist. 37 in Scotus 1997, 204)

Similarly, the commandment involving adultery could have perhaps been different than it is, had God chosen differently. After all, for all we know, God could allow a dispensation from this precept. Mary Beth Ingham and Mechthild Dreyer point out, for example, that "Scotus notes, if there were a devastating epidemic and the survival of the human race were threatened, one might be allowed to practice bigamy. This dispensation from the sixth commandment . . . would be rational in light of the particular circumstance" (Ingham and Dreyer 2004, 135; see also *Ordinatio* IV, dist. 33, q.1 in Scotus 1997, 208–12). But if there are *any* circumstances under which it could ever be rational for God to allow such a dispensation, then the injunction against adultery is not reflective of a necessary truth, and thus is contingent on the divine precept.

Why, then, did God choose the specific set of commandments outlined in the second table, as opposed to some other set of commandments? It is here where some sense of arbitrariness enters the picture again. For Scotus, however, this is not a problematic arbitrariness, precisely because those commandments were still *constrained* or limited, though not entailed, by divine reason: the relevant commandments were still exceedingly harmonious with the first precepts of the natural law in the strict sense. To be sure, some other set (or sets) of commandments could also have been exceedingly harmonious with the first precepts of the natural law, too. Had God so chosen, God could have reasonably ordered the natural law in those ways. This power to reasonably order the universe in ways other than the way

God actually did reasonably order it makes room for contingency, and contingency allows room for the divine will. And recall that, for Scotus, where there is no contingency, there is no will.

It is worth noting that, in making room for the divine will to operate without being fully determined by the divine intellect, Scotus relies on a distinction between the *ordained* and *absolute* power of God. We can think of ordained power as the power to "act in conformity with some right and just law" (*Ordinatio* I, dist. 44 in Scotus 1997, 191).[9] Both God and humans have ordained power. By contrast, we can think of absolute power as the power to "act beyond or against such a law" (*Ordinatio* I, dist. 44 in Scotus 1997, 191). Here again, both God and humans have absolute power. However, while humans might act *inordinately* in exercising their absolute power (i.e., when acting *against* right law), God can only ever act ordinately in exercising God's absolute power. This is because God's acts, by definition, are always ordered and always consistent with right law. So how, then, could God ever exercise absolute power? Scotus explains, "God, therefore, insofar as he is able to act in accord with those right laws he set up previously, is said to act according to his ordained power; but insofar as he is able to do many things that are not in accord with, but go beyond, these preestablished laws, God is said to act according to his absolute power. For God can do anything that is not self-contradictory (and there are many such ways he could act); and then he is said to be acting according to his absolute power" (*Ordinatio* I, dist. 44 in Scotus 1997, 192).

So God could exercise absolute power by ordering creation in one of the multitude of alternate ways that God could have ordered creation, which would have thereby (downstream from that creative act) entailed a different natural law than the one we actually have. Yet no matter how God might have ordered creation, it would have thereby been reasonably ordered, even though it would have been ordered according to some other system or package of laws.

Two Sources of Moral Obligation

Despite the fact that Scotus is sometimes taken to be a reductive voluntarist about the metaphysical foundations of morality, what we actually see in Scotus is not just one but *two* fundamental ontological sources of morality at play. The first source—necessary truth—does not arise from the divine will per se, but rather is infallibly recognized by the divine intellect. The commandments in the first table of the Decalogue reflect, or possess, this necessary truth, and the thought is that by merely understanding that to which the term *God* refers—what is perfectly good and, hence, what is to be loved above all else—we can see that created beings necessarily owe such a being their total devotion and worship. Accordingly, with respect to the obligations identified by the first table of the Decalogue, Scotus says in no uncertain terms, "God could not dispense in regard to these so that someone could do the opposite of what [they] prohibit" (*Ordinatio* III, suppl., dist. 37 in Scotus 1997, 203). The divine will is thereby fully determined by this necessary truth. So not even an omnipotent God could, for example, command that we hate God, or that we put others above God, or that we not worship God.

The second source of obligations is the divine will. In other words, some obligations arise as a result of God's positive commands, which proceed from the divine will. Obligations that arise in connection to the divine will, like those expressed in the second table of the Decalogue, are contingent obligations. They are not necessitated by the dictates of God's perfect perception of necessary truth, though they are exceedingly consonant with it. Hence they are not immutable and, as such, can admit to dispensation.

For example, Scotus takes the infamous acts of the patriarchs (e.g., Abraham's binding of Isaac, the Israelites' despoiling of Egypt, and Hosea's situation with Gomer) to represent clear cases where the commandments of the second table were fully and robustly dispensed from. But notice the sunlight that this puts between the Subtle Doctor and the Angelic Doctor. For Aquinas, the acts of the patriarchs were entailed by the divine reason, and thus were not actually cases of theft

76

or murder or adultery on final analysis. That is, the injunctions against murder and theft and adultery were never revoked—the specific acts of the patriarchs in question, despite appearances to the contrary, were simply *not* cases of murder, theft, or adultery, as indicated by the divine command. Scotus seems to have something like that sort of Thomistic explanation in mind when he writes that if one assumes that the second table of the Decalogue is immutable,

> then one would have to explain away those [biblical] texts where God seems to have given a dispensation. One way of doing this is to claim that, though a dispensation could be granted to an act that falls under a generic description [like killing in general], it could never be given insofar as it is prohibited according to the intention of the commandment [e.g., killing an innocent neighbor], and hence [killing an unjust aggressor, for example] would not be against the prohibition. Put another way, an act that is inordinate cannot become well ordered, but an act insofar as it violates a prohibition is inordinate. Therefore, it cannot be subject to dispensation insofar as it is against a prohibition. (*Ordinatio* III, suppl., dist. 37 in Scotus 1997, 200)

Scotus rejects this way of handling things, precisely because he thinks the biblical texts in question clearly indicate that God made full-stop dispensations from the relevant injunctions, and, thus, rendered specific acts that would have otherwise been impermissibly permissible—and not merely under generic descriptions but also under more specific descriptions. Scotus holds, for example, that Abraham's intention to kill Isaac was an act that, absent the divine command, would have been impermissible. He continues,

> My question is this. Granted that all the circumstance are the same in regard to this act of killing a man except the circumstances of its being prohibited in one case and not prohibited in another, could God cause the act which is circumstantially the same, but performed by different individuals, to be prohibited and illicit

in one case and not prohibited but licit in the other? If so, then he can dispense unconditionally, just as he changed the old law when he gave a new law. . . . But that he did so is clear in the case of Abraham and many other cases. (*Ordinatio* III, suppl., dist. 37 in Scotus 1997, 200–201)

So for Scotus, the commands of the second table of the Decalogue are contingent. Although they are harmonious with the necessary first precepts of the natural law in the strict sense, they are not entailed by them. And the fact that there are other ways God could have commanded us with respect to the matters covered in the second table is demonstrated by the simple fact that there are other ways that God *has* commanded, according to Scotus. The other ways that God could have (and has) commanded would also be (and were) harmonious with the first table of the law. God is constrained only in that the nature of God's goodness and wisdom makes it impossible for God to command in ways that are not exceedingly harmonious with the first precepts. However, God's will is free to choose among any number of possibilities, each of which is consonant with the first precepts of the natural law in the strict sense.

Obviously enough, the second source of moral obligations, from which the second table of the Decalogue arises, is precisely why Scotus is sometimes taken to be a proponent of voluntarism or DCT. And to be sure, it is clear that he at least moves in the direction of DCT. But the first source of moral obligations, from which the first table of the Decalogue arises, is precisely why Scotus is not a proponent of a thoroughgoing or unalloyed DCT, since he does not contend that the first source fully reduces to the second source. Ultimately, then, it seems fair to say that Scotus holds something like a *two-source* theory concerning the metaphysical foundations of morality. And for that reason, if for no other, Scotus represents a clear—if not clean—break from Aquinas's NLT.

Notes

1 All subsequent references to Aquinas's *Summa* will follow the standard citation format [ST #, q. #, a. #] and, additionally, cite page numbers from Aquinas (2002), except where noted otherwise.

2 For more on this point, see also Stillner (1993, 231).

3 To be clear, Idziak does not claim that this argument is endorsed by Aquinas, only that it is found in Aquinas.

4 We acknowledge, with trepidation, that our interpretation appears to conflict with the presentation of a similar matter in Stump (2003, 310–11). There, Stump cites ST IIa–IIae q. 57, a. 2, ad. 3, according to which divine law "has partly to do with those things which are naturally just but whose justice is hidden from human beings, and partly with those things which become just by divine institution. And so divine justice (*ius*) can be divided by these two [categories] in the same way as human justice. For in divine law, there are certain things which are prescribed because they are good and prohibited because they are evil, and certain other things which are good because they are prescribed and evil because they are prohibited."

5 Ultimately, we think that Boyd's reflections about the priority of the divine intellect to the divine will are enough to show why M. V. Dougherty has failed to show that Aquinas affirms a DCT of meta-ethics. Dougherty notes that Aquinas affirms that the obligation to obey God's commands is *per se notum*. See Dougherty (2002, 154ff.). But even though we fully concede this point, that point is not enough to qualify Aquinas as a proponent of DCT: if Boyd is correct, the divine command would simply *reiterate* what is determined by the divine intellect. In other words, the divine command does not cause or constitute or otherwise provide the ontological ground for the moral obligation in question.

6 For more on this connection, see Stump (2003, 92–130; esp. at 127–28).

7 All subsequent references to Scotus's texts will follow the standard citation format of the relevant primary source and, additionally, cite page numbers from Scotus (1997) as well, except where otherwise noted.

8 We remain unclear whether, for Scotus, the multiple human orders or systems that God could have used to direct the commands of the second table all assume that humans have the particular kind of biology and psychology that God created us to have. Supposing God could have made humans with very different bodies and psychological

dispositions, then the range of fitting orders to which God might have directed us increases even further.

9 For a helpful discussion of this distinction, see also Veldhuis (2000, 225).

References

Aquinas, Thomas. 1954. *Questiones Disputatae de Veritate*. Translated by Robert W. Schmidt, SJ. Chicago: Henry Regnery. Available online: https://isidore.co/aquinas/QDdeVer.htm (accessed on 7 March 2022).

———. 2002. *Thomas Aquinas: On Law, Morality, and Politics*. 2nd ed. Translated by Richard J. Regan. Edited by William P. Baumgarth and Richard J. Regan. Indianapolis: Hackett.

Boyd, Craig. 1998. "Is Thomas Aquinas a Divine Command Theorist?" *Modern Schoolman* 75 (3): 209–26.

Dougherty, M. V. 2002. "Thomas Aquinas and Divine Command Theory." *Proceedings of the American Catholic Philosophical Association* 76:153–64.

Hare, John E. 2000. "Scotus on Morality and Nature." *Medieval Philosophy and Theology* 9 (1): 15–38.

———. 2009. *God and Morality: A Philosophical History*. Malden, MA: Wiley-Blackwell.

———. 2015. *God's Command*. New York: Oxford University Press.

Idziak, Janine Marie. 1989. "In Search of 'Good Positive Reasons' in Favor of an Ethics of Divine Command: A Catalog of Arguments." *Faith and Philosophy* 6 (1): 47–64.

Ingham, Mary Beth, and Mechthild Dryer. 2004. *The Philosophical Vision of John Duns Scotus*. Washington, DC: Catholic University of America Press.

Möhle, Hannes. 2003. "Scotus's Theory of Natural Law." In *The Cambridge Companion to Duns Scotus*, edited by Thomas Williams, 312–31. Cambridge: Cambridge University Press.

Quinn, Philip L. 1990. "The Recent Revival of Divine Command Ethics." *Philosophy and Phenomenological Research* 50 (supplement): 345–65.

Rooney, Paul. 1995. "Divine Commands and Arbitrariness." *Religious Studies* 31 (2): 149–65.

Scotus, John Duns. 1997. *Duns Scotus on the Will & Morality*. Translated by Allan B. Wolter, OFM. Edited by William A. Frank. Washington, DC: Catholic University of America Press.

Stillner, Brian. 1993. "Who Can Understand Abraham? The Relation of God and Morality in Kierkegaard and Aquinas." *Journal of Religious Ethics* 21 (2): 221–45.

Stump, Eleonore. 2003. *Aquinas.* New York: Routledge.

Veldhuis, Henri. 2000. "Ordained and Absolute Power in Scotus' Ordinatio I 44." *Vivarium* 38 (2): 222–30.

 CHAPTER 4

God's *Will* as the Foundation of Morality

A Medieval Historical Perspective

Janine Marie Idziak

ABSTRACT: Theological voluntarism places the foundation of morality in the will of God. The formulation of such a thesis warrants further refinement. Different formulations of theological voluntarism were put forward in medieval philosophical theology involving the relation of God's will to the divine intellect (reason) in determining ethical status. The fourteenth-century Franciscan Andrew of Neufchateau maintained a purely voluntaristic theory in which it is God's will alone (and not the divine intellect) that determines ethical status. Subsequently Pierre d'Ailly worked with a divine will that is identical with the divine intellect in a strong sense while still maintaining that it is properly assigned to the divine will to be an obligatory law. Later, Jean Gerson, a student of Pierre d'Ailly, spoke explicitly of God's will and reason together as involved in God's activity in the ethical realm. In this paper, we set out these three different formulations of theological voluntarism, tracing the evolution of medieval formulations of theological voluntarism. Although the paper is historical in nature, we conclude with some reflections on how contemporary philosophers and theologians interested in theological voluntarism might profit from the study of this historical literature.

Introduction

An ethics of divine commands maintains that ethical status is dependent on the commands of God. But to say that ethical status is determined by divine commands is a thesis standing in need of further specification, for we have not yet been told what it is in the divine nature that is responsible for making those determinations. An ethics of divine commands has often been cast as theological voluntarism, in which divine commands are regarded as expressions of some aspect of God's will (Quinn 2006). As Robert Adams has observed, "the two concepts [of 'divine command' and 'God's will'] often seem interchangeable in theistic ethics, and believers may think of their ethical reflection as an attempt to 'discern the will of God'" (1999, 258).

In the contemporary literature, there have been attempts to further refine the description of the role of God's will in determining ethical status (Murphy 1998; Quinn 1999). For example, a distinction has traditionally been made between the *antecedent* and *consequent* wills of God—that is, between "God's preference regarding a particular issue considered rather narrowly in itself, other things being equal" and "God's preference regarding the matter, all things considered" (Quinn 1999, 55). Working within this framework, Quinn has proposed that a sufficiently rich and nuanced conception of God's antecedent will "will allow us to identify the ground of [moral] obligation with some of its activities" (55). Or again, Mark Murphy (1998, 2019) has explored whether theological voluntarism should be formulated in terms of *God willing that the agent be morally obligated to perform a particular action* or in terms of *God willing that the agent perform that action*. Recently some philosophers have explored whether the act of the divine will requisite to determining ethical status is to be understood as some mental act such as choosing, intending, preferring, or wishing (Murphy 2019). Beyond such discussions, Murphy makes an important methodological point: as well as answering objections against the ethical theory in question and providing good positive reasons in support of it, the task of determining the specific formulation of it merits attention (Murphy 1998).

Study of the historical literature reveals that different formulations of theological voluntarism were put forward in medieval philosophical theology, specifically, involving the relation of God's will
to the divine intellect (reason) in determining ethical status. The
fourteenth-century Franciscan Andrew of Neufchateau maintained
a purely voluntaristic theory in which it is God's will alone (and not
the divine intellect) that determines ethical status. Subsequently
Pierre d'Ailly worked with a divine will that is identical with the divine
intellect in a strong sense while still maintaining that it is properly
assigned to the divine will to be an obligatory law. Later, Jean Gerson,
a student of Pierre d'Ailly, spoke explicitly of God's will and reason
together as involved in God's activity in the ethical realm.

This paper will set out the formulations of theological voluntarism developed by Andrew of Neufchateau, Pierre d'Ailly, and
Jean Gerson, tracing the evolution of the formulation of theological
voluntarism that occurred in the medieval literature. Although the
orientation of this paper is historical rather than argumentative,
we will, in the final section of the paper, offer some reflections
on how contemporary philosophers and theologians interested in
theological voluntarism might profit from the study of this historical
literature.

Andrew of Neufchateau

In his treatise *De Veritate*, q. 23, a. 6, Thomas Aquinas considers the
question of whether justice as found among created things depends
simply upon the divine will (1952). In setting out his own position on
this issue, Aquinas maintains that "the will does not have the character of a first rule"; rather, the will is "a rule which has a rule" for the
reason that "it is directed by reason and the intellect" (647). Additionally, according to Aquinas, the direction of the will by reason
and the intellect holds true "not only in us but also in God" (647).
Hence "the first thing upon which the essential character of all justice
depends is the wisdom of the divine intellect" (647). On the other

hand, "to say that justice depends simply upon the will is to say that the divine will does not proceed according to the order of wisdom" (647). To say this, Aquinas asserts, "is blasphemous" (647).

Aquinas's intellectualist position contrasts with a medieval ethical voluntarism described by the Renaissance scholastic Francisco Suárez in *De Legibus ac Deo Legislatore* II.6 (2013). Following Gregory of Rimini's distinction between an *indicative* and an *imperative* precept, prohibition, or law in *Super Primum et Secundum Sententiarum* II, d. 34–37, q. 1, a. 2, corr. 2 (1980), Suárez defines a notion of perceptive law that requires an *act of will* on the part of a superior issuing the command (2013). It is within the context of addressing the issue of whether natural law is *perceptive* law that Suárez describes the position of theological voluntarism: "The second opinion . . . is that the natural law consists entirely in a divine command or prohibition proceeding from the will of God as the Author and Ruler of nature. . . . These authorities also add that the whole basis of good and evil in matters pertaining to the law of nature is in God's will, and not in a judgment of reason, even on the part of God Himself, nor in the very things which are prescribed or forbidden by that law" (2013, 209–10).

The position described by Suárez is an explicit thesis of the fourteenth-century Franciscan Andrew of Neufchateau. In *Primum Scriptum Sententiarum* d. 48, q. 1, a. 1, De Secundo, concl. 1 and d. 48, q. 1, a. 2, concl. 2, Andrew argues that all varieties of goodness are good because the divine will so freely wills and decrees (1997, 9, 27). Subsequently, in d. 48, q. 1, a. 2, concl. 3, Andrew proposes,

THIRD CONCLUSION: For no activity of a rational creature which is simply good and just is it the case that the divine will wills and decrees it to be good and just because it is good and just in itself by nature. In other words, because first it is antecedently dictated and judged to be good and just by the divine intellect, so that it is not the divine will as will but the dictate of the divine intellect which is the first reason and rule or measure of his activity which is simply good and just. (35)

Why Andrew would put forward such a thesis is understandable within the broader context of the intellectual history of the period.

In *Virtues of the Will: The Transformation of Ethics in the Late Thirteenth Century*, Bonnie Kent sets out characteristics of voluntarism regarding the human person that emerged in the latter years of the thirteenth century. According to Kent, "Perhaps the most familiar is that the will is nobler than or superior to the intellect" (1995, 95–96). Kent points out as "other earmarks of voluntarism . . . the claims that beatitude or happiness consists more in an activity of will than in an activity of intellect, that man's freedom derives more from his will than his rationality, that the will is free to act against the intellect's judgment, and that the will, not the intellect, commands the body and the other powers of the soul" (96). Kent suggests that "these doctrines can . . . be taken as points of division between Franciscan thought and Thomism, or more generally, between voluntarism and intellectualism" (96).

This division is vividly illustrated in John Quidort's discussion of the question of whether the will can will and choose against reason's dictate in his commentary on the *Sentences* (Kent 1995). The first opinion reported is "that the will can choose nothing against the judgment of reason, so that when reason proposes two actions and judges that one of them ought to be chosen, it is impossible for the will not to choose that and to will the opposite; and that the will can do nothing against the judgment of reason, because otherwise it would not be a rational appetite. For this reason people say that the will is not free in desiring except because reason is free in judging" (106). The second opinion that Quidort reports is "that however great and firm be the judgment of reason that this thing should be chosen, nevertheless the will can, with its own freedom, choose the opposite, so that the will's freedom comes not from the free judgment of reason but from and on account of [the will] itself" (Kent 1995, 106). As Kent comments, the first opinion is basically that of Thomas Aquinas, while the second represents the voluntarist school of thought (106).

An important piece of the theological and philosophical climate of this period that favored the voluntarist viewpoint is the

Condemnations of 1277 at Paris. One group of condemned propositions appears "to detract from human freedom by regarding the
will as a passive power which must be actualized by something else"
(Wippel 1977, 192). In this group are propositions concerning the
relationship between will and intellect. For the present purposes,
noteworthy is the condemnation of the proposition that "the will of
a human being is necessitated by its knowledge just as is the appetite
of a brute" (Wippel 1995, 256). Also condemned is the proposition that
"will necessarily pursues that which is firmly believed by reason; and
that it cannot withhold consent (lit. abstain) from that which reason
dictates," such being "the nature of the will" (256–57).

Marilyn McCord Adams describes similar voluntarist strains of
thought in William of Ockham and Duns Scotus:

> True to his Aristotelian inspiration, Ockham consistently presents
> will as rational appetite. . . . Nevertheless, Ockham denies that any
> deliverance of reason *determines* the will's action (inaction), for the
> principal systematic reason that then the will's action (inaction)
> would not be within the agent's power and so would not be imput-
> able. Scotus had already challenged Giles of Rome and Godfrey of
> Fontaines precisely on this ground—the determination of the will
> by the intellect would turn the former into a passive rather than an
> active power; for Scotus, no matter what reason dictates, the will
> retains power to act or not. This is not enough control for Ockham,
> who insists that *experience* shows that "no matter how much reason
> dictates something, the will still has power to will or not to will or to
> nill it." Moreover, systematic considerations require it: the power of
> inaction contrary to reason opens the possibility of sins of omission,
> but created will power must extend further to sins of commission.
> In the same vein, Ockham finds it counterintuitive to explain sins
> of incontinence and malice in terms of ignorance; rather they are
> instances of action against full knowledge. (1999, 254–55)

Adams's commentary lays out motivations for holding the position
that reason does not determine the will. First, if this were the case,

"then the will's action (inaction) would not be within the agent's power and so would not be imputable" (1999, 254–55). Kent reports the same line of argument for the voluntarist movement: "Moral responsibility was thought to require freedom of will, and freedom was thought to be incompatible with necessity, including the necessitation of the will by rational judgment" so that "if we are to be held responsible for our actions, we must be able to act against what our own deliberation or judgment tells us to do" (1995, 113). Moreover, it is claimed that the ability of the will to act against reason is required to make sense of the phenomenon of sin. As Kent points out, "Voluntarists worried that if the will were determined to choose in accordance with reason's judgment of what is good, all wrongdoing would stem principally from ignorance or mistake, so that the appropriate response would be not punishment or blame but education" (115). However, as Gonsalvus of Spain argued, no ignorance preceded the sins of Adam and Eve and of Satan; rather, they sinned against conscience and such sins are possible only if the will can act against what reason dictates should be done (143). Indeed, "Gonsalvus suggests that experience establishes the same point" (143). For, "when people act against conscience, they feel remorse; but we would never have grounds for remorse if we always did what we believed at the time to be good *simpliciter*" (143).

In sum, the Franciscan Andrew of Neufchateau formulated his ethical theory within the framework of an intellectual culture that attached great importance to the faculty of will. For our purpose, of particular interest is the contention that the human will is free to act against the intellect's judgment or, in other words, that the human intellect does not determine the actions of the human will—a position not put forward without supporting reasons. One can see Andrew of Neufchateau extrapolating this view of human action into the realm of divine action in his formulation of a divine voluntarist ethical theory.

In fact, In *Primum Scriptum Sententiarum*, d. 48, q. 1, a. 2, concl. 3, Andrew supports his particular formulation of theological voluntarism by posing it as an instance of a broader voluntarist thesis about the nature of divine action in general—namely, that "for no outward activity of God is it the case that the divine will wills and decrees it because first it is antecedently dictated and judged by the divine intellect as it were from reason antecedently moving and stating why it must be done so" (1997, 39). Andrew's supporting arguments for this voluntarist position on divine action in general fall into two categories.

The first set focuses on unacceptable consequences of rejecting the voluntarist position. Andrew argues that "the divine will would [otherwise] be necessitated to act outwardly or it would be inconsistent with and deviate from reason antecedently dictating" (1997, 39). This is actually a shortened version of an argument found in Thomas Bradwardine's *De Causa Dei* I, 21 in arguments given for a negative answer to the question of whether reason moves and directs the divine will: "If reason moves the divine will, that reason is not caused in God by any creature . . . but it is intrinsic and essential to him; therefore it is necessary. And therefore the will of God necessarily agrees with it; for otherwise there could be an opposition of will and reason in God. . . . And so it would be the case that God necessarily acts with respect to things outside himself, whatever he does" ([1618] 1964, 230).

A second argument, likewise a variant of one found in Bradwardine's *De Causa Dei* I, 21 ([1618] 1964), contends that "God could not work otherwise or make better things" (Andrew of Neufchateau 1997, 39). The reason for this consequence is again connected with necessitation versus freedom of the divine will: "For if reason so dictates, the will necessarily will do it; and if reason does not so dictate, the will cannot do it. The dictating, however, will not be free since it is understood prior to every dictate of the free divine will" (39). Thus, a thread running through both lines of argument is opposition to the divine will being necessitated in its activity, specifically, *necessitated* by reason.

The second category of arguments calls our attention to cases in which reason does not decide an issue but the decision falls to will. Andrew makes reference to the biblical text Romans 9:20–21 regarding the potter of clay having the right to make out of the same lump of clay one vessel for noble use and another for ordinary use (Andrew of Neufchateau 1997). Bradwardine's commentary on this text in *De Causa Dei* I, 21 sheds light on its relevance as illustrating "the indifference of reason for different deeds" ([1618] 1964, 231). This concept is a theme continued in the argument that follows: "Fourth, in the case of two things, *a* and *b*, which are producible and equally possible, there is no reason why this one is produced and not that one except primarily because it pleases the divine will" (Andrew of Neufchateau 1997, 39).

This theme is further continued in a line of argument Andrew offers in support of his ethical thesis specifically. Again borrowing from Bradwardine, Andrew puts forward an analogical line of argument pointing out cases in human experience in which reason does not and cannot decide an issue, yet human beings perform just actions from a sheer choice of will. Suppose, for example, that someone has been given the power to pardon one, and only one, of two persons placed under a death sentence, and that no relevant differences can be found between them. In such a case, there is no better reason for pardoning the one than for pardoning the other. Nevertheless, the pardoner justly frees the one whom he chooses to pardon, although reason did not antecedently move his will to make this choice. The same kind of situation occurs when someone is in a position to bestow a gift on only one of two or more persons who are equally worthy of receiving it (Andrew of Neufchateau 1997; Bradwardine [1618] 1964). Thus, since we allow that justness can stem from the human will unmoved by reason, then surely the same can hold true of the divine will in determining what is good and just.

When Andrew considers objections to his formulation of theological voluntarism in d. 48. q. 1, a. 2, concl. 3, the very first objection presented is the intellectualist position on divine action in general—namely, that "God may do nothing unless from reason antecedently dictating and judging and as it were stating why it is that he so acts" (1997, 39). It is noteworthy that subsequent objections, for the most part, do not deal with ethical considerations specifically but focus generically on God acting from reason (39–45). This clearly indicates how Andrew of Neufchateau's ethics is embedded in the medieval debate about voluntarism versus intellectualism.

91

Concomitantly, the plausibility of Andrew's particular formulation of theological voluntarism is related to the plausibility (or implausibility) of the philosophical position of voluntarism.

Pierre d'Ailly

Andrew of Neufchateau commented on the *Sentences* at the University of Paris c. 1358–59 (Idziak 1997). Pierre d'Ailly engaged in the same exercise at the University of Paris in 1377 (Oakley 1964). In *Principium in Primum Sententiarum*, d'Ailly offers an argument in support of God as the foundation of morality that has as its conclusion that the divine will is the first law or rule in the class of obligatory laws (2013). In *Principium in Secundum Sententiarum*, d'Ailly reports that a certain Brother Jacob [of Chiva] took issue with the conclusion of this argument precisely in the respect of representing a *voluntarist* position. This objector claims that "the divine will ought not properly to be called a law or rule" (2013) and brings forward Augustine's descriptions of the first and eternal law to demonstrate that such law belongs to the divine intellect (2013).

When confronting this objection to a divine voluntarist ethics, d'Ailly's response is very different from that of Andrew of Neufchateau. While Andrew is insistent that it is the divine will and not the divine intellect that makes the laws of ethics, d'Ailly invokes the identity of will and intellect in God:

> I will advance four propositions against this Reverend Father.
>
> The first proposition is that the divine will and the divine intellect or reason are, just as much formally as really, the same in every way, nor is there a distinction between them in any way. . . .
>
> The second proposition is that whatever is suitable by its nature to the divine will is suitable to the divine intellect. . . .
>
> The third proposition is that if the divine intellect is an obligatory law or rule, so also is the divine will, and vice versa. . . .

The fourth proposition, not precluded by the previous claims, is this: According to the mode of speaking of saints and teachers, it is more properly assigned to the divine will than to the divine intellect to be an obligatory law. Thus this is true per se, *The divine will is an obligatory law*, and not this, *The divine intellect is an obligatory law*. And this is the reason why: Just as the mode of speaking of teachers is that the divine will, and not the [divine] intellect, is the effective cause of things on account of the fact that whatever the will wills exists or is done, and not whatever the intellect understands, so it is in what is to be proven, viz., whatever the will wills to be obligatory, is obligatory, while this is not so with respect to the intellect. So this inference holds good, *The divine will wills that Socrates be obligated to do A, therefore Socrates is obligated to do A*; nevertheless this one does not hold good, *the divine intellect understands Socrates to be obligated to do A, therefore Socrates is obligated to do A*. And therefore this true per se, *The divine will is an obligatory law*, and not this, *The divine intellect is an obligatory law*, although either one is true. (2013, 56, 58–59)

D'Ailly's response can be understood as having two parts. The first is composed of propositions one, two, and three, and the second part, of proposition four.

D'Ailly begins by pointing out that God is a different kind of being from human beings. While humans are a composite of various parts and faculties, the being of God is a unity. Moreover, this unity obtains in a strong sense. There is no *real* distinction between the divine will and the divine intellect, nor are they even *formally* distinct. In other words, the divine will and the divine intellect are not in actuality separate entities, nor are they in principle separable, even by the divine power itself. Further, the unity of intellect and will in God is such that they do not even possess different definitions; hence, it is not the case that the divine will is conceivable differently from and without the divine intellect, or vice versa (cf. Grajewski 1944).

The objector takes issue with attributing the status of a law or rule to the divine faculty of will. But given the peculiar identity of will and intellect in God, if it turns out that the divine will is an obligatory law, then so is the divine intellect; and if, on the other hand, the divine intellect is to be designated as an obligatory law, then the divine will is also an obligatory law. In fact, given the ontological and definitional identity of the divine will and intellect, there is a sense in which insisting on designating the divine intellect (rather than the divine will) as the first obligatory law, or vice versa, is simply misguided.

D'Ailly refines and complicates this position in the fourth proposition. The meaning of this proposition, and of d'Ailly's accompanying comments, can be elucidated through a subsequent discussion in *Quaestiones super libros sententiarum* I, q. 6, a. 2 (d'Ailly [1490] 1968).[1] Against his claim of the formal identity of intellect and will in God, d'Ailly records the following objection: the divine intellect and the divine will are not formally the same because of the fact that some things are suitable per se to the divine intellect that are not suitable per se to the divine will, or vice versa. For example, God understands through his intellect and not through his will, and God wills through his will and not through his intellect. Or again, God is the efficient cause of things through his will, not through his intellect. And when it comes to the issue of sin, God knows sins but does not will them ([1490] 1968).

D'Ailly replies to this point of objection by distinguishing two senses in which it may be claimed that something is suitable per se to the divine intellect but not to the divine will, or vice versa. First, this contention may be interpreted as the claim that something is in some way suitable to the *thing (res)* that is the divine intellect that is not suitable to the *thing* that is the divine will. This ontological interpretation contrasts with a linguistic interpretation: some proposition in which some predicate is applied to the *term (terminus)* "divine intellect" is true per se while the proposition in which the same predicate is applied to the *term* "divine will" is not true per se (d'Ailly [1490] 1968).

Working on the ontological level, d'Ailly denies that it is ever the case that something is suitable per se to the divine intellect but not to the divine will, or vice versa. Thus, on this level, it must be conceded that God understands through his will, and that he wills through his intellect, and that he is the efficient cause of things through his intellect, and so on (d'Ailly [1490] 1968).

Operating on the linguistic level, however, the situation is different. If it were the case that the terms *intellect, will, to understand, to will*, and so on had as their exact meaning that thing (res) that God is, then such propositions as *God knows evils* and *God wills evils* would be equally true. However, the terms in question are also connotative. To continue with the same example, the proposition *God wills sins* means, *according to our ordinary way of speaking*, that God does something wrongly or as he ought not. In other words, the proposition in question *connotes* that the thing that God is does something wrongly or as he ought not, a kind of behavior that can only belong to a creature. On the other hand, the proposition *God knows evils or sins* does not have this connotation. For this reason, the second proposition has been allowed but the first denied (d'Ailly [1490] 1968).

Against this background, d'Ailly's fourth proposition and his accompanying comments may be understood in the following way. From an ontological point of view, it is just as true that the divine intellect is an obligatory law as that the divine will is an obligatory law. From a linguistic point of view, however, it is more properly assigned to the divine will than to the divine intellect to be an obligatory law. The proposition *The divine will is an obligatory law* is true per se, while the proposition *The divine intellect is an obligatory law* is not. This difference obtains because of the connotative aspect of the terms in question. To say *God wills x to be obligatory* connotes that x is in fact obligatory, for any x whatever. On the other hand, not everything that God may be said to know falls into the category of the ethically obligatory. Hence to say *God knows x* does not connote the obligatoriness of x.

D'Ailly's ethics may be characterized as *voluntarist* in that he wishes to speak of the divine will, and not the divine intellect, as the first obligatory law. For the sake of distinguishing the varieties of theological voluntarism developed by medieval philosophical theologians, it is important to note that d'Ailly's voluntarism is of a different sort than that articulated by Andrew of Neufchateau. While Andrew insists on the priority of the divine will over the divine intellect in the ethical realm, d'Ailly's ethics works with a divine will that is identical with the divine intellect in a strong sense. D'Ailly's designation of the divine will rather than the divine intellect as the first obligatory law is not ontologically grounded but is a choice dictated by linguistic considerations.

Jean Gerson

Jean Gerson was a student of Pierre d'Ailly and, like him, a chancellor at the University of Paris (Connolly 1928). In Gerson's writings can be found passages indicating that he regards God as the foundation of morality.

On some occasions, Gerson speaks of the divine will alone in an ethical context. In *Regulae Morales* 2, he states that "all obligation is finally reduced to the dictate of divine free choice so willing to obligate a creature" (Gerson 1973b, 95).[2] Or again, in *Definitiones Terminorum Theologiae Moralis*, he says that "the first law is the good pleasure or the supreme will of the Lord God prescribing to the things established by it their ends and the movements and operations towards them" (Gerson 1973a, 134). Or yet again, in *De Vita Spirituali Animae*, lectio II, corollarium 5, he states that preceptive natural law gives "notice of the divine will willing a rational human creature to be bound or obliged to the performance or avoidance of something for the attainment of his natural end" (Gerson 1962, 135).

On the other hand, we also find the following affirmation in Gerson's treatise *De Vita Spirituali Animae*, lectio I, corollarium 10: "It is probable that no act of a creature is, of itself and intrinsically, good with moral or meritorious goodness or similarly evil except with respect to the divine reason and will. For clearly the divine will and reason deem a human being worthy for one kind of act and render him unworthy for another. . . . And from this point we are consequently easily able to see how nothing is evil except because it is prohibited by God and how nothing good except because it is accepted by God" (1962, 123–24).

It is clear that Gerson here presents God as determining ethical status. For our purposes, what is noteworthy about this text is that both the divine will and the divine reason are named in God's establishment of ethical status. In a later passage in lectio III of the same treatise, Gerson comments that "it is established that in moral practices right reason is not prior to the will, so that it is not the case that God wills to give his laws to a rational creature because first his right reason judged that this ought to be done, but rather the contrary" (1962, 141). Gerson then goes on to state that "therefore it seems to be a more orthodox and unencumbered position if we say that neither one is prior to the other in God" (141). He supports this position by an analogy: "Just as, in a similar situation, it is not the case that God judges that Socrates will walk because it is so in external reality, nor properly the contrary, but rather, they are correlative and accompany each other in a certain measure by inference" (141).

Moreover, Gerson presents in lectio II of this treatise a definition of "divine law" and a subsequent exegesis of it, which makes very explicit that both God's right reason and God's will are involved in God's obligatory power:

> Preceptive divine law is a true sign revealed to a rational creature which gives notification of divine right reason willing that creature to be held or bound to doing or not doing something for the sake of him being deemed worthy to attain eternal life and to avoid damnation. There follows in the description, 'which gives notification of divine right reason willing that creature to be held or bound to doing or not doing something' because a question is raised by certain persons, *What is the obligatory principle in God, right reason or will*? Here both are affirmed because neither right reason without the will, nor the contrary, constitutes the totality of obligation in God. (1962, 130–31)

Thus, Gerson took a step beyond d'Ailly. While d'Ailly works with a divine will that is identical with the divine intellect in a strong sense, he still maintains that it is more properly assigned to the divine will than to the divine intellect to be an obligatory law. Gerson speaks explicitly of God's will and reason together as involved in God's activity in the ethical realm.

Concluding Reflections

John Haldane authored a paper entitled "Voluntarism and Realism in Medieval Ethics" that focuses on the relationship between God and ethics as presented in the Euthyphro dilemma. He cites Thomas Aquinas, Duns Scotus, and William of Ockham as the main contributors to the voluntarism/realism dispute in the medieval period, with emphasis on Ockham for the voluntarist position (Haldane 1989). *The Cambridge Companion to Medieval Ethics*, published in 2019, includes some consideration of the extent to which the moral law was thought to depend on God's will or intellect (Williams 2019). From the Christian tradition, it is again Aquinas, Scotus, and Ockham who are discussed (Hagedorn 2019). Such sources suffer from a knowledge gap in ignoring the subsequent discussions of Andrew of Neufchateau, Pierre d'Ailly, and Jean Gerson. Thus, this paper serves to point out a lacuna in contemporary understanding of the medieval literature and makes a contribution to medieval scholarship and the history of ethics.

Can contemporary philosophers and theologians who are interested in the position of theological voluntarism gain any insights from the study of this neglected medieval literature?

A recurrent criticism of theological voluntarism is that grounding ethical status in the will of God makes morality arbitrary, capricious, and even irrational (Haldane 1989; Murphy 2019). Andrew of Neufchateau's formulation of theological voluntarism, in which ethical status is determined by God's will alone without an antecedent dictate and judgment of the divine intellect, seems particularly vulnerable to this line of criticism. It is noteworthy that both Pierre d'Ailly and Jean Gerson moved away from this formulation of theological voluntarism.

In the course of his work on Gabriel Biel, the medievalist Heiko Oberman has proposed that the medieval concept of divine simplicity can rescue the theological voluntarist from the objection of arbitrariness:

> Still this does not answer the charge of those who claim that this legal structure of the set order is not an expression of God's holiness and inner being but the result of an arbitrary and changeable decision of God's unguided will . . .
>
> . . . Against the Thomistic emphasis on the priority of God's intellect, the priority of God's will is not stressed as much as the simplicity of God's being and the resulting unity of his intellect and essence. As the simplicity of God's being also implies a unity of essence and will, God's very essence guarantees the unbreakable relation and cooperation of intellect and will in God's *opera ad extra*. Biel constantly tries to make clear that, whereas the will of God is the immediate cause of every act, these acts are certainly no arbitrary products of God's will alone. On the contrary, God's will operates according to God's essential wisdom, though this may be hidden from man. (1983, 98–99)

There has been considerable debate about the doctrine of divine simplicity among contemporary philosophers of religion (Dolezal 2011). Some have questioned its plausibility (Dolezal 2011), but the doctrine has also had its defenders (Stump and Kretzmann 1985; Vallicella 1992; Brower 2008; Dolezal 2011). Indeed, Stump and Kretzmann (1985) have proposed that the divine simplicity can serve as a tool for understanding the relation between God and ethics and for resolving the Euthyphro dilemma.

Prescinding from particular formulations of the doctrine of divine simplicity and problems with them, one can ask a more global question of whether there is a theological insight that the doctrine of divine simplicity is trying to capture. Thomas Morris, for example, while rejecting the thesis of divine "property simplicity," comments that "it is still possible that the doctrine is an attempt to express a true mystery concerning the real metaphysical unity of God" for "it is sensible to think there is a special kind of integrity to the being of God" (2002, 117–18). Or again, Millard Erickson has observed that "as foreign as the concept of divine simplicity seems to modern persons, it was formulated to express an important truth about God: the unity of his nature, the harmony of his attributes, and the fact that his actions involve the whole of what he is" (1998, 232).

D'Ailly captures the sense of the metaphysical unity and integrity of God's being in maintaining that the divine will that we designate as the obligatory moral law is identical with the divine intellect. Similarly, in speaking of God's will and reason together as involved in God's activity in the ethical realm, Gerson reflects the belief that God's actions involve "the whole of what he is."

There may be reason for specifying God's "will" as the foundation of morality (rather than speaking generically of what God commands; Quinn 1999). Nevertheless, the evolution of the formulation of theological voluntarism in the medieval literature may serve to caution us against slicing off God's will from the rest of God's being in formulating the theory. Such an approach does not do justice to the being of God. Any adequate formulation of theological voluntarism must address the relation of God's will to God's intellect (reason), and for that matter, to other attributes of God (Brown 1963), in determining ethical status.[3]

Notes

1 All translations of d'Ailly's text in this chapter are those of the present author.
2 All translations of Gerson's texts in this chapter are those of the present author.
3 Sections of this paper were originally written with the support of grants from the Pontifical Institute of Mediaeval Studies, the National Endowment for the Humanities, and the American Council of Learned Societies.

References

Adams, Marilyn McCord. 1999. "Ockham on Will, Nature, and Morality." In *The Cambridge Companion to Ockham*, edited by Paul Vincent Spade. Cambridge: Cambridge University Press.

Adams, Robert Merrihew. 1999. *Finite and Infinite Goods.* New York: Oxford University Press.

Andrew of Neufchateau. 1997. *Primum Scriptum Sententiarum.* D. 48, q. 1 & 2. In Andrew of Neufchateau, OFM, *Questions on an Ethics of Divine Commands*, edited and translated by Janine Marie Idziak. Notre Dame, IN: University of Notre Dame Press.

Aquinas, Thomas. 1952. *The 29 Questions on Truth.* Translated by Robert W. Mulligan. Available online: https://documentacatholicaomnia.eu/03d/1225-1274,Thomas_Aquinas_The_29_questions_on_Truth_(Mulligan_Translation),_EN.pdf (accessed on 17 April 2021).

Bradwardine, Thomas. (1618) 1964. *De Causa Dei.* London: Ioannis Billius. Reprint, Frankfurt am Main: Minerva GMBH.

Brower, Jeffrey E. 2008. "Making Sense of Divine Simplicity." *Faith and Philosophy* 25:3–30.

Brown, Patterson. 1963. "Religious Morality." *Mind* 72:235–44.

Connolly, James L. 1928. *John Gerson Reformer and Mystic.* St. Louis: Herder.

d'Ailly, Pierre. (1490) 1968. *Quaestiones Super Libros Sententiarum cum Quibusdam in Fine Adjunctis.* Strassburg. Reprint, Frankfurt: Minerva.

———. 2013. *Questiones Super Primum, Tertium and Quartum Librum Sententiarum.* Vol. 1, *Principia et Questio Circa Prologum.* Edited by Monica Brinzei. Turnhout: Brepols.

Dolezal, James E. 2011. *God without Parts Divine Simplicity and the Metaphysics of God's Absoluteness.* Eugene, OR: Pickwick.

Erickson, Millard J. 1998. *God the Father Almighty: A Contemporary Exploration of the Divine Attributes.* Grand Rapids, MI: Baker Books.

Gerson, Jean. 1962. *De Vita Spirituali Animae.* In *Oeuvres Complètes*, vol. 3, edited by Mgr. Glorieux. Paris: Desclées.

———. 1973a. *Definitiones Terminorum Theologiae Moralis.* In *Oeuvres Complètes*, vol. 9, edited by Mgr. Glorieux. Paris: Desclées. Translation of the text is that of the present author.

———. 1973b. *Regulae Morales.* In *Oeuvres Complètes*, vol. 9, edited by Mgr. Glorieux. Paris: Desclées. Translation of the text is that of the present author.

Grajewski, Maurice J. 1944. *The Formal Distinction of Duns Scotus.* Washington, DC: Catholic University of America Press.

Gregory of Rimini. 1980. *Lectura Super Primum et Secundum Sententiarum.* Vol. 6, *Super Secundum.* Dist. 24–44. Edited by A. Damasus Trapp and Venicio Marcolino. New York: Walter de Gruyter.

Hagedorn, Eric W. 2019. "From Thomas Aquinas to the 1350s." In *The Cambridge Companion to Medieval Ethics,* edited by Thomas Williams, 55–77. Cambridge: Cambridge University Press.

Haldane, John. 1989. "Voluntarism and Realism in Medieval Ethics." *Journal of Medical Ethics* 15:39–44.

Idziak, Janine Marie. 1997. "The Disputed Biography of Andreas de Novo Castro." In Andrew of Neufchateau, OFM, *Questions on an Ethics of Divine Commands,* edited and translated by Janine Marie Idziak, 135–47. Notre Dame, IN: University of Notre Dame Press.

Kent, Bonnie. 1995. *Virtues of the Will: The Transformation of Ethics in the Late Thirteenth Century.* Washington, DC: Catholic University of America Press.

Morris, Thomas V. 2002. *Our Idea of God: An Introduction to Philosophical Theology.* Vancouver: Regent College Publishing.

Murphy, Mark C. 1998. "Divine Command, Divine Will, and Moral Obligation." *Faith and Philosophy* 15:3–27.

——. 2019. "Theological Voluntarism." In *Stanford Encyclopedia of Philosophy.* Available online: https://plato.stanford.edu/entries/voluntarism-theological (accessed on 15 March 2021).

Oakley, Francis. 1964. *The Political Thought of Pierre d'Ailly.* New Haven, CT: Yale University Press.

Oberman, Heiko Augustinus. 1983. *The Harvest of Medieval Theology: Gabriel Biel and Late Medieval Nominalism.* Durham, NC: Labyrinth.

Quinn, Philip L. 1999. "Divine Command Theory." In *The Blackwell Guide to Ethical Theory,* edited by Hugh LaFollette, 53–73. Oxford: Blackwell.

——. 2006. "Theological Voluntarism." In *The Oxford Handbook of Ethical Theory,* edited by David Copp, 63–90. New York: Oxford University Press.

Stump, Eleonore, and Norman Kretzmann. 1985. "Absolute Simplicity." *Faith and Philosophy* 2:353–82.

Suárez, Francisco. 2013. *A Treatise on Laws and God the Lawgiver.* In *Selections from Three Works of Francisco Suarez,* edited by Thomas Pink. Liberty Fund. Available online: https://www.libertyfund.org/books/selections-from-three-works (accessed on 17 April 2021).

Vallicella, William F. 1992. "Divine Simplicity: A New Defense." *Faith and Philosophy* 9:508–25.

Williams, Thomas. 2019. "Will and Intellect." In *The Cambridge Companion to Medieval Ethics*, edited by Thomas Williams, 238–56. Cambridge: Cambridge University Press.

Wippel, John F. 1977. "The Condemnations of 1270 and 1299 at Paris." *Journal of Medieval and Renaissance Studies* 7:169–201.

———. 1995. "Thomas Aquinas and the Condemnation of 1277." *Modern Schoolman* 72:233–72.

CHAPTER 5

Does Darwall's Morality of Accountability Require Moral Realism? (And Would It Be Strengthened by Adding God to the Story?)

C. Stephen Evans

ABSTRACT: Stephen Darwall has developed an account of moral obli-gations as grounded in "second-personal reasons," which was devel-oped in conversation with early modern "theological voluntarists" who were divine command theorists. For Darwall, morality does not require accountability to God; humans as autonomous moral agents are the source of moral obligations. In this paper, I try to show that Darwall is vulnerable to some objections made against divine command theories. There are responses Darwall could make that have parallels to those given by divine command theorists. However, those responses require moral realism, while Darwall's project is often seen as being inspired by metaethical constructivism. Finally, I suggest that Darwall's view could be further strengthened by the addition of God to the story.

In the last two decades, Stephen Darwall has developed what he calls a "juridical account" of moral obligations. The account is inspired by themes in Fichte and Kant, but it is also developed in conversation with early modern "theological voluntarists," such as Pufendorf and Locke, who defended a divine command account of moral obligations. Like these early modern thinkers, Darwall wants to hold that moral obligations are grounded in the demands of persons, that moral obligations are linked to being accountable for such demands, and that persons can be held blameworthy when these obligations are not fulfilled. However, for Darwall, no divine commands are necessary for morality. Rather, the foundations of morality lie in a moral community of equal, autonomous human agents who hold each other accountable.[1]

In this paper, I raise the question as to whether the parallels between Darwall's view and a divine command theory might mean that Darwall's view is vulnerable to some of the objections, such as the Euthyphro problem, which are often raised against a divine command theory. I answer the question by comparing Darwall's view to a contemporary divine command theory, that of Robert Adams. It appears that someone might object to Darwall's view in ways that are similar to the manner in which Adams's divine command theory is often criticized. Such criticisms are not necessarily devastating, as can be seen by examining the way Adams himself responds. Darwall's view could be defended by making moves similar to those Adams makes. However, it appears that the responses would require Darwall to embrace a substantial form of moral realism, a view that is not a cost to Adams since he already accepts the existence of objective value. Such a response also seems possible for Darwall; at least it is logically consistent with his view. There is, however, a cost, in that part of the motivation for Darwall's view seems to lie in a metaethical constructivism that grounds morality in human willing and activity. In conclusion, I suggest that Darwall's view not only would be strengthened by embracing moral realism but would be stronger still if God were brought back into the story. Moral obligations would then be grounded in actual demands (assuming God exists, admittedly a big assumption for many), not merely in the hypothetical demands of an idealized moral community.

Darwall's Defense of a "Juridical" View of Moral Obligations

Darwall has made an impressive case for the role of what he calls "second-personal reasons" as the basis of morality (see especially Darwall 2006). The argument begins with a defense of a "juridical" view of moral obligations. On this view, a moral obligation is not simply an act one has a moral reason to do. Rather, moral obligations derive from claims or demands that persons make on each other: "If all this is correct, then the concept of moral obligation must differ from that of what moral reasons recommend, however categorical or overriding these reasons might be. What fills the gap . . . is the concept of accountability and moral blame. Moral obligations are moral *demands*, and moral demands are whatever we are legitimately *held* to or answerable for, that is, where violations are *blameworthy* if the agent lacks a valid excuse" (Darwall 2013, 43).

The plausibility of Darwall's view gains much of its force from examples of demands that individuals make on one another. His favorite example is someone standing on another person's foot (2006, 5–10). A utilitarian might well say that this is morally wrong just because it is an act that causes needless pain. However, even if this is so, the situation changes if the person whose foot is being stood upon makes a request to the offending party to move the foot. If the offender refuses to move the foot, then the act is wrong in a new way and for a new reason: a justified claim has been ignored and this shows a lack of respect for the person who has made the claim.

This seems perfectly right. In this case, there is an actual claimant and an actual claim. However, although Darwall wants to argue that morality is linked to being accountable to others, it turns out that morality does not rest solely on claims made by actual persons. In the example of someone stepping on someone's foot, we have a case of what Darwall calls a "bipolar obligation," in which there is a reciprocal relationship between two people. Person A makes a request of person B, assuming that B has the competence to recognize the legitimacy of the request and accede to it because of its legitimacy. Person A here has what Darwall calls individual authority, which is an authority grounded in the relation the two people have. There is a relation of moral obligation between two actual persons. Person B may be legitimately blamed for wronging A if B fails to respond to the request.

However, Darwall believes there is a difference between wronging a person who has individual authority and doing wrong simpliciter. All cases of wronging a person with individual authority are wrong simpliciter, but not all cases of doing wrong simpliciter are grounded in individual authority (2013, 24). Doing wrong simpliciter is conceptually linked to a demand that one would be blameworthy for not recognizing, but the demand is not one that must be made by anyone: "No moral obligation period, and so no bipolar obligations or moral claim right, can exist unless *non-discretionary* demands exist that do not depend on being made by anyone with the individual authority to make them" (35).

These "non-discretionary demands" are made by everyone and no one, one might say. "Rather, when we blame someone, we add our voice to, or second, . . . a demand that we must presuppose is made of everyone by the moral community or a representative person as such" (Darwall 2013, 37). Thus, there are many moral obligations that are not grounded in actual demands made by anyone. Darwall is quite explicit that "the moral community as I understand it is not any actual community composed of actual human beings," but rather is a "regulative ideal that we employ to make sense of our ethical thought and practice" (2007). I shall try to argue that the fictional character of the moral community poses problems for Darwall if he is understood as a constructivist.

A Problem for Darwall

Although Darwall does not claim that his view requires metaethical constructivism, even saying at one point that his view is compatible with a "recognitional realist" framework, his sympathies seem to be with a "procedural" constructivist view.[2] I am going to assume in what follows that his proposal is intended as a form of constructivism. If one does not view Darwall as a constructivist, this could be considered a thought experiment to test the consistency of constructivism and Darwall's "juridical" view of morality. Constructivism, as I understand it, attempts to justify the objectivity of morality without positing the existence of "stance-independent" moral properties or facts. While Darwall draws on both Kantian and contractualist forms of constructivism, he seems to be offering yet another form by proposing that moral obligations are grounded in the claims human persons make on each other.

However, if Darwall is offering a form of constructivism, it is not a simple form in which morality is rooted in actual claims people make on each other, since we have just seen that the claims that ground morality on his view include claims that may never actually be made, but that are in some way justified or warranted *if* they are made. The claims we make on each other as moral beings must be such that we can understand them as justified and such that we can expect that those we make claims on can recognize them as justified. Otherwise, a moral claim could not be distinguished from the demands of a bully. Obviously, justified or warranted claims are themselves normative in character and it looks as though these normative facts hold antecedently to any claims any actual person makes. A normative framework is thus presupposed by the account given of the claims we make on each other and is not simply the product of those claims. If I am justified when I ask a person who is standing on my foot to move his foot, then I have the moral standing to make the request, a legitimate right not to be stepped on. However, I must have this right even if I do not exercise it, which is a point Darwall supports. So far, I am not criticizing Darwall, but explaining what I take his view to be.

Therefore, it appears that even if some moral obligations are rooted in actual claims or demands, Darwall's account presupposes some other normative truths that do not rest on actual claims or demands since the account requires that we be able to recognize someone as having the authority or normative standing to make a demand. Furthermore, it also must be possible to say when the demands made by someone who has some moral authority are appropriate, given they possess that moral authority. Surely, having moral authority will be a normative matter and thus there must be some account of what it is to have such authority that is normative in character. It is clear that the account will not be one that rests the authority on making a demand because that would be circular. It is having the right kind of authority that makes it possible for one's demands to be moral demands. Merely making a demand is not sufficient to give one moral authority.

This is not necessarily an objection to a view such as Darwall's. There is no reason an account of one moral concept, obligation, cannot presuppose and make use of other normative concepts. A good example of this can be seen in Robert Adams's divine command theory of moral obligations (henceforth DCT). Adams responds to the Euthyphro objection to divine command theories by distinguishing the concept of moral obligation from that of the good. On his account, moral obligations are identical to God's expressed demands but they are not arbitrary, as Euthyphro objections claim is the case, because God is necessarily good and his commands are aimed at the good.

Adams's case is relevant to Darwall's view because, as Darwall himself acknowledges, there is a parallel between Darwall's view and a DCT. Both kinds of views see moral obligations as "what we are responsible or accountable for doing" (2013, 179). Darwall sees early modern divine command theorists, such as Pufendorf and Locke, as holding that "the moral law implicates our accountability to God" (179). He agrees with DCT theorists that morality requires accountability but says that "moral obligations concern our accountability to one another and ourselves as equal moral persons or members of the moral community" (179). The human moral community thus replaces God in Darwall's account.

This parallel between a DCT and Darwall's view suggests a possible problem with Darwall's view. A criticism often made against a DCT is usually called the "prior obligations" objection.[3] This critic of a DCT argues that, even if God's commands are sufficient to create moral obligations, they are not necessary, because we would have an obligation to obey God prior to God giving any commands. Not all obligations are therefore created by divine commands. A parallel objection could be raised against Darwall's view, as follows: "Even if some of our moral obligations rest on the demands people make of each other, not all arise in this way, because there is a prior obligation to respect the legitimate demands of other people even when no demands have been made." It looks as if some obligations must already be in place for the demands humans make on each other to create obligations. Darwall, I take it, understands the necessity of this, and that is why he proposes that, in addition to bipolar obligations between actual individuals, there are moral obligations that exist independently of the claims made by actual persons. These are the claims that people *could* make as representatives of the ideal "moral community."

One may, at this point, wonder what the problem is. After all, the view that there are such obligations is an explicit part of Darwall's view, not an objection to it. My answer is that the distinction between such standing obligations and those created by actual demands is not itself a problem. I agree that some such distinction is necessary to distinguish the bully from someone making a valid moral claim. The problem I want to raise is whether, if Darwall is understood as a constructivist, he has the resources to make sense of the distinction, while continuing to hold that morality is "second-personal" in nature. Are the "prior obligations" that hold antecedently to any actual claims made by actual persons something that the constructivist can explain? Can "the moral community," understood as a "regulative ideal," do

111

the job? If not, then there might seem to be moral obligations that are not second-personal in nature after all.[4]

Darwall could evade the problem by retreating to a weaker position, which claims that the demands made by humans are not the basis of *all* moral obligations, but just some obligations.[5] In a similar way, the proponent of a DCT might retreat to the weaker position that God's commands are sufficient for moral obligations, though not necessary. However, such a response seems more plausible for Adams than for Darwall, at least if Darwall is understood as a meta-ethical constructivist rather than a moral realist since the proponent of a DCT who follows Adams is clearly a moral realist and, thus, could (and does) recognize objective moral truths that are independent of the demands of any person, human, or divine being. Adams is not a voluntarist who tries to ground all moral truths in acts of willing. In fact, Adams roots his divine command account of moral obligation in a Platonic theory of the good that the theory of obligation presupposes.

If Darwall is a constructivist, however, it is not clear that a similar move is open to him. The set of moral facts that hold antecedently to the demands humans make on each other seems to be facts that are independent of any actual demands.[6] Darwall wants these facts to be derived from an ideal moral community, but there are, I believe, several problems in trying to see such obligations as arising in this manner.

One worry is that Darwall's moral community faces its own Euthyphro problem. Can we really say that what makes a moral obligation to be a moral obligation is that it is a claim or demand that *could* be made by someone as a representative of the moral community? Or is it not rather the case that it is because the claim is already moral in character that someone who makes it is representing the moral community? The former alternative appears to lead to the same kind of arbitrariness that those who press a Euthyphro problem against a DCT claim will follow from a DCT, while the latter alternative seems to imply that moral principles are antecedently true independently of any human claim.

One may here respond on Darwall's behalf that constructivism does not assume that moral obligations are constructed by actual humans, but are principles that reasonable human persons would follow. Thus, the "actors" or "contractors" who construct morality can be hypothetical or ideal, just as is the case with Darwall's moral community.

However, I believe there are problems that lurk for constructivism at just this point and that those problems may infect Darwall's view if it is understood as a form of constructivism. It is not clear that actual obligations can be derived from nonactual persons or communities. Suppose, for example, that a person in my situation who was perfectly rational would promise to make a donation to some worthy cause, such as alleviating climate change. If such an idealized version of myself existed, that person would thereby acquire an obligation to do this. It is not at all clear that the fact (if it is a fact) that this (nonexistent) person would make such a promise and thus have an obligation means that I am actually obligated to make such a donation (even if it were a good thing for me to do, I would not be obligated to do it since I have not promised to do so).

Another problem may lie in the indeterminate character of what the "moral community" would do. Is there a fact of the matter as to what representatives of the moral community would claim from each other? Just as it is sometimes claimed that Kant's categorical imperative is too abstract and formal to give rise to determinate moral principles, it may be that the idea of the "moral community" is too abstract and formal to give rise to determinate moral obligations.

Yet another problem stems from the identity of the moral community. How does one know when one is representing the moral community? How do humans achieve this status? Which claims that humans make are justified as moral? Clearly, many of the claims that humans make on each other are not morally valid claims. If we say that the claims humans make on each other are morally valid only if they are in accord with claims that are morally justified, then it looks as if those claims must be antecedently justified. One becomes a representative of the moral community by making claims that are

113

morally justified; it is not the case that claims are morally justified because they are made by representatives of the moral community. The parallel with the Euthyphro objections to a DCT should be clear.

Should Darwall Embrace Moral Realism?

Would it be possible for Darwall to reject constructivism and accept a moral realist framework? Yes, but this would represent a shift that seems inconsistent with some of the motivation for the view. A common theme among constructivists is that moral truths do not exist as independent facts that the human will must simply recognize. Rather, moral facts are in some way constituted by the human will. Moral realism is seen as a threat to the rational autonomy of humans. In a similar spirit, Darwall says that "when you and I make a claim to autonomy that we take to be rooted in the dignity of persons, therefore, we presuppose that we are bound by practical laws and reasons that are valid, not by virtue of any 'object' of volition, whether the value of any outcome or of any act considered in itself" (2013, 131).

Could the reference to "dignity" above as the "root" of the claim to autonomy help? Dignity might be taken to be a kind of intrinsic value that humans have. On this view, the "authority" that humans have to make justified claims on each other is derived from this value and can be reasonably exercised only if this value is respected. However, this kind of appeal to intrinsic value seems to presuppose moral realism. On such a view, the objective value gives rise to the moral status, while the constructivist wants the moral status to be in some way the product of our activity.

There is another problem that a shift to a moral realist framework might solve. I noted above that it is often argued that constructivist-type views that base morality on rational agency are too formal and abstract to provide substantive moral content. The contemporary Kantian Christine Korsgaard recognizes this problem by admitting that the categorical imperative by itself is too formal to give us concrete moral guidance and needs to be supplemented by what she calls a "principle of identity," since "a view of what you ought to do is a view of who you are" (see Korsgaard et al. 1996, 117).

A similar problem faces Darwall's form of constructivism. It is far from clear that we can determine what demands humans are justified in making on each other merely by seeing them as equal participants in the moral community. Darwall says that the authority a free, rational agency is "bound to recognize" stems from "whatever authority one is committed to in making and considering claims in the first place" (2013, 110). Even if this is so, it is not easy to see how one might go from recognizing this authority to deciding what particular claims are justified.

Darwall tries to show that at least one substantive moral principle can be derived merely from recognizing other humans as moral agents. This principle is that we must recognize and value others' autonomy. Darwall supports the value of autonomy by giving the example of parents who pressure a middle-aged child to eat broccoli because it is good for her, even though she does not like broccoli (2013, 128). This example has force; most would agree that it is wrong for parents to try to control the choices of a middle-aged child in this way. However, even if this is so, it does not mean that autonomy's value is unlimited, or that it is the only relevant factor. Suppose the daughter is an alcoholic, and she wants to drink alcohol, even though her liver is failing, and her life is at stake. In that case, her autonomy surely must be lower in value than saving her life. Paternalism is sometimes objectionable, but it also sometimes appears to be justified. The value of autonomy is not absolute, and a reasonable person would have to balance that value against other values. Without a realist moral framework, it is very hard to see how Darwall can derive concrete guidance for dealing with actual moral situations.[7]

Consider again the parallel between an Adams-type DCT and Darwall's view. On the DCT, God gives us obligations, but there must be a framework of values that undergirds his authority to do this. Similarly, perhaps humans create obligations by making demands or claims on each other. However, just as in the case of a DCT, this ability humans have to create obligations by making demands on each other rests on a framework of antecedent values.[8] However, such a view would not be a form of constructivism; it would require a commitment to moral realism in the end.

Does Darwall Need God as Part of the Story for His Account to Work?

Given a realist framework, which undergirds the authority humans have to make justified demands on each other, it does look like humans could generate some moral obligations. However, if one wants to hold firmly to a "juridical" view of moral obligations, which grounds all of them in the claims or demands persons make on each other, it is not clear that idealized demands, which are demands that one makes as a "representative of the moral community," will do the job since such hypothetical demands look just like timeless moral truths of the sort that nonnatural realists accept. They are not actual demands, but rather demands that would be reasonable to accept *if* they were made.

At this point, a DCT actually has an advantage over Darwall's view. The DCT grounds moral obligations in the justified demands God makes on humans. The proponent of a DCT takes God to be an actual being, and the demands or commands that are made by God are not just hypothetical but actual. To see the advantage of a DCT, compare a DCT to an "ideal observer" theory of ethics. Ideal observer theory identifies moral obligations with the judgments of an ideal observer, which is a being who is fully knowledgeable and impartial. However, it is not clear why an actual human should care about what judgments such an ideal observer would make (assuming that such a being could make such judgments and we would know what they are). Why should I care about the judgments of a nonexistent being? However, if God actually exists, God's judgments might matter greatly. For example, it may be argued that humans owe a great debt of gratitude to God as the creator of every good we have, or it might be argued that our ultimate happiness is linked to a loving relationship with God.

In fact, a DCT might provide exactly what Darwall's view needs. The demands that Darwall says we make as "representatives of the moral community" might just be the demands that God wills for us to make on each other. Darwall would then have the antecedent moral truths his theory requires. There would be actual demands, made by an actual person, that undergird the ideal demands we should make on each other, and we would be properly representing the moral community when our demands align with those God wills us to make.

I believe that much of what Darwall says about divine command theory is correct and valuable. For example, he claims that for God's commands to create moral obligations, it would have to be the case that God has authority that human subjects can themselves recognize as legitimate, such that if God sanctions humans for disobeying those commands, God would have to assume that reasonable humans would themselves agree that they deserve the sanctions. Points such as this show that a viable DCT must be rooted in an underlying framework of normative truths that are independent of God's will. However, this is exactly what a DCT such as that provided by Adams offers. Darwall often labels a DCT as a form of "voluntarism." This may, however, be misleading, for if God's commands are constrained by his understanding of the good, it is not clear how much discretion, if any, God has over what he commands.[9]

The theistic framework sketched here fits well with the moral realism Darwall's view seems to need. The dignity or intrinsic value humans have, which the view requires, can be explained by the fact that humans are creatures of God and are made in God's image.[10] This is not a voluntarist framework. Rather, God himself possesses supreme value, and creatures made in his image would participate in that value or share in it because humans can mirror or image God. Humans may indeed create obligations by making demands on each other and holding each other accountable, but they can do that because of the moral status they possess.[11]

Notes

1 Gary Watson explicitly claims that Darwall's whole project can be read as a response to Elizabeth Anscombe's famous complaint against "modern moral philosophy." Anscombe says that the concept of moral obligation only makes sense if there is a lawgiver and urges contemporary philosophers to drop discussions of obligation in favor of virtues. Watson says, rightly in my view, that Darwall attempts to show that human persons can substitute for God and thus that God is not necessary to make sense of morality. See Watson (2007).

2 See the brief discussion of metaethics in Darwall (2006, 293–97). However, in his "Reply to Korsgaard, Wallace, and Watson," Darwall claims his view does not require constructivism, though that is a view he would "happily" embrace (2007, 64).

3 For a clear account of the kind of objection to a DCT, see Wainwright (2005, 80–83).

4 Darwall, in fact, might be open to such a qualified view of not all moral obligations being grounded in second-personal reasons. At one point he says that there might be moral obligations that are "not relational or bi-polar," such as those to take care of the environment. See Darwall (2007, 61).

5 There is another response I will not discuss here, one that could be used both by the advocate of a DCT and by Darwall, in which it is argued that the "prior obligations" are not true obligations, but just good reasons to fulfill the legitimate demands of others. This response still would leave the position vulnerable to the problem discussed below.

6 There is a nice discussion of this problem in Zilberman (2017). Zilberman calls this problem in Darwall the "antecedent problem."

7 In Darwall (2006, 300–320), Darwall suggests that this problem might be solved via contractualism, with his own view providing a kind of foundation for the contractualist view. I think this move is dubious for several reasons; I doubt that a view like Darwall's is consistent with most forms of contractualism. However, this is a subject for another paper.

8 On this point Watson's "Morality as Equal Accountability" is helpful again, in suggesting that Darwall's account of the right is too loosely connected to the good, specifically the good life for humans. See Watson (2007, 46–50).

9 Evans (2013) distinguishes two aspects of a DCT, which he terms the "modal status thesis" and the "divine discretion thesis." Evans argues

that only the former is actually essential to a DCT, which means that nonvoluntaristic forms of a DCT are possible. See 34–37.

10 Here, I shall not attempt the enormous task of explaining how God might be the basis of human dignity or arguing that a religious basis for this dignity is superior to secular accounts. There is an enormous literature on this topic that I cannot do justice to here, but here are a couple of good starting places to explore the issue: For an attempt to argue that human dignity requires a religious foundation, see Wolterstorff (2008, 316–19). For a good discussion of alternative ways of conceiving dignity, including secular alternatives, see again Ariel Zilberman (2017) "Two Second-Personal Conceptions of the Dignity of Persons." The Zilberman article is particularly valuable since it focuses on Darwall.

11 I wish to thank the Templeton Religion Trust, which funded this research by Grant 0171, on "The Virtue of Accountability." The views expressed in the article do not necessarily reflect the views of the Templeton Religion Trust.

References

Darwall, Stephen. 2006. *The Second-Person Standpoint: Morality, Respect, and Accountability*. Cambridge, MA: Harvard University Press.

——. 2007. "Reply to Korsgaard, Wallace, and Watson." *Ethics* 118:64.

——. 2013. *Morality, Authority, and Law*. Oxford: Oxford University Press.

Evans, C. Stephen. 2013. *God and Moral Obligation*. Oxford: Oxford University Press.

Korsgaard, Christine M., G. A. Cohen, Raymond Geuss, Thomas Nagel, and Bernard Williams. 1996. *The Sources of Normativity*. Cambridge: Cambridge University Press.

Wainwright, William. 2005. *Religion and Morality*. Aldershot, UK: Ashgate.

Watson, Gary. 2007. "Morality as Equal Accountability: Comments on Stephen Darwall's *The Second-Person Standpoint*." *Ethics* 118:37–51.

Wolterstorff, Nicholas. 2008. *Justice: Rights and Wrongs*. Princeton: Princeton University Press.

Zilberman, Ariel. 2017. "Two Second-Personal Conceptions of the Dignity of Persons." *European Journal of Philosophy* 25:921–43.

CHAPTER 6

John Calvin's Multiplicity Thesis

Daniel Bonevac

ABSTRACT: John Calvin holds that the fall radically changed human-ity's moral and epistemic capacities. Recognizing that should lead Christian philosophers to see that philosophical questions require at least two sets of answers: one reflecting our nature and capacities before the fall, and the other reflecting our nature and capacities after the fall. Our prelapsarian knowledge of God, the right, and the good is direct and noninferential; our postlapsar-ian knowledge of them is mostly indirect, inferential, and filled with moral and epistemic risk. Only revelation can move us beyond fragmentary and indeterminate moral and theological knowledge.

Introduction

John Calvin is not usually viewed as a philosopher. There is no entry for Calvin in the *Stanford Encyclopedia of Philosophy*. Indeed, Calvin is famously hostile to philosophy: "How lavishly in this respect have the whole body of philosophers betrayed their stupidity and want of sense? To say nothing of the others whose absurdities are of a still grosser description, how completely does Plato, the soberest and most religious of them all, lose himself in his round globe? What must be the case with the rest, when the leaders, who ought to have set them an example, commit such blunders, and labour under such hallucinations?" ([1559] 1989, *Institutes of the Christian Religion* I, 5, 11).[1]

It is easy, however, to overstate the case. Philosophy's problem is that it tends to focus solely on worldly matters, neglecting spiritual dimensions relevant to attaining true wisdom:

> Whatever a man knows and understands, is mere vanity, if it is not grounded in true wisdom; and it is in no degree better fitted for the apprehension of spiritual doctrine than the eye of a blind man is for discriminating colors. We must carefully notice these two things—that a knowledge of all the sciences is mere smoke, where the heavenly science of Christ is wanting; and man, with all his acuteness, is as stupid for obtaining of himself a knowledge of the mysteries of God, as an ass is unqualified for understanding musical harmonies. (Calvin [1546] 1848, 1:20)

Philosophy, in other words, is not intrinsically incapable of attaining truth, knowledge, and wisdom, any more than science is; its difficulty is that it tries to do so without the aid of religion, without "the heavenly science of Christ."[2] We cannot understand by ourselves the mysteries of God; we require revelation. Secular philosophy and even natural theology, in themselves, can do little more than point beyond themselves to something greater:[3] "Reason is intelligent enough to taste something of things above, although it is more careless about investigating these. . . . There is one kind of understanding of earthly things; another of heavenly" (II, 2,13).[4]

In this essay I argue that, despite his disparaging remarks about the subject, Calvin is a philosopher with an innovative and intriguing metaphilosophical position.[5] Calvin offers answers to philosophical questions. In fact, he offers at least two answers to each philosophical question pertaining to ethics, metaethics, epistemology, and the philosophy of mind. He thinks that any Christian philosophy requires multiple answers to central questions of philosophy. I call that Calvin's Multiplicity Thesis.

This opens space for a range of philosophical positions. If Calvin is right, Christian philosophers need not an answer, but at least a pair of answers to basic philosophical questions. We cannot give unified answers to questions such as

Who am I?

What am I?

What can I know?

How can I know?

What should I do?

How should I decide?

They each require n-tuples of answers, one for each stage of our relationship with God.

Recognizing that the fall has deep implications for Calvin's philosophy and theology is commonplace. What I hope to accomplish here is to explicate the nature of its implications and map the space of Christian philosophies that are possible as a consequence.

The Fall

Calvin understands the fall of mankind as an epistemological catastrophe as well as a moral catastrophe. It not only expels us from the Garden; it hobbles us. It damages our cognitive as well as our moral capacities.[6] Prelapsarian epistemology differs from postlapsarian epistemology; prelapsarian ethics differs from postlapsarian ethics. There is such an important divide between these two realms that many philosophical questions require at least two answers—one for each side of the lapsarian divide:

Answer before the fall—when the world was as it was designed to be, and we were as we were designed to be.

Answer after the fall—now that we are less than we were designed to be.

Other answers may be required as well, for there may be other theological divisions that make a philosophical difference. We may need distinct answers before and after redemption, for example, or for the new heaven and new earth that arise when we encounter Christ, not through a glass darkly, but face-to-face. Here, however, I shall focus on the philosophical ramifications of the fall, for it is there that Calvin elaborates those ramifications most clearly.

In discussing philosophical questions, Calvin makes common use of counterfactual conditions such as "if Adam had stayed sinless" (I, 2, 1) and "if the depravity of man's mind did not lead it away from the right approach" (I, 2, 2). He often splits his response into two parts, as here: "It relates firstly, to the condition in which we were originally created and secondly, to our condition immediately after Adam's fall" (III, 15, 1).

The Multiplicity Thesis generates a problem, creating a gap between two kinds of entities, two kinds of norms, two sets of methodologies, two modes of description, two modes of knowledge, and so on. How do things on the sides of the gap relate?

Calvin's answer depends on his analysis of the fall. He sees it as bringing about our corruption and degradation, and not only in a moral or practical sense. It corrupts and degrades our faculties of knowledge. It corrupts our intuitions and our reasoning ability. It corrupts our decision-making capacities. It distances us from God, epistemically as well as morally. As Karl Barth puts it, "Between what is possible in principle and what is possible in fact there inexorably lies the fall."[7]

Calvin famously begins the *Institutes* by saying that our knowledge of God and our knowledge of ourselves are intertwined; we cannot know ourselves without a knowledge of God, and we cannot know God without a knowledge of ourselves.[8] The fall, however, complicates our ability to know both. We not only have to seek such knowledge with impaired faculties; we must recognize our fallen condition and understand that it entails the need for two aspects of self-knowledge. We must know what we were intended to be and were before the fall, as well as what we have become as a result of our own sin: "We cannot clearly and properly know God unless the knowledge of ourselves be added. This knowledge is twofold,—relating, first, to the condition in which we were at first created; and, secondly to our condition such as it began to be immediately after Adam's fall. For it would little avail us to know how we were created if we remained ignorant of the corruption and degradation of our nature in consequence of the fall" (I, 15, 1).

Doing this is difficult for us. "The corruption and degradation of our nature in consequence of the fall" is not just a marring, beclouding, or obscuring of it. The fall corrupts and degrades our epistemic faculties as well as our moral character. There is not only something else to know, something from which we are at a greater distance, though all that is true. We must carry out that more difficult task with weakened, damaged tools. That has implications for epistemology, for what we can know and how we can come to know it. It has implications for who we are, for what we can become, and for how we ought to make decisions. It affects theories of meaning and reference, for it has implications about how our words can relate to the world. It even has implications for political philosophy, for how we can relate to one another.

To say more about these implications, we need to understand the nature and extent of the corruption and degradation of our faculties. Something is retained; Adam is still Adam after the fall.

> On the other hand, soundness of mind and integrity of heart were, at the same time, withdrawn, and it is this which constitutes the corruption of natural gifts. For although there is still some residue of intelligence and judgement as well as will, we cannot call a mind sound and entire which is both weak and immersed in darkness. As to the will, its depravity is but too well known. Therefore, since reason, by which man discerns between good and evil, and by which he understands and judges, is a natural gift, it could not be entirely destroyed; but being partly weakened and partly corrupted, a shapeless ruin is all that remains. (II, 2, 12)

125

We might put Calvin's position this way. Intelligence is retained in a weakened and corrupted form; its soundness is destroyed. Judgment, both theoretical and practical, is retained, but weakened and corrupted; integrity is destroyed. We retain our will, but it too is weakened and corrupted. Our freedom is destroyed. We retain a love of truth, but our ability to attain it is limited within the sphere of the natural world, or gone altogether with regard to the supernatural.

It is worth pausing for a moment to consider Calvin's distinction between weakening and corrupting these faculties. Reason is weak in that it can no longer see what is written on the heart or in the book of the world very clearly. Though he sometimes speaks that way, it is not blind. But its vision is poor.[9] The faculty remains, but in a diminished form, less able to recognize a priori truths, draw inferences, construct and evaluate hypotheses, recognize moral qualities, weigh moral considerations, and, in general, engage in other intellectual tasks. It is corrupted in the sense that it is specifically weak of will; it is tempted to let bias, self-interest, desire, and other inappropriate factors affect its operation.

Calvin's Application of the Multiplicity Thesis

As a result of the fall, Calvin contends, Christian philosophers need at least two answers for each philosophical question:

- one describing how things were before the fall, and would have been now without it—with our original moral and epistemic abilities
- the other, how they are now, after the fall—with our weakened and corrupted moral and epistemic abilities

There is a moral and epistemic gap between our prelapsarian and postlapsarian conditions.

The closest analogue to Calvin's position in later Christian philosophy may be Aquinas's theory of analogical predication.[10] But

Calvin's position is far more radical. There is not merely an epistemic and semantic gap between the natural and the divine, between knowledge, power, wisdom, and other qualities as exemplified in this world and the knowledge, power, and wisdom of God. There is, for Calvin, a vast epistemic, semantic, and moral gap between us and everything—even ourselves—after the fall. All predication, for Calvin, ends up as analogical.

There is another crucial difference between Calvin's view and that of Aquinas: We did this ourselves. We sold ourselves into slavery, damaged our eyes, and went into exile. We cannot get back on our own. Only God has the needed causal power. We cannot redeem ourselves, any more than the slave can purchase his own freedom or the nearsighted can do surgery on their own eyes.

Calvin's own application of the Multiplicity Thesis is sweeping. He uses it to interpret the divide between Platonic and Aristotelian approaches to central questions of philosophy. To put it crudely, Plato, "the most religious of all the philosophers and the most sensible" (I, 5, 11), described how things were before the fall; Aristotle, how they are (or, more accurately, how we are) afterward.

Before the fall, we were capable of attaining a priori knowledge, knowledge written on the heart, including knowledge of God and God's commands. After the fall, we still have knowledge written on the heart, but our ability to discern it is much reduced. We must rely on revelation for our knowledge of God's nature and God's commands. Our knowledge is entirely, or almost entirely, a posteriori knowledge, derived from experience of the world and from revelation.

Calvin is, broadly, in the Platonic tradition, siding with Plato and Augustine against Aristotle and Aquinas.[11] However, he deviates from it in an important way. A way that foreshadows Descartes's evil deceiver. He qualifies the Augustinian resolution of Platonism's epistemological problem. Augustine had put Plato's forms into the mind of God as God's ideas, and maintained that God illumined some of the forms to us, enabling us to anchor our ideas and our language to ideas in the mind of God. That solved the problem of skepticism that had plagued Plato's doctrine of forms, for Plato had left it unclear how it was possible for us to gain knowledge of the forms. Within a generation, the Academy had become a center of skepticism, and "Academic" had become synonymous with "skeptic." Augustine's position is stable, however, for God, who is omnipotent and supplies the causal power linking our minds to the forms.

Calvin takes himself to be explicating Augustine, not disagreeing with him. Calvin's Multiplicity Thesis generates a problem for this view, however, for the Augustinian resolution, in his opinion, is prelapsarian. It works before the fall—but only before the fall. After the fall, our nature has been corrupted and degraded. We do not need something external, such as Descartes's demon, to make us question our access to the truth; we have done it ourselves.

"Our minds are so blinded that they cannot perceive the truth, and all our senses are so corrupt that we wickedly rob God of his glory" (II, 6, 1).

Our minds are no longer illuminated in the same way. God's action is the same, but we are no longer able to receive as clearly. The Augustinian resolution of Platonism's epistemological problem thus breaks down:[12] "Accordingly, Augustine, in speaking of this inability of human reason to understand the things of God, says, that he deems the grace of illumination not less necessary to the mind than the light of the sun to the eye (*August. de Peccat. Merit. et Remiss*. lib. 2 cap. 5). Moreover, not content with this, he modifies his expression, adding, that we open our eyes to behold the light, whereas the mental eye remains shut, until it is opened by the Lord" (II, 2, 25).

Calvin represents an important milestone on the path to Descartes.[13] Descartes, from this perspective, tries to reinforce the Augustinian doctrine of illumination; Calvin seeks to limit it. Descartes tries to combat the skeptic, finding a foundation on which he can rebuild the full structure of human knowledge, including a priori knowledge that Plato would have seen as knowledge of the forms. Calvin would have little hope that it could be done. We can regain that knowledge only with the help and grace of God.

Before the fall, Calvin embraces a strong form of rationalism. We have immediate knowledge of a priori truths, including truths about the forms, about God, about God's commands, and about ethical truths. After the fall, in contrast, we are left with at best a moderate rationalism. Some writing remains on the heart—we still have some capacity for a priori knowledge—but that capacity is limited. Our path to that innate knowledge generally goes through experience or revelation. We can access what is written on the heart only with the help of something a posteriori. Knowledge of the forms is still possible, but it is mediated and inferential rather than direct and immediate.

Augustine's doctrine of illumination, in short, offers us a plausible account of our knowledge of the forms before the fall. After the fall, our minds are not illumined in the same way.

Calvin talks about the diminution of illumination in two ways. Sometimes he suggests that, after the fall, the light of illumination itself no longer shines:

> I feel pleased with the well-known saying which has been bor-
> rowed from the writings of Augustine, that man's natural gifts
> were corrupted by sin, and his supernatural gifts withdrawn;
> meaning by supernatural gifts the light of faith and righteousness,
> which would have been sufficient for the attainment of heavenly
> life and everlasting felicity. Man, when he withdrew his allegiance
> to God, was deprived of the spiritual gifts by which he had been
> raised to the hope of eternal salvation. Hence it follows, that he
> is now an exile from the kingdom of God, so that all things which
> pertain to the blessed life of the soul are extinguished in him until
> he recover them by the grace of regeneration. (II, 2, 12)

Sometimes, however, Calvin speaks as if our minds are still illumined, but we are no longer able to perceive God's light in the same way. The light shines as it did before, but we have drawn the shades: "We open our eyes to behold the light, whereas the mental eye remains shut, until it is opened by the Lord" (II, 2, 25). This points to the possibility that God reopens our mental eyes, that Paul's "new man" can once again see, at least partially, through a glass darkly, perhaps, what God has illumined.[14]

The metaphors of exile and closing of our mental eyes both imply that our capacities, after the fall, are much diminished. There is, however, an important difference. The exile metaphor suggests that God has turned out the light; any effort on our part to open our eyes is fruitless without action from God. The closed-eyes metaphor suggests that the light is still on, but that we have closed our eyes to it. This in turn seems to imply that we could act to restore our ability to see what we had seen before the fall without any further action from God. But these are not as far apart as that makes them sound, for Calvin makes it clear that we cannot open our eyes on our own; we require God's grace.

There is much more to be said about the contrast between our pre- and postlapsarian conditions. We have not yet begun to say anything about the nature of philosophy after our redemption in Christ, much less in the kingdom of God or in the new Jerusalem. Before considering those questions, however, it is important to isolate the core of the Multiplicity Thesis, which is independent of any particular construal of an appropriate pre- or postlapsarian philosophy. Calvin's key contribution is that a Christian philosophy should not rest content with a single philosophical theory or attitude. We cannot simply be realists, or antirealists, or foundationalists, or fallibilists, or moral realists, or constructivists, and so on. We have to recognize that the fall marked a sharp divide. Philosophical theories adequate to our circumstance now, after the fall, do not capture the circumstance in which and for which we were created.

We are, in short, more than we have become. We were meant for more. That must be at the heart of any Christian philosophy.

Knowledge of God

There is not space here to explore all the philosophical implications of Calvin's view thoroughly. I do want to examine one of central interest to Calvin: the possibility of knowledge of God.[15]

Calvin believes that we have some a priori knowledge of God: "Some idea of God always exists in every human mind" (I, 3, 3). Indeed, "a sense of Deity is indelibly engraven on the human heart" (I, 3, 3). This is Calvin's *sensus divinitatis*, the sense of the divine, that remains in us even after the fall:[16] "That there exists in the human minds and indeed by natural instinct, some sense of Deity, we hold to be beyond dispute, since God himself, to prevent any man from pretending ignorance, has endued all men with some idea of his Godhead, the memory of which he constantly renews and occasionally enlarges, that all to a man being aware that there is a God, and that he is their Maker" (I, 3, 1).

Before the fall, our knowledge of God was immediate, direct, and noninferential, though still fragmentary; a finite being cannot fully comprehend an infinite God. We had some knowledge of God as creator, as author of our being, as savior, as "the origin and fountain of all goodness." We understood God's commands and felt a natural love for God.

After the fall, however, our knowledge of God is fleeting and indistinct. It is indeterminate, easily resisted, hard to cultivate, and inferential. The sense of the divine gives us glimpses, but we must, through careful attention, diligent study, and judicious reasoning, build an admittedly incomplete portrait of God from them.[17]

To return to Augustine's metaphor of illumination, our innate sense of the divine gives us flashes of lightning, giving us glimpses of God and the things that God has written on our hearts. But this is nothing like the light that bathed our minds before the fall: "Their discernment was not such as to direct them to the truth, far less to enable them to attain it, but resembled that of the bewildered traveler, who sees the flash of lightning glance far and wide for a moment, and then vanish into the darkness of the night, before he can advance a single step" (II, 2, 18).

We are able to patch together the glimpses that the sense of the divine provides to a limited extent, not merely through what has been traditionally known as natural theology, but also, and even primarily, through the contrast between God and the self and its depravity. We come to know God by coming to know ourselves, and come to know ourselves through knowing God. "Our wisdom, in so far as it ought to be deemed true and solid Wisdom, consists almost entirely of two parts: the knowledge of God and of ourselves" (I, 1, 1). The power of the *sensus divinitatis* is real:[18] "For, in the first place, no man can survey himself without forthwith turning his thoughts towards the God in whom he lives and moves; because it is perfectly obvious, that the endowments which we possess cannot possibly be from ourselves; nay, that our very being is nothing else than subsistence in God alone" (I, 1, 1).

What is true of our faculties, "the endowments which we possess," is also true of the world, "the theater of God's glory" (179, I xiv 20), and its many gifts to us: "In the second place, those blessings which unceasingly distil to us from heaven, are like streams conducting us to the fountain" (I, 1, 1).

So far, these sound like undeveloped cosmological/teleological/criteriological arguments for the existence of God. The excellence we find in ourselves and the world, the argument seems to go, entails the existence of its even more excellent cause. However, the more compelling argument, in Calvin's view, rests not on excellence but on deficiency. The fall obscures God from us but also impels us to seek knowledge of God: "Here, again, the infinitude of good which resides in God becomes more apparent from our poverty. In particular, the miserable ruin into which the revolt of the first man has plunged us, compels us to turn our eyes upwards; not only that while hungry and famishing we may thence ask what we want, but being aroused by fear may learn humility" (I, 1, 1).

In short, wonder and appreciation provide reasons to look for and believe in God, but feelings of inadequacy and shame provide more powerful reasons: "For as there exists in man something like a world of misery, and ever since we were stript of the divine attire our naked shame discloses an immense series of disgraceful properties every man, being stung by the consciousness of his own unhappiness, in this way necessarily obtains at least some knowledge of God" (I, 1, 1).

Calvin's natural theology, then, takes an unusual form. Our negative qualities provide more evidence for God's existence than our positive qualities do. We infer God's existence and excellence not so much from the good qualities of ourselves and the world as from our own negative qualities.

> Thus, our feeling of ignorance, vanity, want, weakness, in short, depravity and corruption, reminds us that in the Lord, and none but He, dwell the true light of wisdom, solid virtue, exuberant goodness. We are accordingly urged by our own evil things to consider the good things of God; and, indeed, we cannot aspire to Him in earnest until we have begun to be displeased with ourselves. . . . Every person, therefore, on coming to the knowledge of himself, is not only urged to seek God, but is also led as by the hand to find him. (I, 1, 1)
>
> Of course, we do not recognize the full extent of our own deficiencies until we form the idea of a perfect God. The gap between our own intelligence, wisdom, virtue, and power and the corresponding qualities in God is not merely vast; it is infinite. Only when we conclude that God exists, therefore, do we truly attain self-knowledge. That greater sense of our own inadequacy impels us toward God even more strongly. (I, 1, 2)[19]

The fall thus creates distance between man and God but also provides the force that impels us toward God. It damages our faculties, impairing our ability to know God. It takes the light with which God had illumined the mind and leaves only occasional flashes of insight. It creates an intervening fog, making it difficult for us to discern God's nature, commands, and call.

Nevertheless, it leaves little room for doubt that there is a God: "We cannot open our eyes without being compelled to behold Him" (I, 5, 1). We cannot comprehend the essence of God, which remains "incomprehensible, utterly transcending all human thought." When we consider ourselves and the world around us, however, we find that "his glory is engraven in characters so bright, so distinct, and so illustrious, that none, however dull and illiterate, can plead ignorance as their excuse" (I, 5, 1).

Calvin's Paradox

The thought that we can know that God is, but not what God is, is hardly original with Calvin. But Calvin develops from this position a paradox that seems to me unique, and to bring us back to the core of the Multiplicity Thesis. The world serves as a mirror of the divine.[20]

> Hence, the author of the Epistle to the Hebrews elegantly describes the visible worlds as images of the invisible (Heb. 11:3), the elegant structure of the world serving us as a kind of mirror, in which we may behold God, though otherwise invisible. Hence it is obvious, that in seeking God, the most direct path and the fittest method is, not to attempt with presumptuous curiosity to pry into his essence, which is rather to be adored than minutely discussed, but to contemplate him in his works, by which he draws near, becomes familiar, and in a manner communicates himself to us. (I, 5, 9)

What is true of the world is also true of us. We are ourselves models of God: "Hence certain of the philosophers have not improperly called man a microcosm (miniature world), as being a rare specimen of divine power, wisdom, and goodness, and containing within himself wonders sufficient to occupy our minds, if we are willing so to employ them" (I, 5, 3).

The view that nature is a mirror of God, and that we ourselves are microcosms of God, would seem to give us hope that we can know far more of God than His mere existence. After all, nature and humanity both have a structure that we can understand, at least in part. If we can attain knowledge of some laws of nature, and nature is a mirror of the divine, can we not therefore attain some knowledge of the laws of God?

With sufficient humility, we might indeed be able to attain such knowledge. Our pride, however, will not let us. We suppress this knowledge because it would presuppose recognition of the depth of our own inadequacy. We prefer to see the mind as a mirror of nature, or even, as in various forms of idealism, antirealism, constructivism, and so on, as the architect, builder, or projector of nature. We feel drawn toward a vision of ourselves as creators. We want to see ourselves as capable, on our own, of understanding the world without reference to something higher.

Calvin calls minds who seek to understand the world and themselves without appealing to God "monster minds." Such minds "are not afraid to employ the seed of Deity deposited in human nature as a means of suppressing the name of God" (I, 5, 4). Calvin has little respect for a person with such a mind; "substituting nature as the architect of the universe, he suppresses the name of God" (I, 5, 4).

Even though the world is a mirror of God, and we ourselves, in a different way, are something like mirrors of God, we fail to recognize the face of God in ourselves and the world around us. We put ourselves or nature in God's place, thinking of one or both as self-sufficient. As soon as we do so, we take our own conceptions, our own mistaken self-images, our own illusions, desires, and confusions, and project them onto the world and onto whatever concept of the divine we manage to form: "Hence that immense flood of error with which the whole world is overflowed. Every individual mind being a kind of labyrinth, it is not wonderful, not only that each nation has adopted a variety of fictions, but that almost every man has had his own god" (I, 5, 12).

Calvin gives us here a classic argument for skepticism, the argument from variability (Striker 1983).

1. Variability—people indulge in varied superstitions, forming various conflicting concepts of God.
2. Undecidability—there is no way to tell who if anyone is right.

135

3. Skepticism—"the human mind, which thus errs in inquiring after God, is dull and blind in heavenly mysteries" (I, 5, 12).

On our own, therefore, we would be left with little more than skepticism.

> Some praise the answer of Simonides, who being asked by King Herod what God was, asked a day to consider. When the king next day repeated the question, he asked two days; and after repeatedly doubling the number of days, at length replied, "The longer I consider, the darker the subject appears." He, no doubt, wisely suspended his opinion, when he did not see clearly: still his answer shows, that if men are only naturally taught, instead of having any distinct, solid, or certain knowledge, they fasten only on contradictory principles, and, in consequence, worship an unknown God. (I, 5, 12)

The reasons that the wonders of the world and the excellences as well as deficiencies of our own nature supply for concluding that God exists, therefore, do not become, for us, reasons to conclude anything in particular about the nature of God. That is not because they do not constitute such reasons; indeed, they should lead us to conclude that both nature and the mind point us toward God and give us knowledge of God just as mirrors point us toward and give us knowledge of the objects reflected in them. But after the fall, we are constitutionally incapable of responding in the way we should and in principle could. The fall has kept us from understanding God's nature: "In vain for us, therefore, does Creation exhibit so many bright lamps lighted up to show forth the glory of its Author. Though they beam upon us from every quarter, they are altogether insufficient of themselves to lead us into the right path. Some sparks, undoubtedly, they do throw out; but these are quenched before they can give forth a brighter effulgence" (I, 5, 14).

Before the fall, then, we see God's glory in the world around us, and can attain a posteriori knowledge of God's nature from the world and from ourselves. After the fall, the world hints toward God, but we can no longer attain determinate knowledge of God from experience of the world or ourselves. The evidence is still there, but we can no longer see it as evidence; we will not allow ourselves to see it. That, in short, is why we need revelation.

Revelation

After the fall, our a priori knowledge of God is fleeting, inferential, and depends on self-knowledge, which is itself entangled with knowledge of God. A posteriori knowledge is indeterminate or impossible for us, even though the evidence is there, if only we could permit ourselves to see it as evidence of God's nature. Without revelation, we would be left with skepticism or at best a vague spirituality, a conjecture that there is a higher being of an unknown and unknowable character, a "something, I know not what," whose relation to the world would remain a mystery.

Revelation changes that picture entirely. We need revelation to know God as redeemer. We need it even to recognize God as creator. We need it for determinacy and for de re knowledge. Otherwise, we would be left with an unclear and indistinct concept of God that could yield only de dicto knowledge, and very little of that: "I am only showing that it is necessary to apply to Scripture, in order to learn the sure marks which distinguish God, as the Creator of the world, from the whole herd of fictitious gods" (I, 6, 1).

Calvin sees revelation as testimony, giving us knowledge as any kind of testimony does. He moreover gives a recursive theory of revelation. We need an account of the acquisition of revealed knowledge as well as an account of the transfer of revealed knowledge in the Word.

Understanding both acquisition and transfer requires us to understand the epistemic role of Christ. To grasp that, it may help to think about the process by which someone might recognize something as a mirror. Imagine a person sitting in a room—a restaurant, say—seeing people in the next room talking, eating, and laughing. The room appears to be large, extending far beyond the edge of the room the diner inhabits. Suddenly, the diner has a gestalt shift, perhaps catching, out of the corner of one eye, a movement on the right side of that room matching a movement clearly observed on the left. The diner realizes that the next room is the same size as this room, and that the people who appear to be on the left are those on the right reflected in a mirror, cleverly placed to make the restaurant appear to be twice its current size. The diner did not naturally recognize the mirror as a mirror. Nor did anything in the mirror itself indicate its nature as a reflection. The diner had to see something on both sides to realize that the mirror was a mirror.

Just so, to see the world and ourselves as mirrors of God, we have to see something on both sides. Viewing one side alone cannot support such a conclusion. Christ supplies that view. Man and God at once, Christ offers us the opportunity for the gestalt shift, the switch to seeing the world and ourselves as mirrors of the divine.

Of course, that shift also offers much more. We learn not only what we can learn from seeing ourselves and the world as microcosms of divinity but also an aspect of God as redeemer that we could not have derived from those sources, no matter how clearly we might be able to see them.

I speak only of that simple and primitive knowledge, to which the mere course of nature would have conducted us, had Adam stood upright. For although no man will now, in the present ruin of the human race, perceive God to be either a father, or the author of salvation, or propitious in any respect, until Christ interpose to make our peace; still it is one thing to perceive that God our Maker supports us by his power, rules us by his providence, fosters us by his goodness, and visits us with all kinds of blessings, and another thing to embrace the grace of reconciliation offered to us in Christ. Since, then, the Lord first appears, as well in the creation of the world as in the general doctrine of Scripture, simply as a Creator, and afterwards as a Redeemer in Christ,— a twofold knowledge of him hence arises. (I, 2, 1)

Calvin's theory of revelation acquisition concerns the rationale for thinking that a first-person experience is actually a case of acquisition of revealed knowledge of God. What justifies Moses in thinking that the burning bush is a sign from God rather than a delusion? What justifies a prophet in thinking that the inspiration he feels comes from God, that the vision of the future he experiences is veridical? Sometimes, as in the case of the resurrection of Jesus, there are multiple witnesses.[21] But in many cases no such confirmation is available. Moses was alone when he saw the burning bush and heard the voice of God. Prophecy is by its very nature private. Calvin sees that an adequate theory of acquisition therefore cannot rely on interpersonal considerations. Nor can it rely on anything about the content of the experience itself. There is no mark distinguishing veridical from illusory experiences in the content of the experience.

Calvin concludes that acquisitions of revelation cannot be distinguished from pretenders by their content or their relations to the experiences of other people. The only option remaining is that we distinguish them by their relations to our other mental states, specifically, by an accompanying feeling of certainty: "Whether God revealed himself to the fathers by oracles and visions, or, by the instrumentality and ministry of men, suggested what they were to hand down to posterity, there cannot be a doubt that the certainty of what he taught them was firmly engraven on their hearts, so that they felt assured and knew that the things which they learnt came forth from God, who invariably accompanied his word with a sure testimony, infinitely superior to mere opinion" (I, 6, 2).

This would seem a dangerous criterion, for false prophets, too, can feel certain that their experiences come from God. But Calvin, I think, means something more than that. The certainty true prophets feel is "firmly engraven on their hearts." Calvin uses this phrase in speaking of the sense of the divine and of the moral law written on the heart. In short, he uses this locution for a priori knowledge, for something innate. An experience of the divine, in the form of a perceptual experience or an inspiration to prophecy, accompanies a certainty that is innate, that reflects something deep in our very natures. We might call it a profound certainty, a certainty that has deep a priori roots. The experience of the divine overpowers the person experiencing it; they cannot but feel certain of its divine origins.

Calvin has little to add to standard accounts of the transmission of knowledge through testimony. He does, however, make two further points. First, the public transmission of scripture plays an important role. The promulgation of the law and the interpretations of the prophets spread revealed knowledge more widely than would have been possible without them (I, 6, 2–3).[22] They create a community that is in important ways self-regulating, preventing divergent private experiences and divergent transfers from corrupting the transmission of revealed knowledge. Second, scripture is self-authenticating by way of the Holy Spirit: "Let it therefore be held as fixed, that those who are inwardly taught by the Holy Spirit acquiesce implicitly in Scripture; that Scripture carrying its own evidence along with it, deigns not to submit to proofs and arguments, but owes the full conviction with which we ought to receive it to the testimony of the Spirit" (I, 7, 5).

The same profound certainty that accompanies an acquisition of revealed knowledge thus also accompanies its transfer through scripture. We accept scripture as revealed because it reaches something deep in us, something powerful, something innate—something "engraven on the heart." But it is not just that its content appeals to something we are by our very natures equipped to receive, accept, and understand. The Holy Spirit supplies its own testimony, acting to impress the Word on us, serving as evidence that the Word is indeed the Word of God. Our revealed knowledge is thus doubly revealed—revealed to the person receiving the direct revelation through experience or inspiration, and again in transfer by way of scripture through the power of the Holy Spirit.

What could we know of God apart from revelation? The answer, for Calvin, is very little: "We should consider that the brightness of the Divine countenance, which even an apostle declares to be inaccessible, (1 Tim. 6:16), is a kind of labyrinth,—a labyrinth to us inextricable, if the Word does not serve us as a thread to guide our path;

and that it is better to limp in the way, than run with the greatest swiftness out of it" (I, 6, 3).

Apart from the revelation of scripture and, especially, of the revelation of the incarnation, we would have no way of escaping a skepticism that would leave the nature of God almost completely indeterminate. We could not recognize the world or ourselves as mirrors or microcosms of God. Even if we did, we would find ourselves unable to understand the world or ourselves well enough to grasp what they could tell us about God's nature. We would be stuck inside the labyrinth—the labyrinth of the world and, just as intricate, the labyrinth of the self.

Moral Knowledge

I have explored Calvin's position on our knowledge of God because it provides a key to his understanding of the nature and possibility of moral knowledge.

Calvin believes that we have some a priori knowledge of the good. The moral law is written on the heart (Romans 2:14–15). Before the fall, our moral knowledge was immediate, direct, and noninferential, just like our knowledge of God, though it too was fragmentary. We had some direct access to the commands of God, and thus some direct knowledge of God as "the origin and fountain of all goodness." We understood God's commands, which were the source of moral truth; we had a natural tendency to follow those commands,[23] but we also had the freedom to break them.

Once we did break them, our moral knowledge became indistinct. The law was still written on the heart, but it became entirely general, indeterminate, and easily resisted. Our innate sense of right and wrong gives us some insight: "That homicide, putting the case in the abstract, is an evil, no man will deny" (II, 2, 23). But we often falter in attempting to apply that knowledge in particular cases. Calvin's analysis here foreshadows Kant's idea that the essence of immorality is making an exception for oneself: "One who is conspiring the death of his enemy deliberates on it as if the thing was good. The adulterer will condemn adultery in the abstract, and yet flatter himself while privately committing it. The ignorance lies here: that man, when he comes to the particular, forgets the rule which he had laid down in the general case" (II, 2, 23).

But Calvin holds that we sometimes fall prey to weakness of will in a different way. Desire overcomes reason; our passions suppress our knowledge of right and wrong in particular cases: "The turpitude of the crime sometimes presses so on the conscience, that the sinner does not impose upon himself by a false semblance of good, but rushes into sin knowingly and willingly. Hence the expression,— I see the better course, and approve it: I follow the worse (Ovid)" (II, 2, 23). We may distinguish weakness of will, *akrasia*, from corruption, *akolasia*, by the fact that only the former leads to regret. The weak-willed person regrets giving in to temptation, and has a disposition to repent. The corrupt person, however, feels no regret, for the desire on which such a person acts is itself corrupted in a way that person cannot recognize. Weakness of will, then, makes us aware of our own failings in a way that can lead us back to God. Corruption does not.

The indistinctness of our moral knowledge, the difficulty of applying it to particular cases, and our tendency to weakness of will and corruption all fill our lives with moral risk. Being good and doing right were easy for us in the Garden. They are not easy now. The fall damaged our moral sense, impairing our ability to know what we ought to do and what we ought to be.

The fact that we are models of God—that we are in a sense mirrors of the divine—gives us some ability to attain moral knowledge. Just as in other respects, however, we want to see ourselves as creators. Our "monster minds" lead us to think of ethics as springing from ourselves rather than springing from God. So although the divine command theory is ultimately correct, and something we understood before the fall, we now resist it, seeing morality as consisting of conventions we devise for the improvement of our lives together. We are not entirely wrong in this; that is mostly what morality, as we now practice it, has become. But just as we were meant to be more than we have become, so morality was meant to be, and is, more than we have let it become. We fail to recognize God as its source and put ourselves in God's place, sometimes directly, as in existentialism or constructivism, and sometimes more subtly.

So long as we retain a purely secular approach to ethics, we are bound to stumble into skeptical traps, at least once we go beyond the few, vague perceptions we retain of the law written on the heart. We see that beyond a few generally accepted moral principles, people form different, conflicting conceptions of the right and the good. Using secular tools, we cannot tell which of these, if any, are correct. The only rational response would be to suspend judgment.

We can move beyond a few vague moral generalities, then, only through revelation. Without revelation, we would be left with little moral knowledge and even less understanding of how to apply it to the situations we face. But revelation allows us to have more than indistinct concepts of the right and the good. This is true in two respects. Scripture develops the law in much greater detail than we are able to discern from our limited grasp of what God has written on our hearts. It provides access to revealed a posteriori knowledge and allows Christians to form a self-regulating community that counteracts the force of skeptical arguments. Scripture's self-authenticating nature, in theory, but sadly not always in practice, prevents an analogous skepticism from afflicting those communities. The picture, then, is this: we have some general and rather indeterminate a priori moral knowledge, arising from our being made in the image of God. We have the ability to attain more precise and more particular a posteriori moral knowledge through the study of scripture.

By itself, however, scripture is not enough. Christ, here too, enables a gestalt shift, allowing us to see the world and ourselves as mirrors of God, made in the image of God, and thus as mirrors of the moral truth. Apart from Christ, we could not recognize the world or ourselves as revealing something of God's nature and the moral truth that arises from it. Even if we somehow did come to that recognition, we still could not understand the world or ourselves well enough to grasp securely what they could reveal about the right and the good and their application to the particular, concrete circumstances of our lives. We would be stuck inside a labyrinth largely of our own creation, with only the vaguest sense of how to navigate it. The labyrinth of the social world, the world that sees moral codes as conventional constructions and in which distinct, competing, conflicting moral codes interact, is even more intricate than the labyrinth of the self.

Conclusions

I have been arguing that Calvin has a distinctive metaphilosophical position. There are distinct stages of our relationship with God, each of which demands its own answers to basic philosophical questions. There are such sharp epistemological and ethical divides between the stages that each demands its own unique answers. Christian philosophers need at least one position reflecting our nature and capacities before the fall, and the other reflecting our nature and capacities after the fall. Calvin thus outlines a criterion—the Multiplicity Thesis—that an adequate Christian philosophy must fulfill.

I would not go so far as Bavinck, who holds that Calvinism yields "a specific view of life and the world; so to speak a philosophy of its own" (1894, 5). As Calvin sees it, our prelapsarian knowledge of God, the right, and the good is direct and noninferential; our postlapsarian knowledge of them is mostly indirect, inferential, and filled with moral and epistemic risk. Christian philosophers, however, might paint different portraits of those two stages.

Nevertheless, Calvin's thought gives us more than "marginal notes on philosophy" (Partee 1977, 21); it implies a metaphilosophy that constrains the philosophical positions available to Christian philosophers. We are more than we have become; morality was meant to be, and is, more than we have let it become. That must be at the heart of any Christian philosophy.

What Calvin sees as essential is this. Apart from the revelation of scripture and the incarnation—in short, apart from Christ—we would have no way of escaping skepticism. We could not recognize the world or ourselves as mirrors of God, as models of God's nature. The glories of nature and the deficiencies we sense in ourselves could point us toward God, but would tell us little about the being to which they were pointing. We could not understand the world or ourselves well enough to conclude anything about God's nature or the nature of the right and the good. We would be stuck inside the labyrinth of the natural world, the social world, and the self without any way to trace a path out. Only God's revelation in scripture and in Christ can allow us to go beyond the most fragmentary and indeterminate moral, philosophical, and theological knowledge.

Notes

1   All references to Calvin hereafter will be to the *Institutes* unless otherwise noted.

2   See Kolfhaus (1939, 12): "Hence all thinking about God outside Christ is a vast abyss which immediately swallows up all our thoughts." But it is important to note that Calvin's opinion of theology is little better; as Helm (2010, 5) observes, he generally uses it "as a term of contempt." Our relation to God is not primarily an intellectual relation; philosophy and theology thus tend to lead away from a proper relationship with God. Still, it is important not to exaggerate, for Calvin refers to his work as "Christian philosophy"; see Niesel (1957) and Partee (1977), contra Schulze (1902) and Mann (1934). Calvin sees philosophy as appropriately confined to "earthly things" (II, 2, 13), so in the phrase "Christian philosophy," "philosophy" must take on a somewhat different meaning Partee (1977, 14–16), based not only on reason but on scripture and the guidance of the Holy Spirit.

3   As Bouwsma (1989, 71) puts Calvin's view, "classical philosophy . . . conjured up for him fears of entrapment in a labyrinth." See also

Bouwsma (1988, 45–48). Of course, Calvin's interpretation, too, "can become a labyrinth in which the unprepared reader quickly becomes lost" (Holder 2006, 2)!

4 Calvin, consequently, eschews what he sees as excessive theorizing even in theology. As de Gruchy (2013, 118) observes, "The *Institutes* were not written as academic systematic theology to impress scholars of the day and engage them in debate, but as a guide for understanding the Scriptures in order to educate people in the Christian faith and help them live the Christian life." As Breen (1968) observes, "Calvin's first purpose was to teach."

5 Partee (1977) is the most extensive treatment of Calvin as a philosopher, and explores Calvin's relation to a variety of philosophical figures, themes, and movements. As Partee (1977, 10) observes, following Bohatec (1950, 30–31), Calvin's opening statement in the *Institutes* tracks Budé's definition of philosophy—the knowledge of God and man—which in turn tracks the Stoic definition as reported by Cicero and Seneca.

6 Most commentators on Calvin stress the moral significance of the Fall and at most hint at its epistemic significance. Consider Karl Barth ([1922] 1995, 33): "Human innocence before the fall consists of a sure combination, free of all friction, between sensuality, understanding, and reason with its vision. Original sin is the absence of righteousness; we have been dealt a wound that is in need of healing." Understanding and reason earn a mention, but Barth's focus throughout is on ethics. An important exception is Warfield (1909).

7 Barth (1934); quoted in Steinmetz (2010, 23).

8 For an argument that this is the central organizing claim of the *Institutes*, see Helm (2004, 2010).

9 Partee (1977, 15) puts it this way: "Although something of the understanding and judgment remains in man after the fall, the mind is not whole and sound but weak and dark." Haas (2004, 94) reconciles the conflicting language this way: "Because of his mercy and grace, God grants to fallen humanity some apprehension of right and wrong, justice and injustice. Appealing to Romans 2:14–15 Calvin notes that God imprints upon human hearts some understanding of his moral law, and God sustains the conscience as the faculty that judges between good and evil, justice and injustice. This knowledge and judgment is always defective and imperfect." In short, we blind ourselves, but God restores and sustains a limited vision so that we have at least some glimmering of the truth we used to see clearly. For a more detailed treatment of this theme, see Haas (1997).

10 That theory, as well as its interpretation, are controversial; see Bonevac (2012).

11 For studies of Calvin in relation to the Platonic tradition, see Battenhouse (1948); Boisset (1959, 1964); McLelland (1965); Babelotzky (1977); Partee (1977); Gerrish (1993). The dominance of Aristotle in Scholastic philosophy after Aquinas, despite the efforts of Renaissance humanists to revive Platonism, might account for some of Calvin's hostility to philosophy in general and to Scholasticism in particular. Calvin's relation to Scholasticism is controversial in its own way; see, for example, Muller (1995, 1996, 2000); Van Asselt and Dekker (2001); Partee (2008).

12 The interpretation I advocate is thus intermediate between the view of Torrance (1964) that Calvin "rejected the basic tenets of the Augustinian philosophy" (402) and the view of, for example, Smits (1957), Lange van Ravenswaay (1990), Lane (1999), and Holder (2006), who see him as essentially Augustinian in his approach to philosophical questions. For other treatments of the complicated relation between Calvin and Augustine, see Warfield (1956) and McGrath (1990).

13 Links between Calvin's thought and philosophical developments in the early modern period have been receiving increasing attention. See, for example, Bouwsma (1988); Zachman (2012); Helm (2020).

14 Grace and faith mark an important transformation of our relationship with God. There are thus at least three stages that require distinct answers to philosophical questions. I explore only the ramifications of the fall here. There are, I think, important parallels between our condition before the fall and our condition after faith has restored some of our capacities. To quote Haas (2004, 94), "The radical transformation of the human heart that enables sinners to understand and embrace God's moral order for their lives is the result of union with Christ. This doctrine lies at the heart of Calvin's teaching on salvation and the Christian life. It is accomplished by faith and the regenerating work of the Holy Spirit."

15 As de Gruchy (2013, 120) stresses, "Calvin's fundamental question is not Luther's—'how to find a gracious God'—but rather how do we know God at all, and how do we discern God's will."

16 The importance of the *sensus divinitatis* for Reformed Epistemology has engendered substantial controversy. Alvin Plantinga argues for its centrality in a number of works, including Plantinga (1993a, 1993b, 2000). Key reactions include Sudduth (1995); Jeffreys (1997); Helm (1998); Clanton (2017); and McAllister and Dougherty (2019).

17 For a subtle analysis of Calvin's epistemology and philosophy of language in relation to Duns Scotus, Ockham, and Richard of St. Victor, see Torrance (1964, 410–16).

18 "Experience teaches that the seed of religion has been divinely planted in all men" (I, 4, 1).

19 For an argument that Descartes pursues a similar strategy in the third Meditation, see Schechtman (2014).

20 See Schreiner (1991) for an extended treatment of the role of nature in Calvin's theology. Kayayan (1996) explores the mirror metaphor in depth.

21 On the importance of multiple witnesses, as well as miracles occurring in series, see Bonevac (2011).

22 The role of law, and the relation between conscience and natural law, in Calvin's thought is a complex topic that I cannot address here. For helpful discussions, see Bohatec (1934) and Backus (2003).

23 Calvin endorses a divine command theory. We should not conclude from this, however, that God's commands are arbitrary. We are in no position to understand justice as God understands it. To quote Bohatec (1934, 90–91; my translation), "We have to presuppose and believe in a justice unknown to us in all God's expressions of will and actions that seem incomprehensible to us."

References

Babelotzky, Gerd. 1977. *Platonische Bilder und Gedankengänge in Calvins Lehre vom Menschen. Veröffentlichungen des Instituts für Europäische Geschichte Mainz.* Wiesbaden: Steiner.

Backus, Irena. 2003. "Calvin's Concept of Natural and Roman Law." *Calvin Theological Journal* 38:7–26.

Barth, Karl. (1922) 1995. *Theology of John Calvin.* Translated by Geoffrey W. Bromiley. Grand Rapids, MI: William B. Eerdmans.

———. 1934. *Nein! Antwort an Emil Brunner.* Munich: C. Kaiser.

Battenhouse, Roy W. 1948. "The Doctrine of Man in Calvin and in Renaissance Platonism." *Journal of the History of Ideas* 9:447–71.

Bavinck, Hermann. 1894. "The Future of Calvinism." Translated by G. Vos. *Presbyterian and Reformed Review* 5 (17): 3, 5.

Bohatec, Josef. 1934. *Calvin Und Das Recht.* Feudingen. Westfalen: Buchdruckerei und Verlagsanstalt GmbH.

——. 1950. *Calvin und Budé*. Graz: Hermann Böhlaus Nachfolger.

Boisset, Jean. 1959. *Sagesse et Sainteté dans la Pensée de Jean Calvin: Essai sur L'humanisme du Reformateur Français*. Paris: Presses universitaires de France.

——. 1964. *Calvin et la Souveraineté de Dieu*. Paris: Seghers.

Bonevac, Daniel. 2011. "The Argument from Miracles." *Oxford Studies in the Philosophy of Religion* 3:16–41.

——. 2012. "Two Theories of Analogical Predication." *Oxford Studies in the Philosophy of Religion* 4:20–42.

Bouwsma, William J. 1988. *John Calvin: A Sixteenth Century Portrait*. Oxford: Oxford University Press.

——. 1989. "Explaining John Calvin." *Wilson Quarterly* 13:68–75.

Breen, Quirinus. 1968. *John Calvin: A Study in French Humanism*. Hamden: Archon Books.

Calvin, John. (1546) 1848. *Commentary on I Corinthians*. Translated by Rev. John Pringle. Grand Rapids, MI: Christian Classics Ethereal Library. Available online: https://www.ccel.org/ccel/c/calvin/calcom39/cache/calcom39.pdf (accessed on 28 May 2021).

——. (1559) 1989. *Institutes of the Christian Religion*. Translated by Henry Beveridge. Grand Rapids, MI: William B. Eerdmans.

Clanton, J. Caleb. 2017. "John Calvin and John Locke on the *Sensus Divinitatis* and Innatism." *Religions* 8:27.

de Gruchy, John W. 2013. *John Calvin: Christian Humanist and Evangelical Reformer*. Eugene, OR: Wipf and Stock.

Gerrish, Brian A. 1993. *Grace and Gratitude: The Eucharistic Theology of John Calvin*. Eugene, OR: Wipf and Stock.

Haas, Guenther H. 1997. *The Concept of Equity in Calvin's Ethics*. Waterloo: Wilfrid Laurier University Press.

——. 2004. "Calvin's Ethics." In *The Cambridge Companion to John Calvin*, edited by Donald K. McKim, 93–105. Cambridge: Cambridge University Press.

Helm, Paul. 1998. "John Calvin, the 'Sensus Divinitatis,' and the Noetic Effects of Sin." *International Journal for Philosophy of Religion* 43:87–107.

——. 2004. *John Calvin's Ideas*. Oxford: Oxford University Press.

——. 2010. *Calvin at the Centre*. Oxford: Oxford University Press.

——. 2020. "Calvin, Calvinism, and Philosophy." In *Cultures of Calvinism in Early Modern Europe*, edited by Gribben Crawford and Murdock Graeme. Oxford: Oxford University Press.

Holder, Ward R. 2006. *John Calvin and the Grounding of Interpretation: Calvin's First Commentaries*. Leiden: E. J. Brill.

Jeffreys, Derek S. 1997. "How Reformed Is Reformed Epistemology? Alvin Plantinga and Calvin's 'Sensus Divinitatis.'" *Religious Studies* 33:419–31.

Kayayan, Eric. 1996. "The Mirror Metaphor in Calvin's *Institutes*: A Central Epistemological Notion?" *In die Skriflig* 30 (4): 419–41.

Kolfhaus, W. 1939. *Christusgemeinschaft bei Johannes Calvin*. Neukirchen-Vluyn: Kr. Moers.

Lane, Anthony N. S. 1999. *John Calvin: Student of the Church Fathers*. Grand Rapids, MI: Baker.

Lange van Ravenswaay, J. Marius J. 1990. *Augustinus Totus Noster Das August-inverständnis Bei Johannes Calvin*. Göttingen: Vandenhoeck & Ruprecht.

Mann, Margaret. 1934. *Erasmé et les Débuts de la Réforme Française*. Paris: Honoré Champion.

McAllister, Blake, and Trent Dougherty. 2019. "Reforming Reformed Epistemology: A New Take on the Sensus Divinitatis." *Religious Studies* 55:537–57.

McGrath, Alister. 1990. *A Life of John Calvin: A Study in the Shaping of Western Culture*. Cambridge: Blackwell.

McLelland, Joseph C. 1965. "Calvin and Philosophy." *Canadian Journal of Theology* 11:42–53.

Muller, Richard A. 1995. "Calvin and the Calvinists: Assessing Continuities and Discontinuities between Reformation and Orthodoxy." Part 1. *Calvin Theological Journal* 30:345–75.

——. 1996. "Calvin and the Calvinists: Assessing Continuities and Discontinuities between Reformation and Orthodoxy." Part 2. *Calvin Theological Journal* 31:125–60.

——. 2000. *The Unaccommodated Calvin: Studies in the Foundation of a Theological Tradition*. Oxford: Oxford University Press.

Niesel, Wilhelm. 1957. *Die Theologie Calvins*. Munich: Chr. Kaiser Verlag.

Partee, Charles. 1977. "Calvin and Classical Philosophy." In *Studies in the History of Christian Thought* 14. Leiden: E. J. Brill.

——. 1987. "Calvin's Central Dogma Again." *Sixteenth Century Journal* 18 (2): 191–200.

——. 2008. *The Theology of John Calvin*. Louisville, KY: Westminster John Knox.

Plantinga, Alvin. 1993a. *Warrant: The Current Debate*. New York: Oxford University Press.

——. 1993b. *Warrant and Proper Function*. New York: Oxford University Press.

——. 2000. *Warranted Christian Belief*. New York: Oxford University Press.

Schechtman, Anat. 2014. "Descartes's Argument for the Existence of the Idea of an Infinite Being." *Journal of the History of Philosophy* 52:487–518.

Schreiner, Susan. 1991. *The Theater of His Glory: Nature and Natural Order in the Thought of John Calvin*. Durham, NC: Labyrinth.

Schulze, Martin. 1902. *Calvins Jenseitschristentum in seinem Verhältnisse zu religiösen Schriften des Erasmus*. Gorlitz: Rudolf Dulfcr.

Smits, Luchesius. 1957. *Saint Augustin Dans l'Oevre de Jean Calvin*. Assen: Van Gorcum.

Steinmetz, David C. 2010. *Calvin in Context*. Oxford: Oxford University Press.

Striker, Gisela. 1983. "The Ten Tropes of Aenesidemus." In *The Skeptical Tradition*, edited by Myles Burnyeat, 95–115. Berkeley: University of California Press.

Sudduth, Michael L. Czapkay. 1995. "The Prospects for 'Mediate' Natural Theology in John Calvin." *Religious Studies* 31:53–68.

Torrance, T. F. 1964. "Knowledge of God and Speech about Him according to John Calvin." *Revue d'Histoire et de Philosophie religieuses Année* (1964): 402–22.

Van Asselt, Willem J., and Eef Dekker, eds. 2001. *Reformation and Scholasticism: An Ecumenical Enterprise*. Grand Rapids, MI: Baker Academic.

Warfield, Benjamin Breckinridge. 1909. "Calvin's Doctrine of the Knowledge of God." *Princeton Theological Review* 7:219–325.

———. 1956. *Calvin and Augustine*. Philadelphia: Presbyterian and Reformed.

Zachman, Randall C. 2012. *Reconsidering John Calvin*. Cambridge: Cambridge University Press.

 CHAPTER 7

Understanding Moral Disagreement

A Christian Perspectivalist Approach

Blake McAllister

ABSTRACT: Deep moral disagreements exist between Christians and non-Christians. I argue that Christians should resist the temptation to pin all such disagreements on the irrationality of their disputants. To this end, I develop an epistemological framework on which both parties can be rational—the key being that their beliefs are formed from different perspectives and, hence, on the basis of different sets of evidence. I then alleviate concerns that such moral perspectivalism leads to relativism or skepticism, or that it prohibits rational discourse. I end by exploring new avenues for resolving deep moral disagreements opened up by the perspectivalist approach.

Introduction

It is a platitude, I take it, that moral disagreements exist between those who keep the historic and apostolic Christian faith, who I will call "Christians," and those who do not, who I will call "non-Christians."[1] Neither of these groups is monolithic, naturally. My opening observation is simply that certain moral beliefs are prevalent among (important subsets of) Christians and non-Christians, respectively, and that these beliefs sometimes contradict one another. The extent to which these parties disagree should not be overstated, of course. Many moral principles enjoy widespread endorsement within and without the Christian community. Additionally, many of the disagreements that do exist are only surface deep—that is, the disagreement stems from a discrepancy concerning nonmoral facts such that were the interlocutors to come to an agreement on these nonmoral facts, the disagreement would be resolved. Abortion is often taken to be an example of surface disagreement, and perhaps it sometimes is: if Christians and non-Christians came to an agreement on when life or personhood originates, then they might also reach agreement on the morality of abortion. In some instances, however, the disagreement is not so readily resolved.

For example, following Judith Jarvis Thompson (1971), many non-Christians maintain that abortion is moral even if the fetus is a human person, insisting that the woman's bodily autonomy frees her from any obligation to lend herself in sustaining the life of another. Others, following Peter Singer, argue that the moral significance of any person is directly proportioned to the level of sentience it has attained. Hence persons in utero (or even infants) can be permissibly killed if their continued existence significantly harms those with a greater capacity for pleasure or pain (Singer 1979). Thus we see that agreement on the biological and even metaphysical facts of the situation does not always resolve disagreement on the morality of abortion. Such cases—ones where there is a dispute over moral principles, not just their application—are instances of deep moral disagreement.

Deep moral disagreements are more common than one might think, often being obscured by the use of similar terminology. *Love*, for instance, is a virtue ostensibly championed by Christians and (many) non-Christians alike. However, it becomes readily apparent in application that the Christian and non-Christian conceptions of love can differ greatly from one another. On the latter conception, the loving thing may be that which promotes the fulfillment of one's sincerely held desires, whatever they may be. While on the former conception, loving someone may require encouraging them to relinquish certain desires in pursuit of sanctification. Such differences are rooted in rival accounts of human well-being. Here, terminological similarities hide deep moral disagreement.

Deep disagreement can also be obscured by the pervasive influence of Christianity on Western culture. How easy it is to forget that certain moral principles taken for granted in the West today were not so obvious to those of a different time or place. Belief in the inherent dignity and equality of all men and women, for instance, was present in few if any pagan cultures. Indeed, Nietzsche applauds the vigor of an elitist society that "accepts in good conscience the sacrifice of countless people who have to be pushed down and shrunk into incomplete human beings, into slaves, into tools, all for the sake of the aristocracy" (1886, 152). Or consider Singer's position that infanticide is sometimes morally permissible. Those who would claim that this position is evidently false to any morally sane individual should consider that the greatest moral theorists of antiquity, Plato and Aristotle, licensed the exposing of deformed infants. Singer insightfully writes, "If these conclusions appear too shocking to take seriously, it may be worth remembering that our present absolute protection of the lives of infants is a distinctively Christian attitude rather than a universal ethical value" (1979, 172). We must not mistake the moral insights of Christianity for truisms. Thinkers like Singer and Nietzsche are helpful in breaking the illusion of banality.

There is a temptation for Christians to pin such disagreements on irrationality. After all, if moral disagreements can be both deep and *reasonable*, then uncomfortable questions are raised. Does the existence of reasonable disagreement imply moral relativism? More plausibly, does it undermine justification for our own moral beliefs? Does it stifle hope that the disagreement can be resolved through moral discourse?

It is surely the case that many deep disagreements stem from bias, fallacious reasoning, or other failures in one's duty to pursue truth and avoid falsehood. However, Christians should avoid the temptation of charging all who dissent with irrationality of this sort. I will assume here that at least some non-Christians are justified in their moral beliefs, even when those beliefs directly contradict the Christian position. This is a fact about moral disagreement that Christians must face squarely. My goal in this paper is to develop an epistemological approach that charitably acknowledges the possibility of reasonable moral disagreement while avoiding the worries sometimes thought to accompany it.[2] It leads to neither relativism nor skepticism, nor does it deny the possibility of fruitful moral discourse. What it does do is illuminate why ordinary moral discourse between reasonable individuals can often reach something of an impasse, as well as shed light on how such apparent impasses may in fact be resolved. The crux is that a reorientation in perspective is needed—discursive reasoning alone is not enough.

The approach that I defend is a version of moral perspectivalism. The name signifies that the justification of one's moral beliefs is ultimately determined by the perspective from which one makes those judgments; thus, differences in perspective explain how conflicting moral beliefs can both be justified. My particular version of moral perspectivalism is grounded in an epistemological framework I call "seemings foundationalism." I address common concerns with moral perspectivalism in section two, and draw out important lessons for resolving disagreement in section three.

Seemings Foundationalism

The purpose of this section is to introduce a rough sketch of seemings foundationalism and show how it accounts for deep and reasonable moral disagreement. As a form of foundationalism, seemings foundationalism maintains that all inferential justification ultimately arises from the noninferential justification afforded to basic beliefs. Different forms of foundationalism differ concerning what provides noninferential justification and how. True to its name, seemings foundationalism says that noninferential justification derives entirely from how things seem to the subject. This breaks down into two epistemic principles. The first is phenomenal conservatism:

PC: If it seems to S that p, then, in the absence of defeaters, S thereby has at least some degree of justification for believing that p.[3]

The second is seemings exclusivism:

SE: S has some degree of immediate justification for believing that p only if it seems to S that p.

In short, all and only appearances, or "seemings," provide non-inferential justification. I do not have the space to argue for seemings foundationalism here, though I will seek to make it plausible. To do so, let us first turn our attention to these mental states, seemings, that supposedly ground all justification.

Seemings are a kind of experience—one in which a propositional content is presented to the subject as true.[4] Consider a case where you are in pain. You attend to that pain and think, "I am in pain." How do you know that thought to be true? The answer is that you can simply see that it is—you are directly acquainted with the correspondence between that content and the state of affairs it represents. There is a certain kind of feeling, or phenomenal character, that accompanies one's thought in such situations. The thought's content feels true. When a proposition feels this way, we call it "obvious," or "evident," or "manifest," or we might simply say "it seems true."

Introspection is not the only area in which things seem true. In perception, for instance, one's perceptual experiences feel as though they are accurately representing the way things are in one's immediate physical environment. There is a feeling of correspondence between the content of our perceptual experience and the world that it describes. Something similar is true in cases of rational intuition. It feels as though there is a correspondence between the content of some thought and the logical, mathematical, or metaphysical facts at issue. Importantly for us, there are also moral intuitions that display these same characteristics. For instance, it may seem evident to you that infanticide is a grave moral evil. Here, as before, there is a felt correspondence between some thought and a fact in the world (in this case, a moral fact). These are all different varieties of the same basic kind of state—namely, seemings.

A rough argument for seemings foundationalism goes as follows. Beliefs are noninferentially justified only if the mental state that causes them psychologically also justifies them epistemically. This is the nature of doxastic justification—that is, a belief is justified only if it is properly based on that which propositionally justifies its content. Furthermore, since this is a case of noninferential justification, the state that causes and justifies belief must do so immediately, without reliance on a larger system of justified background beliefs. Notice that, on foundationalism, some beliefs or others must be immediately justified in this way lest there be nothing justified at all. The question to ask then is, What kind of states are capable of both psychologically motivating and epistemically justifying belief in this immediate manner?

There are really only two basic ways to psychologically motivate belief: by indicating that some content is true or by indicating that it is good that it be true. States that motivate in the latter way (emotions, desires, and other affective states) are not capable of justifying.[5] Therefore, whatever mental states immediately justify basic beliefs must do so by indicating that the content is true. Such indication must be intrinsic as well—that is, the mental state M cannot indicate the truth of proposition p only because the subject has some surrounding framework of justified background beliefs that inform her that M makes p likely.

Seemings fit the bill here. By phenomenally presenting their content as true, seemings intrinsically indicate the truth of their content. They are the kind of state that not only does motivate belief but should motivate belief for those concerned to pursue truth and avoid falsehood. Since all seemings share this same phenomenological character, albeit in differing strengths, all seemings thereby provide some degree of immediate justification for their content. This is phenomenal conservatism.

Are any other kinds of states capable of intrinsically indicating the truth of some content? It seems not. If they lack propositional content, then the subject will not be able to appreciate the connection between that mental state and the content to be believed without a system of justified background beliefs in place. If they possess propositional content, but lack the feel of truth, then they will not intrinsically indicate the truth of that content in the right kind of way. A thought that p, if it does not feel true, only indicates the truth of p if one has reason to believe that the possession of that thought is in some way a sign of p's truth; but that relies on a system of justified background beliefs and so is not an intrinsic indication of p's truth. Finally, if the states at issue possess propositional content and the feel of truth, then they are just species of seemings. Thus, it seems that only seemings are capable of immediately justifying their content. This is seemings exclusivism.

It is important to note that seemings foundationalism is about internalist justification or rationality. This is distinct from warrant, which pertains more to knowledge. A belief is internally justified if, given all of the evidence available to the subject, the content of that belief is on balance indicated to be true. What is available to the subject is just what features within one's conscious awareness. The focus, then, is on the subject's first-person point of view and whether one's beliefs line up with what is indicated to be true from that perspective. Externalist statuses such as warrant look at things from more of a third-person point of view. The details differ by theory, but in outline, a belief is warranted if there is the right kind of connection between one's belief and the matter at hand. For instance, the belief-forming process may need to be reliable (i.e., statistically likely to produce true beliefs), or the belief may need to be produced in a way that tracks the truth (i.e., that is safe or sensitive) or that manifests virtue. The crucial discrepancy here is that warrant does not confine itself to the purview of the subject. One may have no indication whatsoever that one's belief is unreliable, or unsafe, or unvirtuous—even so, one's belief is thereby unwarranted. Our primary focus in this paper will be on internal justification and rationality, although familiarity with warrant will be helpful as well.

Seemings foundationalism can help us understand the origins and significance of deep moral disagreement. The first thing to note is that all of our justified moral beliefs (and any other belief, for that matter) will ultimately be based on seemings. If the moral belief is basic, then it is based directly on moral intuition. For instance, the belief that it is wrong to deliberately harm others when there is no greater good gained nor evil avoided is plausibly believed simply because it seems obviously true. If the moral belief is nonbasic, then one's belief is based on other beliefs, usually some combination of moral and nonmoral beliefs. For instance, say you conclude that it is wrong to torture another person for fun. Presumably, you will have inferred this from the foundational principle that it is wrong to deliberately harm others when there is no greater good gained nor evil avoided, along with the beliefs that torture causes harm, that the fun of the torturer is not a greater good, and so on. What are these other beliefs based on? Eventually, we must trace the inferential chain back to basic beliefs that are based on how things appear.[6]

The next thing to note is that how things appear can differ considerably from person to person. What seems obviously wrong to a Christian may not to a non-Christian. We can describe this by saying that different people have different moral perspectives. A perspective is a set of firm and lasting dispositions for things to seem a certain way. Effectively, one's perspective determines which seemings one counts as possessing.

All of this leads to a natural explanation for deep moral disagreement. Moral beliefs differ because moral intuitions do—because Christians and non-Christians are operating from different moral perspectives. Furthermore, where intuitions differ there is some possibility that both parties to the dispute are proceeding rationally in accordance with how things seem to them. This is not guaranteed, of course. It will often be the case that one or more of the disputants is failing to recognize a conflict between their beliefs, or lending too much or too little weight to some intuition, or making one of many possible errors.[7] The point is that it is possible that neither party is making any mistake at all. They simply see things differently and, from those different moral perspectives, rationally reach different conclusions. Thus, seemings foundationalism accounts for deep and reasonable moral disagreement.

Now if seemings can differ in these opposing ways, then some of them must be wrong. This should not be surprising. Seemings are fallible. It is to be expected, then, that some people's seemings align better with reality than others. This does not change the fact that, from an internal point of view, we must give appearances the benefit of the doubt in our theorizing. Thus, unless we have some indication that they are misleading, the rational thing is to believe in accordance with one's moral intuitions, even if they are (from a more external point of view) flawed.

That being said, if one's beliefs are based on faulty appearances, then that will likely affect the warrant of the resulting beliefs. The beliefs may be rational (internally) but unwarranted (externally). In such cases, there is indeed something wrong with one's beliefs, but the problem is not irrationality per se. One has not feigned one's duties in the pursuit of truth or stupidly miscalculated. The error lies not in the subject's handling of the evidence but in the unreliable or misleading nature of the evidence itself.

This provides us with a charitable way of diagnosing errors within those who disagree with the Christian community. We can, if called for, acknowledge the rationality of their beliefs. They have, we can concede, reached precisely the conclusion that makes the most sense given their moral perspective. The problem, rather, is that the way things seem to them is out of joint with how things really are. Their perspective is skewed. Moreover, this need not be due to any deep flaw within them (though in some cases that may be part of the explanation), but could simply be the result of participating in a flawed tradition.

Common Objections to Moral Perspectivalism

The perspectivalist explanation of disagreement makes some Christians feel uncomfortable. It smells like relativism to some. Or if not relativism, then at least skepticism. How can we acknowledge the rationality of non-Christians in reaching different conclusions and still be reasonably confident that we are getting it right and not them? Allow me to quell these fears.

First is the charge of relativism. The worry here is that acknowledging the rationality of Christians and non-Christians in believing p and not-p, respectively, implies that there is no objective fact of the matter. However, that does not follow at all. The following argument is plainly a bad one:

1. Some Christians rationally believe p, and some non-Christians rationally believe not-p.

2. Thus, there is no objective truth about whether p.

The mere fact that there is reasonable disagreement about something does not entail anything about its objectivity. This is especially obvious when we begin comparing reasonable disagreement across history. An ancient Mesopotamian may have been perfectly rational in believing that the earth was flat, but this in no way suggests that the shape of the earth is relative. One may protest that the ancient Mesopotamians had an entirely different set of evidence than us; what is disturbing, however, is when people living at the same time reasonably disagree. This response misses the key insight of seemings foundationalism, which is that people today are also working with different sets of evidence—in some cases quite different—because they see the world from different perspectives. In this way, the disagreement between people today is not that disanalogous from the disagreement between us and the Mesopotamians.

The only way to connect the lack of agreement to the lack of objective truth is by introducing some expectation concerning our access to objective truth. The idea here is that if there were an objective truth about p, then everyone would have unproblematic cognitive access to that truth such that reasonable disagreement would not be possible. In simply stating such a principle, one cannot help but see its implausibility. Why should we expect the world to be transparent to us? We might like it if that were the case, and perhaps some upstart youths manage to convince themselves that they have a perfect cognitive grasp of everything, but age and experience are humbling (humiliating?) and readily convict us of our finitude.

A more understandable concern is that moral perspectivalism shows our access to objective truth to be problematic, perhaps in insuperable ways. This is the threat of skepticism, and it can be developed in a few different ways. The first arises most notably from Kant and the philosophical tradition that follows him. The suggestion here is that acknowledgment of the ways in which our perspectives necessarily infiltrate the belief-forming process (there is no view from nowhere) shows that what we have access to is the world as we perceive it, not the world as it really is. Thus, while objective reality may be "out there" in some sense, it is not accessible to us. The second concern is that the existence of disagreement shows the Christian moral perspective to be unreliable. The third is that we have no good reason to think the Christian perspective more reliable than any other, in which case we should conciliate and become agnostic on points of disagreement. I will address each of these in turn.

The Kantian argument (though Kant would not have framed things in these terms) begins by recognizing that our moral beliefs are always formed from a certain perspective. Kant himself might emphasize the ways in which the concepts and assumptions underlying our perspectives arise necessarily from the nature of rationality and the structure of rational cognition; others may emphasize the contingency of our perspectives and the ways in which they are shaped by our various cultures, linguistic frameworks, and lived-experiences. In either case, the argument says that because we can only approach reality from a particular perspective, what we are grasping is not objective reality itself but at most a subjective reality molded by our perspective.

This line of reasoning faces numerous difficulties. For one, it is self-undermining. Am I to accept the conclusion as something that is known to be true about the world as it really is? If so, then the conclusion refutes itself. If not, then why should I believe it? A similar point could be made about the reasoning leading to that conclusion. As Thomas Reid says, "He must either be a fool, or want to make a fool of me, that would reason me out of my reason" (1785, essay 1, chap. 8, 24).

Second, the argument rests on a fundamental conflation between the object grasped and the means of grasping it. Consider the analogy of looking through glasses at a tree. The Kantian argument suggests that, when you look through the lenses, what you see is not actually the tree but rather something like an image of the tree projected onto the lenses. The means by which you are supposed to access reality—the lens—becomes the object of perception. To the contrary, as C. S. Lewis writes, "the whole point of seeing through something is to see something through it" (1944, 40).[8] What is perceived in this situation is the tree—an object whose existence and character are completely independent of the lenses through which you are looking. The lenses simply serve as the medium through which you become acquainted with that lens-independent object. In the same way, one's perspective on the world is simply the way in which one's intellect comes into cognitive contact with mind-independent reality. Our reliance on perspectives does not shut us out from knowing that reality any more than someone's wearing glasses prevents him from seeing the world around him.

The Kantian line is tempting, however, for something like the following reason. The glasses through which I am viewing the tree might have a distorting effect. Perhaps the tree appears blurry or fuzzy. The tree itself is not fuzzy, but what I am perceiving is fuzzy, so what I am perceiving cannot be the tree itself. The error here is thinking that what you are perceiving is fuzzy. What you are perceiving is a tree, and trees (around here at least) are not fuzzy. The tree appears fuzzy to you, granted, but that is different from saying that the object of your perception is, in fact, a fuzzy object. Even if one's perspective presents objective reality as being different than it actually is, the point remains that *objective reality is what is being presented to you*. That is what you are forming beliefs about, be they true or false. There is no sense in which the requirement that objective reality be presented through a perspective cuts you off from that reality.

Fine, but the question remains, does the Christian moral perspective present the world to us as it really is or, like a bad pair of glasses, does it distort our view of reality? We might simplify matters by simply asking: Is the Christian perspective reliable? You might think the existence of many different moral perspectives shows that it is not. But how is this argument supposed to go? Acknowledging that the Christian perspective is one among others entails nothing about its reliability. Returning to the glasses analogy, note that glasses do not *have* to have a distorting effect. To the contrary, those with the right prescription will experience clarification, bringing the world as it really is into sharper focus. The fact that other people with different glasses see things differently does not mean that your glasses are distorting things. Perhaps it is they that have the wrong prescriptions while you have met a skilled optometrist and had your sight corrected. In short, even among disagreement, it remains possible that Christians are seeing things reliably.

Even if disagreement does not entail unreliability, it may still provide evidence of it. The burden, however, is on objectors to specify how it is supposed to do so. Perhaps their thinking is as follows:

3. The moral beliefs of Christians and non-Christians, though stemming from different perspectives, ultimately arise from the same basic cognitive processes (the same kinds of rational faculties operating in roughly equivalent ways).

4. Many of the beliefs resulting from these cognitive processes are false, since they contradict one another.

5. If many of the beliefs produced by these cognitive processes are false, then those cognitive processes are unreliable.

6. Therefore, the cognitive processes resulting in Christian moral beliefs are unreliable.

This reasoning contains a number of errors. To see that there must be something wrong, notice that the same line of reasoning could be used to undermine many other kinds of beliefs that we take to be reliable. For instance, the various scientific beliefs that people have held across history seem to stem from the same basic cognitive processes, but many of those scientific beliefs (even most of them) have been false. Does that prove that the faculties under-lying our scientific beliefs are unreliable? Presumably not. (If so, then we are dealing with a much larger crisis that is not unique to moral beliefs.)

One error is that the argument plays up disagreement too much. There is far more agreement than disagreement concerning moral matters. Thus, even if we grant that "many" of our moral beliefs are false in some sense, premise 5 understood in that same sense would not be plausible. A reliable process might produce many false beliefs so long as it produces many more true ones. For premise 5 to be plausible, we would need to understand the antecedent as stating that some large percentage of the total beliefs produced by those cognitive processes are false, but that interpretation (on any reasonable read-ing of "large") renders premise 4 implausible given the predominant agreement in moral beliefs.

The objector may try to refocus the argument on the specific cogni-tive processes at use in areas of disagreement. The cognitive processes underlying contentious moral beliefs may be unreliable even if the general cognitive processes underlying most moral beliefs are not. Narrowing the argument in this way highlights a flaw with premise 3. In areas of deep disagreement, what evidence is there that Christians and non-Christians are relying on the same cognitive processes? If Christianity is true, then the cognitive processes at work in Christians and non-Christians are exceedingly different. In Romans 1, the apostle Paul describes the cognitive processes at work in fallen man: "[18]For the wrath of God is revealed from heaven against all ungodliness and unrighteousness of men, who by their unrighteousness suppress the truth. . . . [21]For although they knew God, they did not honor him as God or give thanks to him, but they became futile in their thinking, and their foolish hearts were darkened" (Romans 1:18, 21 ESV). Elsewhere, he contrasts this fallen manner of thinking with the one present in Christians.

> [17]Now this I say and testify in the Lord, that you must no longer walk as the Gentiles do, in the futility of their minds. [18]They are darkened in their understanding, alienated from the life of God because of the ignorance that is in them, due to their hardness of heart. . . . [20]But that is not the way you learned Christ!—[21]assuming that you have heard about him and were taught in him, as the truth is in Jesus, [22]to put off your old self, which belongs to your former manner of life and is corrupt through deceitful desires, [23]and to be renewed in the spirit of your minds, [24]and to put on the new self, created after the likeness of God in true righteousness and holiness. (Ephesians 4:17–18, 20–24 ESV)

The supposed cause of this renewed mind is the Holy Spirit and his work in the minds of believers: "[12]Now we have received not the spirit of the world, but the Spirit who is from God, that we might understand the things freely given us by God. [13]And we impart this in words not taught by human wisdom but taught by the Spirit, interpreting spiritual truths to those who are spiritual. [14]The natural person does not accept the things of the Spirit of God, for they are folly to him, and he is not able to understand them because they are spiritually discerned" (1 Corinthians 2:12–14 ESV).

If scripture tells truly, then the cognitive processes underlying Christian and non-Christian moral beliefs (at least in these key areas of disagreement) could not be more different. Either the mechanisms themselves are different, with the Holy Spirit functioning as a new kind of cognitive mechanism, or else the operation of one's rational faculties is different, with the Christian's being "renewed" in some way. I have suggested elsewhere that this renewal, which is plausibly a part of faith, may just be the onset of a proper perspective—one that allows the Christian to see the world rightly (McAllister 2018a, forthcoming; Gage and McAllister 2020).

It is also worth noting that the way in which the Spirit might be working is through one's tradition of inquiry. That is, the Spirit may choose to initiate one into a Christian perspective not through mystical experience or miraculous intervention (though those are certainly on the table), but by educating one in the Christian tradition and manner of life. This is carried out through scripture, sermons, and theological training, yes, but also through the liturgy, forms of worship, and witnessing the lives of other Christians.

The essential point is that premise 3 remains doubtful, and in fact contradicts Christian teaching. Nor is there going to be any easy way of shoring up the argument in light of these doubts. If Christianity is true, then the processes underlying Christian moral beliefs are reliable. Thus, establishing the unreliability of those processes will require showing that Christianity is false. This is simply an extension of Alvin Plantinga's (2000) thesis concerning belief in Christian doctrine more generally.

The final skeptical worry does not depend on the unreliability of the Christian perspective; rather it proposes that we lack any good reason for thinking that the Christian perspective is more reliable than (some of) the alternatives. According to this objection, Christians and non-Christians are epistemic peers, being in roughly equivalent epistemic positions with respect to moral matters and therefore equally likely to get at the truth. Learning that one disagrees with epistemic peers should, it seems, lead one to conciliate or, at least, to greatly lower one's confidence in the Christian position (see, e.g., Christensen 2007).

This argument runs into the same problem as the last one. If Christianity is true, then Christians and non-Christians are not epistemic peers. Thus, the Christian who believes in Christian teaching will have reason for thinking that her moral beliefs are more likely to be true. The objector may think such a reason illegitimate. After all, the belief that non-Christian perspectives should be downgraded is itself the product of the Christian perspective. Christians are using the Christian perspective to assure themselves of its special reliability. Is this not like taking a witness's word that she is more trustworthy than some other witness who disagrees? What we need, the objector claims, is independent reason for thinking that the Christian perspective is especially reliable.

As natural as it sounds, the objector's demand is unreasonable. First off, what does it mean to have an "independent reason" for thinking the Christian perspective more reliable? All beliefs are formed from a particular perspective. Thus, what is meant by an "independent reason" could only be a reason formed from some non-Christian perspective. But of course, we must then ask why we should think that particular non-Christian perspective to be especially reliable with respect to the matter at hand. Why think it more reliable than the Christian perspective for judging such things (or from some other non-Christian perspective for that matter)? By the objector's criteria, that dispute could only be adjudicated by some additional perspective that is different from the first two, and we quickly embark on an infinite regress. The result is skepticism, since the objector's demand for an "independent reason" can never be legitimately fulfilled.

Is there an alternative? There is. It is, in fact, the approach dictated by seemings foundationalism and its commitment to phenomenal conservatism. It begins with the recognition that one does not need to prove the reliability of one's perspective prior to trusting it. The rational default is to assume the reliability of one's perspective—to proceed in belief-formation as if it is reliable—and only to question it when challenges arise. Thus, first-order beliefs about the world are accepted prior to "independent" verification. When serious challenges to one's perspective arise (serious challenges require more than the mere possibility of error), one forms beliefs about the merits of those challenges in the same way as before. That is, one thinks about the matter and forms second-order beliefs about the reliability of one's first-order beliefs on the basis of how things seem. You trust your perspective in the formation of these second-order beliefs just as you do on the first order. If that reflective process leads you to conclude that your first-order beliefs are unreliable, or even that there is a good chance they are unreliable, then you have defeaters for those beliefs. On the other hand, if this reflective process reassures you of the reliability of your first-order beliefs, then you maintain them as before. (You then repeat this pattern as serious challenges to the reliability of your higher-order beliefs arise.)

If we apply this to the case at hand, we see that Christians can be perfectly rational in maintaining their Christian moral beliefs in light of moral disagreement. Imagine a Christian who, with all care and earnestness, reflects on the diversity of moral perspectives. As she reflects, it seems evident to her that the Christian perspective reveals the moral dimensions of reality better than any other, and she realizes that this is exactly what is predicted by Christian teaching and its promise of the Holy Spirit. Based on how things seem to her, she is reassured in the reliability of her original moral beliefs. The rational thing for her to do is to trust that reflective assessment, just as she trusted her moral intuitions in originally forming those beliefs, until there is some reason for thinking otherwise. Say that the reliability of that reflective assessment is itself challenged. Once again, there is nothing else for her to do but reflect on the matter and go with what seems true. So long as the reliability of her lower-order judgments continues to be confirmed, then maintaining her original beliefs continues to be rational. There really is not any other way of proceeding that does not end in skepticism.

Still, the whole process seems circular, which is bothersome. Ultimately, this is something one simply has to get over, though the following observations might help. First, note that there is nothing explicitly circular here—one is not relying on the premise "My perspective is reliable" in reasoning to that conclusion. One is simply proceeding as if one's perspective is reliable by believing in accordance with how things seem. Second, note that proceeding on such an assumption is absolutely necessary for rational inquiry more generally. How is anyone to prove the reliability of his perspective (or its unreliability for that matter!) without trusting in how things seem, and thus proceeding as if his perspective is reliable?[9]

In the end, there does not seem to be any good argument from the existence of deep and reasonable moral disagreement to the conclusion that Christian moral beliefs are subjective or unreliable or rationally ought to be abandoned. At least, there is no argument that should persuade Christians of such things.

Resolving Deep Disagreements

A final worry for moral perspectivalism centers on the prospects (or the lack thereof) for resolving disagreement. Does perspectivalism eliminate the possibility of fruitful dialogue between Christians and non-Christians? The first thing to note is that this is not an objection to the truth of moral perspectivalism. Some disagreements may be unresolvable. Perhaps that is our lot as finite creatures that know the world in a mediated way. The fact that we do not like these limitations does not mean we do not have them. Unresolvability becomes an objection only when (i) we have reason to believe that certain disputes are resolvable and (ii) moral perspectivalism leads us to expect that they are not. However, no dispute has clearly met both conditions. That is, some disagreements actually are resolvable on moral perspectivalism, and those that are not are not ones that we can reasonably expect to be resolvable.

There are several ways in which rational discourse between those of different perspectives—in this case, Christians and non-Christians—can continue to be fruitful. Even if the data (the appearances) are almost entirely different for non-Christians, the Christian can still point out an internal flaw in their attempt to explain those data. There may, in other words, be internal inconsistencies or tensions within the non-Christian belief system that the Christian can exploit.

Thankfully, however, the appearances are almost never entirely different. There is usually significant commonality in our moral intuitions that can be leveraged into arguments for the Christian position. Human nature is disposed from the get-go to see certain things as good (e.g., life, knowledge, friendship, benevolence, justice, pleasure) and other things as bad (e.g., death, ignorance, loneliness, misanthropy, injustice, pain). While one's appreciation of such things can sometimes be occluded, it is rarely altogether extinguished. Human nature has a way of reasserting itself given enough time. There are, of course, outliers—psychopaths who suffer from a kind of moral blindness—but here the exception proves the rule. Moral traditions, moreover, have mostly arisen out of these natural intuitions, and so preserve them into reflective maturity. One's moral tradition will undoubtedly reshape one's natural intuitions, recasting them in their own particular likeness, but the larger point remains. We should expect to find, and usually do see, significant commonality between those of different moral perspectives. This is often enough for rational dialogue in some form to continue.[10]

The previous two strategies operate in a straightforward manner. One simply formulates an argument using only premises that one's interlocutor, on his or her perspective, already accepts. There is, however, another path to resolving disagreement; and that is to alter the perspective itself. You may still give your interlocutor an argument, but it is an argument the premises of which are rationally acceptable only if a shift in perspective occurs. The key, then, is to initiate a gestalt shift within one's interlocutor—to get him to see the world in a new way—and by so doing position him to see the superiority of one's own position to the position previously held. If successful, this stratagem generates evidence for the Christian position rather than simply appealing to evidence one already has.

The transition to the Christian perspective can be encouraged in a variety of ways. Generally speaking, the goal is to get one's interlocutor to "try on" the Christian perspective.

This is not merely to inspect the Christian point of view from the outside, but to imaginatively enter into it, temporarily considering the world as though Christianity were true. C. S. Lewis (1970) gets at something close to this distinction with the following example:

> I was standing today in a dark toolshed. The sun was shining outside and through the crack at the top of the door there came a sunbeam. From where I stood that beam of light, with the specks of dust floating in it, was the most striking thing in the place. Everything else was almost pitch-black. I was seeing the beam, not seeing things by it. Then I moved, so that the beam fell on my eyes. Instantly the whole previous picture vanished. I saw no toolshed, and (above all) no beam. Instead I saw, framed in the irregular cranny at the top of the door, green leaves moving on the branches of a tree outside and beyond that, 90 odd million miles away, the sun. Looking along the beam, and looking at the beam are very different experiences.

When you get someone to see things through the Christian perspective, rather than just looking at it, the perspective has a tendency to stick. The Christian answers to life's fundamental questions, not to mention the framing of those questions themselves, prove intellectually satisfying. It just makes sense to some people. The result is that their own intuitions begin to align more closely with that of the Christian perspective, either gradually or all at once.

You can invite someone into the Christian perspective in multiple ways. Simply stating the Christian position in a cogent theological treatise, if read carefully and charitably, may do the trick. Of course, treatises are rarely read (not to mention carefully or charitably), and so more accessible and intuitive presentations of Christianity—such as C. S. Lewis's *Mere Christianity*—are often more effective.

Narratives also constitute a powerful tool. Stories engage the imagination and so possess great potential for shaping the perspectives of their readers. This is a point explored persuasively by Eleonore Stump (2010) in *Wandering in Darkness*. Christians, then, might simply invite their conversational partners to read scripture, or other Christian literature by the likes of Lewis, Tolkien, or Dostoyevsky.

There are other strategies that deserve mentioning. Increased attention is being given to the philosophical study of liturgy (see, e.g., Cuneo 2016). One aspect that must surely be considered is the ability of liturgy, through careful selection of language, symbol, and gesture, to coax one into a Christian perspective. Finally, the personal example of Christians is one of our most powerful tools. Empathy allows one to project herself inside the mind of another—to look at the world as someone else sees it—in order to make sense of his or her actions and judgments. Empathizing with a Christian, then, requires trying on the Christian perspective; and this, I have suggested, creates an opportunity for that perspective to become one's own.

One may worry whether this is a rational and altogether respectable form of persuasion. It smells of sophistry—empty rhetoric that appeals to the appetites rather than reason. No doubt one can initiate a perspective shift through appeal to the appetites, but that need not be the way of it. Consider Plato. Plato zealously condemns sophistry, yet the dramatic portrayals of Socrates recounted in his dialogues are best understood as attempts not only to engage the audience in reasoning but also to foster within that audience a perspective that acknowledges the authority of reason (for, as Polemarchus says in reply to Socrates, "But could you persuade us if we won't listen?"). Thus, one who reads Plato's *Republic* receives not only arguments for the superiority of the just life but a grand Platonic vision of reality from which the strength of these arguments can be appreciated. The attempt is to initiate the reader into a Platonic perspective, which is perhaps one reason why Plato chose to write dialogues rather than treatises (the former being generally more effective in triggering perspective shifts). What Plato is doing here is something more than straightforward, discursive argumentation, but whatever it is, it is not mere sophistry.

On further inspection, one sees that what I have suggested in "trying on" the Christian perspective is not altogether different from what happens all of the time in inference to the best explanation. When one considers the quality of an explanation, one does so by projecting oneself into a perspective from which that explanation is taken to be true. For instance, the detective considers whether the butler committed the murder by envisioning a scenario in which the butler does it and then asking himself whether this scenario makes sense: Is it intrinsically plausible? Does it account for all the evidence? How does it stack up against alternative explanations? If the envisioned scenario is a compelling one, the detective may undergo a perspective shift and find himself suspecting the butler. This is essentially what the above strategies do. Whether through prose, narrative, liturgy, or personal example, each invites the subject to consider the world through the Christian perspective. What makes it stick, however, is when that perspective makes sense to the person, and this is just as rational and respectable a way of being persuaded as any other.

There is, of course, no guarantee that the desired perspective shift will occur. There are many and varied reasons why one's interlocutor might decline to try on the Christian perspective or else fail to be convinced by it—factors encompassing the will as well as the intellect.[11] The disappointing fact is that there is no cure-all for moral disagreement. Sometimes the parties in a discussion hold different perspectives leading to different conclusions, and neither of those perspectives will budge. However, this provides no objection to moral perspectivalism. To the contrary, it would be a surprise if all moral debates could be resolved simply through more and better reasoning.

The Christian in particular has no reason to object to moral perspectivalism on the basis of irresolvable disagreements. Paul says, "The cross is foolishness to those who are perishing" (1 Corinthians 1:18) and that "the wisdom of this world is foolishness in God's sight" (1 Corinthians 3:19). The stark difference between the mindset of Christians and non-Christians should, it seems, lead to instances in which the disagreements between them cannot be argued away.

It may be, as suggested earlier, that the onset of the Christian perspective (or certain elements of it) is an integral part of having faith in God. If so, then these perspective-shifting strategies can be understood as creating opportunities for the dispensation of faith. Ultimately, faith is a gift from the Spirit, and the Spirit distributes gifts as he wills (1 Corinthians 12:8–11). This confirms our verdict that the persuasion of non-Christian interlocutors cannot be guaranteed—at least not by any effort on our part. We can do our best to present the Christian position in the manner most conducive to faith, but we can do no more than this. We wait on God for the rest.

Conclusions

I began this paper by acknowledging the reality of deep and reasonable moral disagreement between Christians and non-Christians. The rest of the paper explains why acknowledging this reality need not cause any serious worry to the Christian. Seemings foundationalism, and the kind of moral perspectivalism that arises from it, provides an explanation of the disagreement that avoids both relativism and skepticism. Nor does it close off the possibility of rational resolution. What it does do is help us better understand the nature of our disagreements and, in turn, how they stand the greatest chance of being resolved.

Notes

1 Admittedly, these labels are somewhat infelicitous as nontraditional Christians are sorted into the non-Christian camp. The choice is simply a matter of convenience—it is easier to say "non-Christians" than "those who are not traditional Christians, including non-traditional Christians and those who are not Christian at all." Why focus on traditional Christians rather than on all Christians? For one, the moral judgments of nontraditional Christians are generally more in line with non-Christians than with their traditional brethren. For another, the

resolution to the problem of religious disagreement developed in section 3 will only be acceptable to traditional Christians. Finally, only traditional Christians are likely to be concerned about the challenges to resolving disagreement, since nontraditional Christians are generally indifferent, at best, toward attempts at conversion. Thus, traditional Christians (TC) and not-TC are the relevant contrast classes.

2 While my focus is on how Christians should respond to moral disagreement with non-Christians, much of what I say will have obvious application to non-Christians (who should also resist the temptation to charge all of their disputants with irrationality) as well as to in-house disagreements within each camp.

3 This formulation of phenomenal conservatism is from Huemer (2007). Huemer first introduces phenomenal conservatism to the literature in Huemer (2001).

4 See McAllister (2018b) for an argument for this view of seemings.

5 At least, emotions are not capable of justifying insofar as they are emotions. Plausibly, some token emotions also constitute token seemings, in which case those emotions would be capable of justifying. They simply would do so by virtue of that which makes them seemings rather than that which makes them emotions.

6 Note that this does not commit anyone to ethical intuitionism as a metaethical theory. That theory makes specific claims about the nature of goodness (such as its being nonnatural) and how we intuit things about it that go far beyond what I am claiming here.

7 See Huemer (2005) for some of the many ways in which moral beliefs might still be irrational even if moral intuitions grant *prima facie* justification.

8 Lewis is talking about something else, but the line fits nonetheless.

9 Alston (1991) argues persuasively that no fundamental belief-forming practices can be verified without reliance on those very practices. For more on the use of one's Christian beliefs to dismiss potential challenges to the reliability of those Christian beliefs, see Moon (2021).

10 It is worth pointing toward MacIntyre's work on this point. Even when we acknowledge the pervasive differences between traditions, it is still possible for an adherent of one tradition to come to recognize the superiority of another tradition. This occurs when one recognizes how the alternative tradition frames things in such a way that better explains anomalies, avoids dead ends, and handles problems that plague the former tradition. See MacIntyre (1977, 1988).

11 Kierkegaard makes this point as effectively as anyone. See Evans (1998).

References

Alston, William P. 1991. *Perceiving God: The Epistemology of Religious Experience*. Ithaca: Cornell University Press.

Christensen, David. 2007. "Epistemology of Disagreement: The Good News." *Philosophical Review* 116:187–217.

Cuneo, Terence. 2016. *Ritualized Faith: Essays on the Philosophy of Liturgy*. Oxford: Oxford University Press.

Evans, C. Stephen. 1998. *Faith beyond Reason*. Grand Rapids, MI: William B. Eerdmans.

Gage, Logan Paul, and Blake McAllister. 2020. "The Phenomenal Conservative Approach to Religious Epistemology." In *Debating Christian Religious Epistemology: An Introduction to Five Views on the Knowledge of God*, edited by John M. DePoe and Tyler McNabb, 61–81. New York: Bloomsbury Academic.

Huemer, Michael. 2001. *Skepticism and the Veil of Perception*. Lanham: Rowman & Littlefield.

———. 2005. *Ethical Intuitionism*. London: Palgrave Macmillan.

———. 2007. "Compassionate Phenomenal Conservatism." *Philosophy and Phenomenological Research* 74:30–55.

Lewis, C. S. 1944. *The Abolition of Man*. New York: HarperCollins.

———. 1970. "Meditation in a Toolshed." In *God in the Dock*, 212–15. Grand Rapids, MI: William B. Eerdmans.

MacIntyre, Alasdair. 1977. "Epistemological Crises, Dramatic Narrative and the Philosophy of Science." *Monist* 60:453–72.

———. 1988. *Whose Justice? Which Rationality?* Notre Dame, IN: University of Notre Dame Press.

McAllister, Blake. 2018a. "The Perspective of Faith: Its Nature and Epistemic Implications." *American Catholic Philosophical Quarterly* 92:515–33.

———. 2018b. "Seemings as Sui Generis." *Synthese* 195:3079–96.

———. Forthcoming. "The Partiality of Faith." *Australasian Philosophical Review*.

Moon, Andrew. 2021. "Circular and Question-Begging Responses to Religious Disagreement and Debunking Arguments." *Philosophical Studies* 178:785–809.

Nietzsche, Friedrich. 1886. *Beyond Good and Evil*. Translated by Judith Norman. Cambridge: Cambridge University Press.

Plantinga, Alvin. 2000. *Warranted Christian Belief*. Oxford: Oxford University Press.

Reid, Thomas. 1785. *Essays on the Intellectual Powers of Man*. Edited by Derek R. Brookes. University Park: Pennsylvania State University Press.

Singer, Peter. 1979. *Practical Ethics*. Cambridge: Cambridge University Press.

Stump, Eleonore. 2010. *Wandering in Darkness: Narrative and the Problem of Suffering*. Oxford: Oxford University Press.

Thomson, Judith Jarvis. 1971. "A Defense of Abortion." *Philosophy & Public Affairs* 1:47–66.

CHAPTER 8

Epistemological Crisis in the Free Church Tradition

Michael Beaty

ABSTRACT: Alasdair MacIntyre contends that rationality is tradition-based and tradition-constituted. The free church tradition is an important tradition of thought and practice, very much at the center of the democratization of the United States. In this essay, I identify some of its primary commitments and discuss one of its practical challenges: how to resolve fundamental disagreements about what the Bible teaches and what it requires of those who identify as Christians. In particular, I discuss same-sex marriage in light of the following important features of the free church tradition: sola scriptura, priesthood of the believer, soul competency, the autonomy of the local church, a commitment to democratic practices, a minimally organized church polity, and restorationism.

My identity and formation as a Christian have been mediated, principally, by Baptist churches, their ministers and teachers, and their faithful members. I have been formed and nurtured by an intellectual tradition and its practices that unite a variety of diverse Baptist churches and their ecclesial associations—the free church tradition. In this essay, I discuss some of its primary characteristics and a general problem faced by those of us who adhere to the free church tradition. The problem is this: how to resolve fundamental disagreements about what the Bible enjoins and teaches for those who intend to faithfully follow Jesus, while affirming several key ideas identified with the free church tradition. As an adherent of the free church tradition, I am concerned that implications of some of its essential features make local churches, their members, or the educational institutions that serve these churches subject to a certain kind of intellectual crisis. I will refer to it as an *epistemological crisis*, following Alasdair MacIntyre. In an effort to motivate the reader's interest in the general problem, I focus on the specific question: How should Christians think about marriage between individuals who identify as homosexuals?[1] I focus my attention on Baptists and our challenges as a cautionary tale, perhaps, for those who actively and historically identify with the free church tradition.

My thesis is succinct: Baptists face an epistemological crisis with respect to the issue of same-sex marriages. The crisis forces opponents and proponents of same-sex marriages to prioritize which of the several free church tradition's principles are most fundamental. I have two secondary theses: (1) proponents of the free church tradition who affirm biblical authority will contend that same-sex marriages are morally impermissible; (2) proponents of same-sex marriages elevate soul competency and autonomy of the local church over biblical authority.

The Free Church Tradition and Baptists

In his book *The Free Church through the Ages*, Gunnar Westin observes, "The primitive Christian congregation in Jerusalem—as well as similar congregations in Antioch, Ephesus, Corinth, and Rome—was a free church. . . . It can be established that the primitive Christian assembly was a free church in that it had no relationship, subordinate or coordinate, with any constituted authority or state. For these churches there was a clear line of demarcation between the church and the 'world'" (1958, 1, 2). By free church tradition, I mean that tradition of individual churches (and kinds of Protestant denominations) that share a set of fundamental characteristics. For a very robust set of characteristics of the free church tradition, see *For Such a Time as This: Identity, Mission, and the Future of Abilene Christian University*, a special report of the ACU Board of Regents.[2] The document identifies (at least) sixteen characteristics of the free church tradition.

My primary focus will be on a subset of characteristics of churches that identify with the free church tradition: *sola scriptura* (the authority of the scriptures alone or biblical authority), soul competency, the priesthood of all believers / the priesthood of the believer, the autonomy of the local church, restorationism, and the commitment to general democratic practices and structures with a minimally organized church polity.

An additional feature of churches or denominations that identify with the free church tradition is worth noting. J. S. Whale claims that Protestantism has an impenitent sectarian temper (1962, 177). By sectarian temper Whale means a disposition or tendency toward mutation and schism rather than an ability to sustain one unified body of believers. The temptation toward schism for a tradition is this: intellectual disagreements over doctrine or practices are addressed by separation and rejection. One of the parties with a differing view leaves the church and joins another church or starts another church or denomination. In his splendid *A History of Christianity in the United States and Canada*, Mark Noll identifies eleven different varieties of Baptists. Wikipedia identifies sixty-three different Baptist bodies, denominations or kinds of Baptists.[3] We will revisit this sectarian disposition later in the essay.

MacIntyre on Rationality as Tradition Based

Famously, MacIntyre insists that all reasoning (theological, moral, political, or scientific) takes place within a tradition of thought, belief, and practice. A healthy intellectual tradition contains within itself conflict and continuities of conflict, yet it is capable of transcending, through criticism and invention, its own limitations and

shortcomings. Indeed, claims MacIntyre, a living tradition is a historically extended, socially embodied argument, in part about the
goods and practices that constitute (or ought to constitute) the tradition itself (2007, 222). When I speak of the Christian tradition or free
church tradition or Baptist tradition I assume MacIntyre's understanding of a living tradition.

The richest account and defense of tradition-constituted inquiry
is found in *Whose Justice? Which Rationality?* For my purposes, the most
important chapter is "The Rationality of Traditions" (MacIntyre 2007,
349–69). There MacIntyre insists that a rationally well-ordered tradition involves "the kind of progress which makes it through a number
of well-defined types of stages" (1988, 354). At the first stage, the
beliefs, institutions, and practices of some particular community
constitute a given in such a way that "authority is conferred on certain texts, certain voices, and certain persons. The tradition has not
been put to the question" (355). At the second stage, the authoritative
texts or utterances and their associated truth claims are subject to
"alternative and incompatible interpretations, which justify incompatible courses of action" (355). MacIntyre identifies this moment in
a tradition-constituted narrative as "an epistemological crisis" (1989,
139). In the third stage, a response to the inadequacies identified in
stage two results in "a set of reformulations, reevaluations and new
formulations, and evaluations designed to remedy or overcome the
initial limitations" (139). A tradition may or may not resolve its epistemological crisis. It is resolved when the community that is constituted by a narrative reformulates its narrative, making coherent what
was incoherent (140). MacIntyre argues that traditions are healthy if
they respond adequately to any epistemological crisis they face; and
unhealthy if their responses are inadequate (1988, 366).

Free Church Tradition, Baptists, and Same-Sex Practices

To draw attention to possible internal conflicts among the fundamental commitments of churches that identify with the free church tradition, let us look at one particular issue and the commitments of four Baptist bodies with respect to the issue. The four Baptists organizations are the Baptist General Convention of Texas (BGCT), the Southern Baptist Convention (SBC), the Cooperative Baptist Fellowship (CBF), and the Alliance of Baptists.

The separatist trajectory in Baptist life in the South (and North) is well documented. In his comprehensive and insightful *A History of Christianity in the United States and Canada*, Noll speaks favorably of the "burst of Baptist growth" in the nineteenth century (1992, 178). Noll notes that Baptists "were intense localists" who valued congregational freedom "only slightly less than the authority of the Bible" (179). Because of this disposition to dissent and separate over disagreements about doctrine or practice, numerous new Baptist bodies formed in the nineteenth and twentieth centuries. Noll observes that while "the Southern Baptist Convention eventually became the largest Protestant denomination in America, . . . that body has always been outnumbered by the Baptists who chose not to affiliate with the SBC" (180).

It is no surprise that this separatist disposition has been recapitulated over whether or not a Christian marriage is permissible for homosexual couples. On the one hand, both the BGCT and the SBC have expressed the firm conviction that the Bible teaches, authoritatively, that sexual activity between homosexual individuals is morally impermissible and outside of God's will. Thus, no Christian marriage is permissible for such couples.[4] In contrast, the Alliance of Baptists[5] asserts that marriage is morally permissible for homosexual couples.[6] Furthermore, they regard as unethical the view that Christian marriages are impermissible for homosexual couples because it is discrimination, thus, a form of injustice. Some regard the denial of Christian marriage to homosexual couples as theologically mistaken because it is outside the liberating arc of the biblical story.[7] Unsurprisingly, when the CBF lifted its absolute ban on the hiring of homosexual (and transgender) individuals in 2018, some churches from both the traditionalist and progressivist identities chose to withdraw from CBF.[8] The decision by the CBF Governing Board opened some positions to Christians who identify as LGBT but restricted leadership positions in ministry and missionary roles to those who practice the traditional Christian sexual ethic. The BGCT, which allows its churches to contribute a portion of their monetary gifts to CBF, was especially sharp in its written response to the decision by CBF. A spokesperson for the BGCT said, "While we understand the decision-making process undertaken, our position remains unchanged. We believe the Bible teaches that any sexual relationship outside the bounds of a marriage between a man and a woman is sin."[9] Howie Batson, the pastor of the First Baptist Church in Amarillo, Texas, a church in fellowship with the BGCT, remarked, "CBF's position is completely confusing. If same-gender sexual behavior is wrong—and Scripture says that it is wrong—then it is wrong for all employees, not just certain employees. The double standard is a sure formula for failure that treats staff members as second-class citizens."[10] Note that Batson states, without qualification, that same-sex activity is morally impermissible, given what the scriptures say and teach.[11]

How does CBF justify its decision? Here is one possibility. From the CBF website, we find, "Our understanding of Baptist faith and practice is expressed by our emphasis on freedom in biblical interpretation and congregational governance, the participation of women and men in all aspects of church leadership and Christian ministry, and religious liberty for all people."[12] The authors of the statement of CBF's Baptist identity ground its identity in the freedom of the individual with respect to biblical interpretation and in congregational governance—that is, the autonomy of the local church. This is not the freedom imagined and defended by early English Baptists. Jason Whitt summarizes their view succinctly and well:

> For early Baptists freedom is first God's nature, and only derivatively are human beings free as God calls them from bondage to sin

that is characteristic of the world, and into God's own freedom that characterizes the Church. This freedom for human beings comes by God's gracious activity: when they are oriented to God as their end, they can enjoy lives that rightly exhibit the practices of God's kingdom. The Church must be a disciplining body that forms in its members those practices of living that do not inhibit this freedom, but are consistent with that kingdom ethic. (2011, 39–40)

A more revealing explanation of CBF's self-understanding is provided by the following four core values, which are endorsed as intrinsic to Baptist principles of faith and practice by the CBF.[13]

1. *Soul Freedom*—We believe in the priesthood of all believers and affirm the freedom and responsibility of every person to relate directly to God without the imposition of creed or the control of clergy or government.

2. *Bible Freedom*—We believe in the authority of Scripture. We believe the Bible, under the Lordship of Christ, is central to the life of the individual and the church. We affirm the freedom and right of every Christian to interpret and apply scripture under the leadership of the Holy Spirit.

3. *Church Freedom*—We believe in the autonomy of every local church. We believe Baptist churches are free, under the Lordship of Christ, to determine their membership and leadership, to order their worship and work, to ordain whomever they perceive as gifted for ministry, and to participate as they deem appropriate in the larger body of Christ.

4. *Religious Freedom*—We believe in the freedom of religion, freedom for religion, and freedom from religion. We support the separation of church and state.[14]

A version of these four axioms is identified and defended by Walter Shurden (1993) in *The Baptist Identity: Four Fragile Freedoms*.

However, in contrast to CBF's ordering of the four freedoms, Shurden lists Bible freedom first, rather than soul freedom. Growing up in a Baptist church, the teaching I received from the pulpit and Sunday school classes made it clear that the believer's foundation was God's revelation *via* the Bible. The natural way to read CBF's decision to begin with soul freedom is that "freedom in biblical interpretation" is given priority over biblical authority.

Notice how CBF's affirmation and explanation of Bible freedom differ from the traditional way of understanding *sola scriptura*, that "the scriptures alone are the sole source of authority with respect to Christian belief and practice." In Bible freedom, while CBF affirms the authority of the scriptures, they appear to affirm that each individual's interpretation of scripture is equally authoritative by saying, "We affirm the freedom and right of every Christian to interpret and apply scripture under the leadership of the Holy Spirit." The quoted material is a way of reading the "priesthood of all believers," which makes it equivalent to the "priesthood of each believer." That is, each individual Christian believer is licensed to interpret the scriptures, independently of the church, the local gathered body of believers, or larger ecclesial structures. This way of interpreting the "priesthood of all believers" is worrisome for it undermines the possibility of the scriptures correcting the subjective judgments of individual believers. Indeed, CBF's unwillingness to identify consensual same-sex practices as morally impermissible and to make nonparticipation in consensual, same-sex practices a requirement of all CBF staff elevates a subjectivist understanding of soul freedom and Bible freedom over the traditional way of understanding biblical authority or *sola scriptura*. That CBF speaks of Bible freedom rather than biblical authority or *sola scriptura* is unsurprising. A certain understanding of soul freedom is made weightier than the other core commitments of CBF and influences one's understanding of the other three freedoms. How did (some) Baptists migrate intellectually to elevating the subjective judgments of individual believers over the objective texts of the scriptures and God's revelation *via* those scriptures?[15]

The Genealogy of Soul Competency: Francis Wayland, E. Y. Mullins, and Walter Shurden

To answer, let us begin with *The Axioms of Religion* by E. Y. Mullins (1908). At the beginning of the twentieth century, for nearly three decades, Mullins was the most influential Baptist theologian in the United States. Described by many as the "best known Baptist in the world" and "unsurpassed in influence by any man in his denomination," he was the author of numerous books and essays (see Humphreys 1990, 332). Arguably, his most famous is *The Axioms of Religion*. In it, Mullins identifies six axioms:

1. The Theological Axiom: The holy and loving God has a right to be sovereign.
2. The Religious Axiom: All souls have an equal right to direct access to God.
3. The Ecclesiastical Axiom: All believers have a right to equal privileges in the Church.
4. The Moral Axiom: To be responsible man must be free.
5. The Religio-Civic Axiom: A free church in a free state.
6. The Social Axiom: Love your neighbor as you love yourself. (1908, 73–74)

Of the Religious Axiom, Mullins says, "There is little to be said in explanation of the terms of our religious axiom. It will scarcely be denied by any. It simply asserts the inalienable right of every soul to deal with God for itself. It implies of course man's capacity to commune with God. It assumes the likeness between God and man. It is based on the principle of the soul's competency in religion" (92). Notice that Mullins identifies the Religious Axiom with *soul competency* and not *sola scriptura*. In fact, there is no direct reference to *sola scriptura* or biblical authority. Of *soul competency*, Mullins says that, "The axiom, of course, asserts *the principle of individualism* in religion. Primarily, the relation is between God and the individual man" (93).

Mullins explains its implications: "Since the Reformation this axiom has found expression in nothing more than in the exercise of the individual's right of private interpretation of the Scriptures. It guarantees the right of examining God's revelation each man for himself, and of answering directly to God in belief and conduct" (94). For Mullins, "The sufficient statement of the historical significance of the Baptists is this: The competency of the soul in religion" (53). That is, the right of the individual to his or her own interpretation of the scriptures, or soul competency, is the defining characteristic of Baptists. According to Mullins, soul competency is more fundamental than *sola scriptura* for Baptist Christians.

Importantly, the historian of Christianity Winthrop Hudson claims that this individualistic account endorsed by Mullins was a nineteenth-century innovation among Baptists in the United States and "derived from the general cultural and religious climate of the nineteenth century rather than a serious study of the Bible" (1959, 215). According to the editors of *Baptist Roots: A Reader in the Theology of a Christian People*, "No one was more responsible for so defining and popularizing this version of the Baptist heritage than Francis Wayland (1796–1865)" (Freeman, McClendon, and da Silva 1999, 220). Wayland was pastor of the historic First Baptist Church of Boston and for twenty-eight years served as the president of Brown University. In his *Notes on Principles and Practices of Baptist Churches*, Wayland claims that "Another Truth which has been inscribed on our banner is the absolute right of private judgment in all matters of Religion" (220).

If Mullins is an heir of Wayland, the heir to Mullins's *The Axioms of Religion* is Walter B. Shurden's *The Baptist Identity: Four Fragile Freedoms* (1993). Shurden insists that his aim is not to identify what makes Baptists distinctive, but rather to describe the Baptist mood, posture, or style of faith (1993, 1–2). Shurden summarizes the Baptist style of faith with three concepts: *freedom*, *choice*, and *voluntarism* (2). That Shurden chooses these concepts is predictable, given the previous quotes from Mullins and Wayland, each of whom emphasizes the right of every individual to his or her own interpretation of the scriptures. The Baptist posture is summed up, claims Shurden, by four fragile freedoms, those freedoms endorsed by CBF: *Bible freedom* (9), *soul freedom* (23), *church freedom* (33), and *religious freedom* (45).

While Shurden lists Bible freedom first, in Shurden's exposition of soul freedom he makes clear the centrality of the individual and his or her interpretation of the biblical materials. Like Wayland and Mullins, Shurden both identifies and celebrates the "freedom of individual interpretation of the Bible" as an essential feature of Baptist tradition, affirming an individualist, subjectivist approach to reading the Bible. This is evidence of an epistemological, thus, intellectual crisis for Baptists. For our English Baptist forbearers, the point of affirming the Bible as access to God's revelation is to have objective access to truth about God's nature and redemptive activities, to truths about the human condition and its prospects, and to what God-initiated remedies are available to address our deplorable condition. To affirm the "freedom of individual interpretation of the Bible" as an epistemological principle rather than a political freedom (that there be no established church to whom allegiance is a political duty) is a misrepresentation of the Baptist tradition prior to certain nineteenth- and twentieth-century inventions by some Baptists in the United States.

In August 2015, the First Baptist Church in Greenville, South Carolina, began welcoming same-sex couples as members. The church's six-month-long discussion did not address whether same-sex relationships are morally right or wrong or sanctioned or forbidden by biblical teachings. Rather, the report merely expresses an agreement among its members that individuals may hold divergent personal beliefs about homosexual practice and still worship and serve together.[16] That the membership of FBC Greenville voted as they did is not surprising, given Shurden's understanding of the Baptist posture. But is this posture consistent with Baptists' free church origins? In his *Free Church through the Ages*, Westin notes that "churches and fellowships which follow the free church heritage have regarded the New Testament as being authoritative in matters of organization as

191

well as belief" (1958, 8). In short, adherents of the free church tradition originally affirmed biblical authority as axiomatic with respect to Christian beliefs and practices.

If we were in a position to ask for an argument in support of the decision by the FBC Greenville, it is easy to imagine its membership appealing to Bible freedom, church freedom, or soul freedom to provide their justification. But from printed reports, no arguments were offered on either side of the issue. If an argument had been offered to support the decision of the membership of FBC Greenville, would it acknowledge that there is a legitimate appeal to the scriptures, a plain, clear reading of the relevant Bible texts that provides an argument from scripture that same-sex practices are morally impermissible?[17] Or would their argument appeal only to the right of every individual to interpret the scriptures for herself or himself, which is an appeal to Mullins's understanding of soul competency or Shurden's understanding of Bible freedom? If either of these latter strategies were employed, then their use of Mullins's soul competency or Shurden's Bible freedom provide no opportunity for an epistemological crisis to emerge for that particular church. Why? Because a certain understanding of soul competency or Bible freedom is the axiom by virtue of which both the scriptures are being appropriated for their purposes and, also, the other "axioms" of freedom are being understood. However, this reading of soul competency or Bible freedom undermines the Protestant reformers' more fundamental axiom—namely, *sola scriptura*: that Christian beliefs and practices are properly grounded only when they are expressions of God's revelation that are found in the texts that constitute the scriptures.

In contrast to the leadership of FBC Greenville, Pastor Batson argued that CBF's decision to permit individuals who are committed to same-sex practices to occupy some positions but not others is a confusing decision because it is self-contradictory. That is, anyone who affirms that the Bible is authoritative for belief and practice (*sola scriptura*) and who is also a defender of the view that same-sex practices are morally permissible for Christians owes us an explanation of the apparent contradiction between what the Biblical texts say about marriage and morally permissible sexual practices and the affirmation of homosexual practices as morally acceptable. Their narrative must enable us to understand both how we could have held our original beliefs and how we could have come to endorse these misbeliefs. And how, for example, other Christian denominations were misled, also.[18] The account by the leadership of FBC Greenville of their decision to allow practicing gays and lesbians to serve in positions of leadership in their church provides no such explanation. It merely reflects a vote, whose outcome was democratically administered and determined. According to Mullins, the requirement of democratic decision-making processes is a corollary of the axiom of soul competency (1908, 55). Despite Mullins's affirmation of democratic decision-making processes on contested issues, it is unimaginable that he intended that voting be initiated independently of churchwide discussion of what the Bible teaches, when the contested issue is what Christians ought to believe and how Christians ought to act. And it is unimaginable because of the centrality of scriptures to the free church tradition, in general, and Baptists, in particular. Surely, these facts point to a tradition in disrepair—that is, if FBC Greenville is an apt representative of contemporary Baptist congregational approaches to decision-making with respect to ethical issues.

Important questions arise. What democratic mechanisms are available for resolutions of deep disagreements concerning the scriptures' teachings about what is permissible, impermissible, or required of those who freely identify themselves as Christians? How should congregations in the free church tradition resolve fundamental disagreements about how to regard marriage for homosexual couples who express a monogamous commitment to one another? Or how should they resolve disagreements about whether or not a practicing homosexual is permitted to serve on the church staff or teach Sunday school or serve in the role of deacon or elder of the church?

I can imagine two similar but different democratic-like methodologies to settle disagreements with respect to this issue. Since the polity of Baptist churches is both congregational and democratic, the pastor, in conjunction with other members of the church staff, organizes a study of the controversial issue. Organizing the event includes identifying the relevant passages from the Bible that are essential to understanding the issues and choosing helpful and relevant nonbiblical reading materials. Additionally, it includes decisions about when and how often to meet to discuss the matter. At stake is providing a reasonable amount of time to allow a process of discernment for each individual and for the church, collectively. At its conclusion, the adult members of the church vote, with the outcome of the vote establishing its policy. If some members disagree with the decision the majority of its members approved, then they may choose to join another church. The method I describe above is explicitly endorsed by Mullins in his explanation of *The Ecclesiastical Axiom: All Believers Have a Right to Equal Privileges in the Church*. He says, "Because men have an equal right to direct access to God they are entitled to equal privileges in the church. . . . Because the individual deals directly with his Lord and is immediately responsible to him, the spiritual society needs to be a democracy. . . . Every form of polity other than democracy somewhere infringes upon the lordship of Christ. I mean a direct Lordship" (1908, 127, 129).

A second method may appeal to the biblical model (or practice) of resting important decisions with the deacons or the elders of the church. To the extent that some Baptists privilege the Bible as their "sole authority" with respect to belief and practice, it is unsurprising that some Baptist churches appeal to elders or deacons in such decision-making settings.[19] Consider the following source on *biblical eldership*: "Biblically, the focal point of all church leadership is the elder. An elder is one of a plurality of biblically qualified men who jointly shepherd and oversee a local body of believers. The word translated 'elder' is used nearly twenty times in Acts and the epistles in reference to this unique group of leaders who have responsibility for overseeing the people of God."[20] John MacArthur notes that the consistent pattern of the New Testament church is a local body of believers that is shepherded by a plurality of elders. Presumably, elders are selected because each is recognized to exemplify, in word and deed, Apostle-like qualities in practice, in character, and in wisdom. That some Baptist churches employ the democratically inspired methodologies to settle disagreements may be explained by (1) the fact that direct democracy seems more consistent with a nonhierarchical ecclesiology, (2) the continued influence of the "democratic" mindset expressed by Wayland and Mullins on contemporary Baptist life, and (3) the fact that churches that retain an emphasis on elders tend to limit the occupant of this role to men.

Because the free church tradition emphasis on *sola scriptura* makes what the Bible teaches essential to what Christians ought to believe and which behaviors are permissible or impermissible or obligatory, below I provide two allegedly scriptural responses to the question of whether monogamous homosexual marriages are permissible for Christians. They provide opposite answers to our question. At stake is biblical interpretation. In his book *The Doctrine of Biblical Authority*, Russell Dilday—a former Baptist pastor, scholar, teacher, and administrator—identifies and discusses four principles of biblical interpretation:[21]

1. The Linguistic Principle: Since the Bible was written in several different languages and translated into other languages (such as English), it is important to understand the words, sentence structure and grammar of the relevant languages. It includes the careful use of good translations.

2. The Historical Principle: Knowledge of historical background of the biblical passages is important in understanding the text. This includes knowledge of biblical geography, culture, customs, patterns of family life, national events.

3. The Theological Principle: Since the main purpose of the Bible is to convey knowledge about God and God's will for human beings, it is important to allow the principles and truths about God and God's will for human beings to emerge from a careful reading of the text. The theological principle includes the following interpretative strategies: that difficult verses be understood in light of clearer passages; that incidental passages

be interpreted in light of systematic passages; that Old Testament passages receive the ultimate meaning in light of the New Testament; that the primary criterion to interpret the Bible is Jesus Christ.

4. The Practical Principle: Having determined what the biblical passage meant then, the interpreter must next determine what it means now.

Another, more contemporary biblical scholar, Robin Scroggs, offers the following three principles for the purposes of biblical interpretation and application:

1. Do the work of exegesis to understand the meaning of the biblical statements in their historical and literary context.
2. Compare the specific meaning of the texts with the major theological and ethical themes of the Bible.
3. Determine whether the cultural context addressed in the text bears a reasonable similarity to the modern context in which it is to be applied. (1983, 123)

I find it helpful to use the combination of these interpretative principles for our purposes in this essay. After presenting the two contradictory positions with respect to the biblical witness on same-sex practices, we will ask whether the principles of Biblical interpretation as identified by Dilday or Scroggs allow us to adjudicate which of the two positions fits best with an appeal to biblical authority—*sola scriptura*. Not being a biblical scholar, I rely on the work of biblical scholars to make my arguments.

The Scriptures Say Yes to Homosexual Marriages

What can be said on behalf of the view that same-sex practices are morally permissible for Christians?[22] Of course, the literature on this topic is very large. To provide a manageable response, I focus on William Stacy Johnson's *A Time to Embrace: Same-Sex Relationships in Religion, Law, and Politics*, especially chapter 3, "Becoming Family: The Consecration of Same-Sex Love" (2012, 115–62). There, Johnson argues that there is a strong biblical and theological case for regarding homosexual marriages as morally permissible for Christians. While endorsing the view that the scriptures are both a unique and authoritative witness to Jesus, the Divine Word, and that it is a reliable guide to matters of faith, morals, and practice, Johnson, first, asserts, "Supporting exclusively committed gay unions represents not a departure from our biblical and theological traditions but rather a deepening of it" (115–62). Second, he insists that the scriptures are not a collection of abstract propositions but a living word and a living conversation partner with us. Finally, Johnson claims that marriage is primarily about transformation, and it functions as a means of grace. It mediates God's delight in human beings and God's affirmation of two people's desire for intimate companionship, long-term commitment, and community. On these "three fundamental realities . . . we see that gay couples are just as capable as straight couples of embracing these ideas" (115–62).

Not surprisingly, Johnson rejects the claim that Genesis 1 and Genesis 2 definitively reject homosexual marriages. Genesis 1, claims Johnson, underscores that each of us is created in the image of God. These passages imply that each of us has the capacity and the desire to enter into deep and enduring relationships with God and with our fellow human beings. Marriage is ordained to nurture and order this desire for intimacy and union with another human being while enhancing our relationship with God. In contrast to the traditional way of reading Genesis 1, "male and female" need not refer to biological complementarity, but the complementarity possible for gays and lesbians as they seek deep and enduring human relationships within a covenanted relationship (Johnson 2012, 121): "In short, both male and female are created in God's image whether or not they conform to culturally conditioned norms. They were *all* created in God's image regardless of gender, gender orientation, or any other condition anyone might choose to lessen their humanity" (122).

According to Johnson, the most important verse with respect to the gay marriage debate is Genesis 2:18: "Then the Lord God said, 'It is not good for the man to be alone; I will make him a helper suitable for him.'"[23] Johnson argues that "a suitable helper or partner" implies something other than an "anatomically correct sexual companion." Rather it implies someone "who is a life-giving, nurturing, and sustaining presence" (2012, 124). If so, "then, what kind of suitable, redemptive companion is appropriate for the person who is gay or lesbian? . . . Does it not make more sense for the gay or lesbian person to find a companion suitable to his or her own sexual orientation?" (124). More controversially, Johnson asserts,

This second creation account . . . suggests that marriage is not merely an order of creation but most especially an order of redemption. . . . Marriage becomes a vehicle of redemption. . . . Marriage already gives a foretaste of the divine reordering that is breaking into the world. . . . What do we make of the cry of delight that comes from the lips of Adam when he first catches sight of Eve? . . . The joy expressed by Adam arises because he has found his sexual "other," . . . but . . . there is no emphasis on difference or complementarity. . . . When Adam sees Eve, he does not celebrate her otherness but her sameness. . . . What strikes him is that she is bone of my bone, flesh of my flesh. . . . For gay and lesbian people, a person of opposite sex is simply not able to provide this sort of fitting companionship. The best way for a gay or lesbian person to find a help suitable, an appropriate partner, is a committed union with a person of the same gender. There is nothing explicit in the Genesis texts that prohibits this and much more that supports it. (126)

The second traditional purpose of marriage is to provide a context within which to live out a meaningfully ordered commitment to another person, argues Johnson (2012, 127). The reason we honor the commitment of spouses is that their commitment serves to bear visible witness to the commitment God makes to the people of God. The joy of intimacy and the companionship it nourishes lead to lifelong commitment. In short, the sexual energy of the *Song of Songs* points to something beyond itself, something more enduring and more holy (127). It points to a genuine love based on a rich and joyful companionship that includes physical intimacy and should be celebrated and supported. The possibility of this kind of committed lifelong love, claims Johnson, should be the lens by virtue of which we see and discuss long-term, monogamous marriages, including homosexual ones.

Johnson distinguishes three types of homoeroticism: (1) age-differentiated, intergenerational same-sex practices, (2) status-defined same-sex practices, and (3) egalitarian same-sex practices (2012, 16–17).[24] The scriptures reject the first two types, but they do not reject the egalitarian, covenantal same-sex practices that exhibit constancy and fidelity, he argues. For these characteristics may be exhibited not only in heterosexual marriages but also in homosexual marriages (129). Johnson concludes his discussions of the Old Testament scriptures in this way:

Our sexuality is good when it exhibits context, commitment, and constancy—in short, covenant. . . . The reason such covenantal love [marriage] is blessed by religious communities is to give thanks for God's faithfulness and to lift up the hope that this same faithfulness will be reflected, however inadequately, in human covenant relationships. The goodness of sexuality finds its purposes in the particularity of sexuality within a covenantal context. Goodness seeks holiness as its fulfillment. If love must be consecrated to be

considered holy, then finding a consecrated context for the love
of gays and lesbians should become a moral imperative. (135)

Thus, following Johnson, we might conclude that individual congregations that deny marriage to homosexuals who seek a Christian marriage both (1) ignore what is theologically primary—the celebration of
monogamous sexuality within a covenanted framework—and (2) act
unjustly by failing to assist in the liberation of the oppressed. They fail
in these ways because they deny homosexuals a consecrated context,
one sanctioned by the Christian church, to express their mutual love.

However, Johnson recognizes that he must address and defeat
Paul's proscriptions against homosexual practices.[25] His central thesis
is that Paul is principally condemning the homosexual acts between
an older male or female and a much younger male or female (pederasty) and, more generally, same-sex practices performed by social
superiors on their social inferiors. Paul's frame of reference for his
rejection of homosexual practices "was the passive-active asymmetry
of homoerotic acts in the Roman world. . . . Covenantal relationships
between equals were not envisioned within Paul's culture" (Johnson 2012, 291n15). His treatment of Paul largely recapitulates Robin
Scroggs's thesis in his groundbreaking book, *The New Testament and
Homosexuality* (1983). Both claimed that pederasty, love of boys, was the
only form of homosexual relationships known in the Greco-Roman
world. Paul condemned it primarily because of its inherent inequality,
impermanence, and humiliating characteristics. Thus, Paul's condemnation of homosexuality was condemnation of pederasty alone
(Johnson 2012, 127–28).

The Scriptures Say No to
Same-Sex Practices: Appeal to Hays

Is a biblically grounded denial of Scroggs's and Johnson's shared thesis
that monogamous homosexual marriages are sanctioned by a proper
interpretation of the relevant biblical materials possible? It is.

New Testament scholar and ethicist, Richard Hays, observes that the Bible rarely discusses homosexual behavior, identifying it as a minor concern when compared to Bible's emphasis on the treatment of the poor by the wealthy. However, Hays declares that the small number of biblical passages that address homosexual practices are "unambiguously and unremittingly negative in their judgment" (1996, 381). In Leviticus 18:22, we read, "You shall not lie with a male as one lies with a female; it is an abomination." Leviticus 20:13 provides a strongly worded condemnation of male same-sex practices: "If there is a man who lies with a male as those who lie with a woman, both of them have committed a detestable act; they shall surely be put to death. Their bloodguiltiness is upon them."[26] In several passages from 1 and 2 Kings, we find strong condemnations of male homosexuality as expressed by reference to the Temple male prostitutes and one that may include a condemnation of the Temple female prostitutes.[27]

Hays addresses the objection that the prohibitions of homosexual practices are no longer binding because they were instances of the Old Testament ritual purity laws. Examples include rules concerning circumcision and dietary practices, which many argue are no longer morally or religiously relevant for Christians today. Hays's response is direct. The early church consistently adopted the Old Testament's teachings on sexual morality, including homosexual acts (1996, 382).

In 1 Corinthians 6:9–11, Paul confronts his interlocutors, some of whom believe that they are so spiritually advanced that the customary moral rules do not apply to them. He asks, "Or do you know that the unrighteous shall not inherit the kingdom of God?" He gives a list of the wrongdoers, which include "fornicators, idolators, adulterers, . . . the greedy, drunkards, revilers, robbers and *malakoi* and *arsenokoitai*" (Hays 1996, 382). Hays notes that *malakoi* appears often in Hellenistic Greek as a pejorative slang to describe the passive partners in homosexual activity (382). Hays acknowledges that some scholars suggest that the meaning of *arsenokoitai* is uncertain. Still, Scroggs has shown that it is a translation of the Hebrew *mishkav zakur*, which means lying with a male, insists Hays (382). He concludes,

"Thus Paul's use of the term *arsenokoitai* presupposes and reaffirms the holiness code's condemnation of homosexual acts" (382).

Perhaps the most well-known passage condemning homosexual activities is from Paul's letter to the Romans 1:18–28.[28] Hays says that it is "the most crucial text for Christian ethics concerning homosexuality . . . because this is the only passage in the New Testament that explains the condemnation of homosexual behavior in an explicitly theological context" (1996, 383). To be sure, Paul is condemning the rejection of God that is implicit in so many of the practices of the Roman world. Nonetheless, in Romans 1:22–27, Paul identifies homosexual relationships as at odds with God's rule and the righteousness (right living) expected of Christians.

> Professing to be wise, they became fools, and exchanged the glory of God for an image in the form of corruptible man and of birds and four-footed animals and crawling creatures. Therefore, God gave them over in the lusts of their hearts to impurity, that their bodies might be dishonored among them. For they exchanged the truth of God for a lie, and worshipped and served the creature rather than the Creator, who is blessed forever. Amen. For this reason, God gave them over to degrading passions, for their women exchanged the natural function for that which is unnatural, and in the same way also the men abandoned the natural function of woman and burned in their desire toward one another, men with men committing indecent acts and receiving in their own persons the due penalty of their error.[29]

A plain reading of this New Testament text, especially within its larger context, suggests the following points:[30]

- That God exists and reigns is evident to the wise, but many human beings have suppressed this knowledge with disastrous consequences.
- Among those consequences are the ways in which human beings embraced the unnatural for the natural passions and appetites.

- Paul accepts as ethically normative the anatomical and procreative complementarity of male and female.[31]
- And thus, independently of divine revelation as expressed, for example, in Leviticus, human beings have access to the knowledge that homosexual relationships are morally impermissible and against God's will.

That Paul accepts as ethically normative the anatomical and procreative complementarity of males and females is explained and defended by Hays. He says,

> In describing what it is that straying humans have "exchanged," Paul for the first time introduces the concept of "nature" (*physis*) into the argument (Romans 1:26): they have exchanged (translating literally) "the natural use for that which is contrary to nature." . . . There are abundant instances, both in the work of Greco-Roman moral philosophy and in literary texts, of the opposition between "natural" (*kata physin*) and "unnatural" (*para physin*) behavior. . . . The opposition between "natural" and "unnatural" is very frequently used . . . as a way of distinguishing between heterosexual and homosexual behavior. . . . Though he offers no explicit reflection on the concept of "nature," it appears that in this passage Paul identifies "nature" with the created order. . . . It appeals to the conception of what ought to be, of the world designed by God and revealed by the laws and stories of Scripture. Those who indulge in sexual practices *para physin* are defying the Creator and demonstrating their own alienation from him. (Hays 1996, 387)

In sum, Hays claims that the scriptures speak forthrightly that homosexual practices are outside God's will for human beings. They are morally impermissible acts.[32]

Paul and Pederasty: Appeal to Smith

A possible rejoinder from Johnson and Scroggs is that Paul is rejecting homosexual practices because he identifies such practices with
pederasty. In "Ancient Bisexuality and the Interpretation of Romans
1:26–27," Mark D. Smith (1996) argues that Johnson and Scroggs are
mistaken. Monogamous homosexual marriages are proscribed by the
Christian scriptures. First, Smith shows that Paul would have known
of a wide range of homosexual practices that were not forms of pederasty. Smith sums up his initial evidence by saying that

> the extant source of Greco-Roman homosexual practices dem-
> onstrates many exceptions to pederasty and a decline in the
> prominence of pederasty in the last three centuries immediately
> preceding Paul. Very few references to specifically pederastic activ-
> ity occurs in the literature and art of the last century before Paul's
> era. Considerations of space prevent us from exploring the evi-
> dence of homosexual use of male slave (which was commonplace)
> and the role of male homosexual prostitutes (both active and
> passive) for which there was apparently a viable market. Suffice
> it to say that they offer a yet more varied picture of homosexual
> life in the ancient world, and none of these can be construed to
> conform to the "model" of pederasty. (238)

After demonstrating that Scroggs's account of pederasty is woefully
inadequate, Smith turns next to female homosexuality of which
Scroggs had said that the evidence does not permit one to say much
about it. However, Smith points out that "the evidence shows that
female homosexual practices were known, perhaps from Sappho's
time until well after Paul's, in Greek and Latin literature, in eastern
provinces and Italy, and even among Jewish rabbis" (242). Smith insists
that Paul's references to homosexual practices in Romans 1 show that
he knows about same-sex practices among males and females and
includes both in his condemnation. Since there is little evidence that
female homosexual practices were influenced by pederasty, Paul's

condemnation of same-sex practices is not primarily a rejection of the humiliating character often associated with it. Smith says, "I believe the only interpretation that does justice to the literary and historical context is that Paul probably did know of at least several different types of homosexual practices among both men and women. He used the general language in Romans 1 because he intended his proscription to apply in a general way to all homosexual behavior, as he understood it." Smith adds, "Paul's proscription must be taken in the context in which it is presented. For him, humanity is full of corruption, as is evident in the lives of all persons, and Paul . . . does not place any special emphasis on censuring homosexual activity; rather, the opposite is the case. Paul devotes many more pages to the unjust use of money than to homoerotic activity. Nevertheless, I do not think there is any avoiding the conclusion that Paul considers homosexual behavior to be sinful" (1996, 247).

Let me remind the reader of my aim in sections six and seven [of this essay]. While Johnson and Scroggs acknowledge that the Hebrew and Christian scriptures include passages that condemn same-sex practices, they contend that these passages are proscriptions against pederasty alone. I appealed to Richard Hays's discussion of homosexuality in his *The Moral Vision of the New Testament* to remind the reader that the biblical texts, both Old and New Testaments, unqualifiedly reject all homosexual practices as morally impermissible. I appealed to Mark Smith's work because he refutes the claim that the biblical prohibitions against homosexual practices are only a rejection of pederasty, with special attention to Paul's worldview.

Central to my argument is that *sola scriptura* is the most fundamental principle to those Christians who historically identify with the free church tradition. This axiom declares that Christian beliefs and practices find their origin and correct understanding in the Bible—the Hebrew and Christian scriptures. So for those Christians who affirm *sola scriptura*, Paul's understanding of homosexual practices as morally impermissible expresses God's will for human beings on same-sex relationships.

A Reformulated Narrative, Epistemological Crisis, and the Restorationist Impulse

The features of the free church tradition on which I have focused attention in this essay are *sola scriptura*, soul competency, priesthood of the believers/believer, autonomy of local church, the restorationist impulse, and a democratic polity. My narrative pays special attention to the tension between two features: a commitment to the scriptures as an objective source of knowledge about God and God's will for Christians (*sola scriptura*) and appeals to soul competency (usually aligned with autonomy of the local church).[33] Typically, appeals to soul competency affirm each individual as the final arbiter for understanding what the scriptures teach about God's will. There is no doubt that the Protestant reformers who became proponents of the free church tradition regarded the Bible as a repository of objective truths about God and God's will for human beings. However, the emphasis on private judgment in religious matters by Wayland, Mullins, and Shurden makes Baptists vulnerable to radically subjectivist accounts of religious belief and practice.[34] Contemporary Baptists who endorse soul competency understood in a subjectivist fashion may avoid an apparent contradiction between what the Bible teaches about same-sex practices and their own permissive attitudes toward them by claiming that each individual (and the local churches of which they are members) is the final arbiter of the truth about this kind of behavior. Yet if one affirms that the Bible provides access to objective truths about God, our own human nature, and God's will for human beings, then one will be skeptical that soul competency as understood by Mullins and Shurden provides an adequate account of our access to these biblical truths.

According to the Theological Principle (articulated by Dilday), the main purpose of the biblical texts is to convey knowledge about God and God's will for human beings. According to Hays and Smith, the scriptures teach that God's will with respect to homosexual practices is "No." While Johnson presents a rhetorically attractive counternarrative, especially in light of our culture's current dispositions, it fails to address the early church's adoption of the Old Testament teachings regarding homosexual practices and Paul's clear position on the issue. Additionally, that homosexual practices are morally impermissible has long been the stance of not only the Catholic and Orthodox positions on human sexuality but most Protestant denominations or churches on this issue until fairly recently. Put another way, the cultural context addressed in the biblical texts cited are sufficiently similar to our modern context in which the texts are being applied, which is Scroggs's third principle of biblical interpretation.

A critic might object by appealing to what MacIntyre says about the standards of rational justification via traditions. The critic may say that traditions are rationally vindicated only if they transcend their limitations and provide remedies for those limitations. One does this by reformulating the tradition in such a way to show a fundamental continuity between the new understanding of the tradition and its previous understanding. The critic may insist that individuals who find themselves sexually attracted to members of their own gender, as Johnson underscores, are not willfully seeking to thwart God's will. They are honoring one's natural, God-given desire for intimacy and complementarity within the divinely commanded commitment to monogamy. Thus, marriage between same-sex partners honors a variety of natural and theological goods. In short, the traditional understanding of marriage is reformulated to include monogamous homosexual marriages without discarding its most fundamental God-ordained goods. However, this argument requires one to explain away the injunctions against homosexual relationships found in the Hebrew and Christian scriptures. I am skeptical that this end can be achieved without undermining a commitment to *sola scriptura* or biblical authority.

One of the features of the free church tradition, something emphasized much more among some churches within the free church tradition than among some Baptist churches these days, is the restorationist impulse.[35] Restorationism is the ideal that the local church should imitate the churches described in the New Testament in form, organization, roles, and message(s). Indeed, its defenders may claim that a commitment to the restorationism is an obvious implication of the more foundational principle—*sola scriptura*.

According to James McClendon, the Baptist vision is a basic stance and a hermeneutic in which "the church now is the primitive church; we are Jesus' followers; the commands are addressed directly to us" (1986, 33). Thus, churches that embrace the restorationist ideal are unlikely to accept same-sex practices as normatively permissible. Likewise, they are unlikely to be open to women occupying the roles of preacher, deacon, or elder. Some Baptist congregations that are open to women occupying these roles find it difficult to defend doing so while holding that monogamous marriages of homosexual couples are morally impermissible. A proponent of both women in ministry and the acceptance of homosexual monogamous marriages may argue that just as circumcision and the dietary laws of the Old Testament are no longer binding on Christians, so the near absolute prohibitions against women in leadership positions over men and the absolute prohibitions against homosexual marriages are no longer in place, given the liberating gospel of Jesus Christ. I am not convinced that there are absolute prohibitions against women occupying leadership positions in the church, but this thesis cannot be defended adequately, in this essay. So I recognize I end this essay with a tension: either endorse restorationism full-stop and reject both same-sex practices and the practice of opening the roles of preacher, deacon, and elder to women, or accept the place of women in ministry and reject restorationism. However, even if one rejects restorationism, the biblical arguments presented in this essay are sufficient for the members of churches within the free church tradition to establish how one ought to view monogamous homosexual marriages.[36]

Concluding Remarks

One aspect of this essay has been an appeal to MacIntyre's thesis that a tradition is well-ordered if it is able to overcome any alternative and incompatible interpretations of its authoritative concepts, persons, and texts. While no doubt simmering for some time, in 1979 Baptists who identified with the Southern Baptist tradition experienced just this kind of contest of conflicting and rival interpretations in a very public way. Alternatively identified as a "conservative resurgence" or a "fundamentalist take-over," the relatively stable understanding of Baptist Christianity as voiced by, among others, Wayland, Mullins, and Shurden was called into question, with a vengeance.[37] Those who overthrew the previous Baptist orthodoxy endorsed biblical authority and identified it with inerrant or infallible scriptures. In my view, most of the biblical scholars attacked by those who identified with the conservative resurgence endorsed the thesis that the Bible gives one access to objective truths about God, our vexed nature as human beings, and our prospects via the life, death and resurrection of Jesus Christ, and how to live as Christians bound together in a communion called the Christian church. Yet these scholars endorsed a variety of hermeneutical reading strategies whose point is truth, but eschewed calling the scriptures inerrant or infallible. The extent to which groups of Baptists, once formerly identified with the SBC, have achieved a satisfactory reformulation of Baptist identity, one designed to overcome or remedy the causes of the 1979 crisis, is an open question.

Second, my essay seeks to explain why some churches in the free church tradition do not endorse homosexual marriages and others do. In my view, those churches that have a strong view of biblical authority, and take seriously the biblical passages to which I have alluded, will conclude that the scriptures do not affirm homosexual marriages as morally permissible for Christians. Within the Baptist tradition, the Southern Baptist Convention, the National Baptist Convention USA, and the Australia Baptist Ministries accept the traditional understanding of Christian marriage as between a man and a woman. And yet it is no surprise that many churches that affirm the autonomy of the local church and the right and competency of every Christian to interpret the Holy Scriptures as he or she is directed by the Holy Spirit will endorse same-sex practices as morally permissible for faithful Christians. The American Baptist Church USA, the Progressive National Baptist Convention and the Cooperative Baptist

Fellowship defer to individual congregations to set their own policy on this issue. The Alliance of Baptists and the Association of Welcoming and Affirming Baptists accept practicing gay, lesbian, bisexual and transgender individuals for church membership.

Clearly, I am troubled by the insistence of Wayland, Mullins, and Shurden that "the right of private interpretation of the scripture" is a defining and essential characteristic of Baptist Christians (Shurden 1993, 18).[38] I find it worrisome because this epistemic stance can become a license for endorsing one's subjective preferences. I endorse the importance of this principle as one expression of religious liberty and as a feature of a liberal democratic culture. In contrast, my Baptist upbringing suggests that to embrace biblical authority is to endorse practices of reading, studying, teaching, and preaching that permit the scriptures to correct our hearts and minds, objectively speaking, toward the truth. So I worry that appeals to the priesthood of the believer and soul competency are too easily dodged for the hard work of becoming biblically and theologically literate. Additionally, I implied that those who affirm both the authority of the scriptures and the moral legitimacy of same-sex practices don't have a coherent position. They have resolved an epistemological crisis by elevating certain understandings of the conjunction of soul competency, priesthood of the believer, and the autonomy of the local church, while diminishing the importance and power of the appeal to the scriptures. Still, to be fair, there are serious biblical scholars who argue that the Bible permits same-sex practices for committed married gays or lesbians.[39] In this essay, I gave reasons why I find their arguments unpersuasive or unsound. Nonetheless, it is clear that some serious Christian scholars attempt to provide theologically and biblically compelling arguments for their position, without appeals to soul competency or priesthood of the believer.

How should churches that embrace the free church tradition reformulate their narrative to avoid the worries I highlight? I have argued that *sola scriptura* is more fundamental than other Baptist freedoms, including soul competency and the priesthood of the believer(s). So greater attention must be given to objectively fitting principles of biblical exegesis and interpretation as a matter of the educational practices of churches that identify with the free church tradition, since we honor both biblical authority and soul competency. One need not be a professionally trained biblical scholar to be a good reader of the biblical texts. (Some practices common among Christian biblical scholars are helpful; others are not.) If each adult Christian is to read, interpret, and understand God's revelation in the scriptures competently, then Bible study and discussion as a communal activity and communal good must be taken very seriously. Being priest to one another is like being a physician to one's patients. Just as we require a high level of competency from those who take care of our bodies, we should insist on a high level of competency from those that offer their judgments about what the biblical materials require, permit, and forbid. Having an opinion is not enough. Assisting the members of local churches to become good readers of the biblical texts remains an imperative for those who serve as leaders in churches that identify with the free church tradition.

A final thought: Those of us who are firmly convinced that the scriptures speak against homosexual practices are often tone-deaf to the struggles of our Christian brothers and sisters who have such pervasive and deep-seated attractions. We heterosexuals must take seriously the reflections of our brothers and sisters who struggle to accept their homosexual attractions while living out their faith. A beginning in addressing our failings in this regard is to read empathetically, for example, *Washed and Waiting: Reflections on Christian Faithfulness and Homosexuality* (2010) by Wesley Hill (male, evangelical Christian) and *Gay and Catholic: Accepting My Sexuality, Finding Community, Living My Faith* (2014) by Eve Tushnet (female, Catholic Christian). Both Hill and Tushnet are celibate, same-sex attracted individuals. Their books are edifying accounts of their own struggles to be faithful and chaste while being honest, both privately and publicly, about their orientations. An intrinsic characteristic of the free church tradition is the aspiration to be disciplined students of the Bible and of other texts relevant to the task of deepening our faith and enhancing mission-aimed efforts. These two texts, among many others, are worthy of our attention.

Also, we must respond with compassion and with friendship to those who reject the Christian understanding of human sexuality as we "traditionalists" understand it. In so doing, we love our neighbors as we love ourselves. The Christian ethic was countercultural in the Roman Empire. In much of the world, it is today. To take seriously the free church tradition is to work hard to become a well-informed and thoughtful agent, a person who exercises his or her freedom admirably, in a community of fellow Christian believers, who collectively bear witness to the Triune God revealed in the Bible. That community is larger than our local church and larger than the Baptist tradition. My friend and colleague Barry Harvey sums up our Baptist, free church situation with insight:

> As we (Baptists) embark on this journey into lands as yet unknown to us, we will need provisions that are not available solely with the baptistic heritage. We must therefore learn once again what it means to travel with a host of sisters and brothers in a communal way of life that has a center but ultimately no boundary, for God has summed up all things in that center which is Christ. We will need to cultivate a generosity that is humble enough to accept that, precisely as dissenting movement, our tradition as Baptists is not self-sufficient, and therefore we must reconnect with the larger Catholic whole. We will also need to develop good relations with those we meet along the way, and give to them what we have to offer. (Harvey 2008, 21)[40]

Notes

1 In this paper, I will use the term *homosexual* to identify those that are sexually attracted to individuals that are biologically alike with respect to their sexual equipment. Sometimes I may use *gay* or *lesbian* because

it fits the context better. I know that the categories and ways of self-identifying are more complex than these, but these terms are sufficient for my purposes in this paper.

2 See https://cdno1.acu.edu/content/dam/acu_2016/documents/acu-mission-identity-2.pdf. See especially 31–32.

3 See https://en.wikipedia.org/wiki/Baptists_in_the_United_States.

4 See "Stances of Faiths on LGBTQ Issue: Southern Baptist Convention." Available at https://baptistnews.com/article/sbc-resolution-challenges-christians-who-self-identify-as-gay/#.YGoMrS2caqA.

5 https://allianceofbaptists.org.

6 https://www.hrc.org/resources/stances-of-faiths-on-lgbt-issues-alliance-of-baptists.

7 The website of the Alliance of Baptists makes clear that one important dimension of its identity is located in a commitment to justice. Their conception of justice includes racial equality, the opening of ministerial positions (and other positions of economic and political power in the state) to women, and an affirmation of same-sex marriages and relationships. See https://allianceofbaptists.org.

8 https://www.baptistpress.com/resource-library/news/lgbt-hiring-policy-highlights-cbf-factions/.

9 https://www.baptistpress.com/resource-library/news/lgbt-hiring-policy-highlights-cbf-factions/.

10 https://www.baptiststandard.com/news/baptists/cbf-revises-hiring-policy-lifts-lgbt-ban-posts/.

11 In a subsequent section of the paper, I provide a biblically based argument for Batson's assertion.

12 https://cbf.net/who-we-are.

13 The four axioms identified by CBF were identified and defended in Shurden (1993).

14 https://cbf.net/who-we-are.

15 The appeal to the "scriptures alone" is often both misunderstood and misused in the story of the free church tradition(s). Of *sola scriptura*, D. H. Williams says, "One of the unintended hazards of 'Scripture alone' is that it typifies Scripture as an isolated authority, completely independent of the church from which it emerged. Thus, *sola scriptura* has been construed by many Protestants as if finding the truth of Scripture is an enterprise best done without the church or even in spite of the church. . . . This was, of course, not at all what the early Reformers sought to do with this theological principle" (2005, 96–97).

16 https://www.gracechurch.org/about/distinctives/biblical-eldership.

17 I realize that Biblical exegesis or interpretation is sometimes a complicated activity. Yet sometimes it is relatively straightforward. According
to James McClendon, the Baptist vision includes the way the Bible is read
by those who (1) accept the plain sense of the scripture as its dominant
sense and recognize their continuity with the story it tells and who
(2) acknowledge that finding the point of that story leads them to its
application. See McClendon (1994, 45).

18 In the above, once again, I am paraphrasing a portion of MacIntyre's
discussion of "narrative and epistemological crises." MacIntyre, "Epistemological Crises, Narrative, and Philosophy of Science," in Hauerwas
and Jones (1989, 140).

19 I have not studied this issue carefully, so I am unsure of the number of
Baptist churches whose decision-making includes an elder system. In
Waco, Texas, Harris Creek Baptist Church does rely on elders. See this
site: http://www.harriscreek.org/staff-elders/.

20 https://www.gracechurch.org/about/distinctives/biblical-eldership.

21 Dr. Russell H. Dilday was a former president of Southwestern Baptist
Theological Seminary (1978–94). He also served as the pastor of several
Baptist churches in Georgia and in Texas. The four principles are discussed in Dilday (1982, 120–25). I have provided a summary of what I
take to be the essential themes of each point.

22 Of course, an enormous literature is available on this topic. For the
purposes of this paper, I have selected a few aptly representative interlocutors to permit a straightforward and concise discussion of the
central issues. My primary interlocutors assume the Bible provides
a secure basis for what we ought to believe about God and human
beings (doctrine) and how we ought to behave (ethics). So for example,
I don't consider the arguments of Dale B. Martin because he rejects this
assumption, which he calls textual foundationalism. On my understanding, most Baptists and other free church adherents are committed
to some version of textual foundationalism. For an account of textual
foundationalism, see Martin (2006, 1–3).

23 *New American Standard Bible*. In the *New Oxford Annotated Bible, New Revised
Standard Version*, we find, "Then the Lord God said, 'It is not good that
man should be alone; I will make him a helper as his partner.'"

24 Age-differentiated, intergenerational same-sex practices are those
associated with rites of passage from adolescence to adulthood. Status-
defined relationships are those in which one person is active and the
other passive, sexually. The passive is typically or often a stigmatized
role because of the sexual ethos of submission versus domination.

25 Under the heading "The Case for Prohibition," Johnson discusses four kinds of arguments whose conclusion is that same-sex practices are morally forbidden. The four are (1) arguments from scripture, (2) marriage as an order of creation, (3) arguments from nature, and (4) arguments from tradition. For the purposes of this paper, I am interested only in his arguments from scripture. See Johnson (2012, 50–53).

26 *Holy Bible: New American Standard.*

27 *Holy Bible: New American Standard*, 1 Kings 14:24; 1 Kings 15:12; 2 Kings 23:7.

28 Hays discusses 1 Timothy 1:10 and Acts 15:28–29, also. In the Timothy passage *arsenokotai* is included in a list of forbidden activities, though sexual immorality is not the main theme of the passage. In Acts 15:28–29, *porneia* may well include all the sexual transgressions listed in Leviticus 18:6–30, including "You shall not lie with a male as one lies with a female; it is an abomination" (Hays 1996, 382–83).

29 *Holy Bible: New American Standard*, Romans 1:22–27. Note that this passage makes explicit reference to sexual relations among women.

30 I find especially helpful Robert Gagnon, "The Witness of Paul and Deutero-Paul," in Gagnon (2001, 229–39)

31 For more on complementarity, see Gagnon (2001, 254).

32 Hays begins his chapter on homosexuality with a story about his close friend, Gary, who died from AIDS in May of 1990. In 1989, he and Gary had agreed to write complementary essays on homosexuality and the biblical materials. Gary expressed his disappointment in much that had been written about same-sex relationships, contending that they did justice neither to the biblical materials nor to his own experience as a gay person, in and out of the gay community for over twenty years. See Hays (1996, 380).

33 One could just as easily focus attention on the "priesthood of the believer." These two phrases are often used interchangeably.

34 For an insightful exposition and critique of Mullins's main ideas and also his impact on Baptists see Al Mohler, https://albertmohler.com/2009/07/16/e-y-mullins-the-axioms-of-religion?_ga=2.57136298.1856010680.1621015768-323541392.1621015768.

35 This restorationist theme is exhibited quite clearly in *A Short History of Baptists*, Vedder (1907, 13–70).

36 D. H. Williams worries about "a restorationist view of church history that depicts Protestantism as a means of returning to the pure and original church of the apostles and thus legitimizing itself against the Roman Catholic claim to apostolic authority." He clearly thinks this presents a

false dichotomy of scriptural authority (*sola scriptura*) vs. the tradition of the church, especially the early church. See Williams (2005, 86–88).

37 For a brief but helpful overview of the controversy, see https://en .wikipedia.org/wiki/Southern_Baptist_Convention_conservative _resurgence. It provides a helpful bibliography for those interested in its history.

38 I think that "soul competency" has a nonsubjective interpretation, one consonant with the confidence the free church tradition has in encouraging biblical literacy among the members of local congregations. But exploration of this thesis is beyond the scope of this essay.

39 See Martin (2006, 50), who argues that "all appeals to what the Bible says" are "ideologically and problematic," thus "all appeals . . . must submit to the test of love." I don't think that the wholesale dismissal of "what the Bible says" can be accepted by those who endorse the centrality of *sola scriptura* within the free church tradition.

40 I am grateful to my colleague, Dr. Barry Harvey, both for sharing the paper here cited and for helpful suggestions about how to improve my arguments in the essay itself.

References

Dilday, Russell H. 1982. *The Doctrine of Biblical Authority*. Nashville: Convention Press.

Freeman, Curtis W., James William McClendon Jr., and C. Rosalee Velloso da Silva, eds. 1999. *Baptist Roots: A Reader in the Theology of a Christian People*. Valley Forge, PA: Judson.

Gagnon, Robert A. J. 2001. *The Bible and Homosexual Practice: Texts and Hermeneutics*. Nashville: Abingdon.

Harvey, Barry. 2008. "Where Do We Stand? Imagination, Memory and Tradition." Lecture 1, 2008 Cousin Lectures. Baptist Theological Seminary at Richmond. Richmond, VA.

Hays, Richard B. 1996. *The Moral Vision of the New Testament: Community, Cross, New Creation*. New York: HarperCollins.

Hill, Wesley. 2010. *Washed and Waiting: Reflections on Christian Faithfulness and Homosexuality*. Grand Rapids, MI: Zondervan.

Hudson, Winthrop, ed. 1959. *Baptist Concepts of the Church*. Chicago: Judson.

Humphreys, Fisher. 1990. "E. Y. Mullins." In *Baptist Theologians*, edited by Timothy George and David S. Dockery. Nashville: Broadman.

Johnson, William Stacy. 2012. *A Time to Embrace: Same-Sex Relationships in Religion, Law, and Politics*. 2nd ed. Grand Rapids, MI: William B. Eerdmans.

MacIntyre, Alasdair. 1988. *Whose Justice? Which Rationality?* Notre Dame, IN: University of Notre Dame Press.

———. 1989. "Epistemological Crises, Narrative, and Philosophy of Science." In *Why Narrative? Readings in Narrative Theology*, edited by Stanley Hauerwas and L. Gregory Jones. Grand Rapids, MI: William B. Eerdmans.

———. 2007. *After Virtue: A Study in Moral Theory*. 3rd ed. Notre Dame, IN: University of Notre Dame Press.

Martin, Dale B. 2006. *Sex and the Single Savior: Gender and Sexuality in Biblical Interpretation*. Louisville, KY: Westminster John Knox.

McClendon, James William, Jr. 1986. *Ethics: Systematic Theology*. Vol. 1. Nashville: Abingdon.

———. 1994. *Doctrine: Systematic Theology*. Vol. 2. Nashville: Abingdon.

Mullins, E. Y. 1908. *The Axioms of Religion*. Philadelphia: American Baptist Publication Society.

Noll, Mark. 1992. *A History of Christianity in the United States and Canada*. Grand Rapids, MI: William B. Eerdmans.

Otto, Tim. 2014. *Oriented to Faith: Transforming the Conflict over Gay Relationships*. Eugene, OR: Cascade.

Scroggs, Roger. 1983. *The New Testament and Homosexuality*. Philadelphia: Fortress.

Shurden, Walter B. 1993. *The Baptist Identity: Four Fragile Freedoms*. Macon, GA: Smyth and Helwys.

Smith, Mark D. 1996. "Ancient Bisexuality and the Interpretation of Romans 1:26–27." *Journal of the American Academy of Religion* 64 (2): 223–56.

Tushnet, Eve. 2014. *Gay and Catholic: Accepting My Sexuality, Finding Community, Living My Faith*. Notre Dame, IN: Ava Maria.

Vedder, H. C. 1907. *A Short History of Baptists*. Philadelphia: American Baptist Publication Society.

Westin, Gunnar. 1958. *The Free Church through the Ages*. Nashville: Broadman.

Whale, J. S. 1962. *The Protestant Tradition*. New York: Cambridge University Press.

Whitt, Jason. 2011. "The Baptist Contribution to Liberty." Waco, TX: Center for Christian Ethics at Baylor University. https://www.baylor.edu/content/services/document.php/139884.pdf.

Williams, D. H. 2005. *Evangelicals and Tradition: The Formative Influence of the Early Church*. Grand Rapids, MI: Baker Academic.

CHAPTER 9

Love and Do What You Want

Augustine's Pneumatological Love Ethics

Mac S. Sandlin

ABSTRACT: Augustine famously summarizes all of ethics in the maxim "Love and do what you want" in his *Homilies on the First Epistle of John* but also describes sin as misdirected love and humanity as characterized by sin. This raises the question as to how Augustine can offer such a maxim given humanity's tendency to love so poorly. Aimed at ethicists and theologians with only a general knowledge of Augustine, this paper examines Augustine's approach to ethics and its relationship to his theology of the Holy Spirit. By exploring the *ordo amoris*, the *uti/frui* distinction, and the doctrine of the Spirit as the inner-Trinitarian Love of the Father and the Son, I attempt to show how Augustine's maxim can fit with his hamartiology.

> . . . though every inclination of the human heart is evil from childhood.
>
> —Genesis 8:21

> You shall love the Lord your God with all your heart and with all your soul and with all your mind. This is the great and first commandment. And a second is like it: You shall love your neighbor as yourself. On these two commandments depend all the Law and the Prophets.
>
> —Matthew 22:37–40 ESV

God's love has been poured out into our hearts through the Holy Spirit who has been given to us.

—Romans 5:5

Beloved, let us love one another, for love is from God, and whoever loves has been born of God and knows God. Anyone who does not love does not know God, because God is love.

—1 John 4:7–8 ESV

Introduction

Augustine was as aware of his own sinfulness as perhaps anyone who has ever lived. He imparted to the West the doctrine of original sin and the groundwork for later Calvinistic notions of total depravity. He tells the story of his life as a series of confessions to God, and he invites his readers to join him in contemplating the manifold wickedness of his own sinfulness. "Woe, woe, by what steps I was dragged down to 'the depths of Hell'—toiling and fuming because of my lack of the truth, even when I was seeking after thee, my God!" (Augustine 2012, 11). Even after his conversion and years of service as a bishop and theologian, when his last illness came, Augustine chose to meet death alone, lying in bed and reading the penitential Psalms while weeping over his sins (Brown 1960, 432).[1]

Despite what one might think in light of such a strong interest in guilt and sinfulness, Augustine was not a man plagued by insecurity and self-loathing, not one who thought his sins were especially wicked. Rather, he saw himself as he saw all humanity—broken and in need of repair, lost and in need of salvation. In his descriptions of his own sin, we see his view of sin and human sinfulness in general.[2]

Human sinfulness, Augustine believed, resulted from misdirected or disordered love, making a sharp distinction between that which we ought to *use* and that which we ought to *enjoy* (1996, 20).[3] Sin comes from enjoying that which ought to be used and thereby becoming entangled in disordered loves. Given the ease with which humanity falls into this trap of loving the wrong thing or loving in the wrong way, one might expect Augustinian ethics to take the form of a theory in which right is named and judged by static external rules grounded in eternity rather than arising from individual conscience or social norms—divine command theory or some sort of legalism perhaps. And so, it is surprising to find the same man who teaches us that sinfulness results from our misdirected loves summing up his entire ethical thought in these five short words: *dilige, et quod vis fac*—"Love, and do what you want" (Augustine 2008, 7.8). How can Augustine, who believes that humanity is so sinful and that sin is disordered love, advise us to "love and do what you want" without abandoning his view of sin and human sinfulness? When one loves rightly, right actions will result, but how are we to rightly order our loves? By what means will our loves be transformed? The answer lies not in Augustine's anthropology but in his Pneumatology, for the good is not merely a principle or a power for Augustine; it is the living person of the Holy Spirit. This Pneumatological love ethic helps unite his moral and theological doctrines and provides important clarification for some of Augustine's more controversial ethical positions as well as correctives and helpful direction for contemporary virtue ethics.

This [essay] will therefore offer an overview of Augustine's *ethica caritatis* as a moral theory and then examine his doctrine of the Holy Spirit as the divine love of God and the implications of such a doctrine for his moral theology. The first section will outline the basic shape of Augustine's *ethica caritatis*. It concludes with a discussion of why it is difficult to fit Augustine into any of the major ethical systems embraced by his intellectual heirs and students. The major primary sources engaged in part one include *On the Moral Teaching of the Catholic Church*, *City of God*, and *Teaching Christianity*. The second section looks at Augustine's trinitarian and Pneumatological theology and the importance of *caritas* in Augustine's thinking about God. It draws primarily from *On the Trinity*. Woven throughout both sections of the paper and uniting them are Augustine's *Homilies on First John*, the source from which our driving question comes and also where it finds its answer. I conclude with a brief discussion of implications of Augustine's Pneumatological love ethics for further research in theology proper and theological ethics.

My goal in this essay is not to uncover new insights in Augustinian theology or ethics but to show the connection between Augustine's Pneumatology and his ethics, which may not be obvious to nonexperts, especially those from traditions like my own (Churches of Christ, Stone-Campbell Movement) in which Augustine and his famous maxim, "Love and do what you want," are viewed with suspicion and hostility. To explore either Augustine's doctrine of the Spirit or his approach to ethics fully is clearly beyond the scope of this [essay], but I hope that breadth and consequent lack of depth of my topic is appropriate for a [volume] such as this one.

Augustine's *Ethica Caritatis*

If the early church fathers had been asked for a scriptural summary of Christian ethics, they would likely have pointed to the Sermon on the Mount (Johnson 2000, 654). This was among the most quoted and most referenced passage of scripture in the writings of the early church, and the patristic commentary tended to emphasize themes like obedience, visible action, and radical countercultural witness (Greenman et al. 2007). With Augustine, the emphasis shifts from Matthew 5–7 to Matthew 22, from the Sermon on the Mount to the Greatest Commands.[4] O'Donovan notes, "It is surprising how little attention is paid to the 'summary of the law,' the 'two commands,' of love-of-God and love-of-neighbor, in either the Western or the Eastern Fathers [before Augustine]" (2006, 4). Augustine, he argues, is responsible for the place of primacy the "summary" takes on in Western Christian ethics. For generations, it displaced or reinterpreted not only the earlier emphasis on countercultural witness but also the standard philosophical approaches to ethics.

This emphasis on love is discernable in Augustine's work from the beginning. His treatise *On the Moral Teaching of the Catholic Church* (*De Moribus*) is an early work written against the Manichees. In it, Augustine follows a traditional philosophical line of questioning as he seeks to identify humanity's chief good and to determine how this *summum bonum* might be apprehended. However, *De Moribus* is stridently antiphilosophical in its rhetoric. Augustine's answers are explicitly theological and biblical rather than philosophical, so it is not surprising that in that work he identifies the *summum bonum* as God. "The perfection of all our good things and our perfect good is God. We must neither come short of this nor go beyond it: the one is dangerous, the other impossible" (Augustine 1990, 1.15.8). The way to apprehend this highest good, he asserts, is by love.

What exactly Augustine means by love is not always clear, but some generalizations can still be made: (1) Love always involves the will. (2) There is a hierarchy of value among things that are to be loved, an "*ordo amorum*" with God at the top, other human beings in the middle, and nonhuman things at the bottom. (3) Love can be misdirected or disordered, and this distortion results in sin.

LOVE AND THE WILL

Phillip Cary argues that Augustine invents the concept of the will and bequeaths it to all of later Western philosophy (2013). Augustine's doctrine of the will emerges from his exploration of the origin and nature of evil. Since evil for Augustine is not a thing with substance but rather a privation or perversion of goodness—a turning from the real and the good—it can only come about by the use of some power or cause that allows that turning to take place: "When the will abandons what is above itself, and turns to what is lower, it becomes evil—not because that is evil to which it turns, but because the turning itself is wicked. Therefore, it is not an inferior thing which has made the will evil, but it is itself which has become so by wickedly and inordinately desiring an inferior thing" (Augustine 2013).[5] This ability to turn, to act upon or move toward desire is the essence of love and therefore

the essence of ethics for Augustine. Love and the will are tightly connected whether in sin or in righteousness. As Pratt notes, all sinfulness is a sinfulness of the will, but Augustine is also clear in *The Spirit
and Letter* that God's grace makes us righteous precisely because it
frees the will to love righteousness (1903, 224).[6]

THE ORDER OF LOVES

The famous Augustinian doctrine of the order of loves (*ordo amorum*)
teaches that things are to be loved according to their proper ordering. One key text for this doctrine is Matthew 22 with its discussion
of the greatest commands.

> Now God, our master, teaches two chief precepts, love of God
> [and] love of neighbor; and in them man finds three objects for his
> love: God, himself, and his neighbor; and a man who loves God is
> not wrong in loving himself. It follows, therefore, that he will be
> concerned also that his neighbor should love God, since he is told
> to love his neighbor as himself; and the same is true of his con-
> cern for his wife, his children, for the members of his household,
> and for all other men, so far as is possible. (Augustine 2013, 19.14)

Augustine points out that the greatest commands teach us that
there exists a hierarchy of loves and that having that hierarchy firmly
in place is essential for any proper ethical act. If we love God properly,
we will also love our neighbor and ourselves properly. As Chappell
argues, "Character cannot be good without being truly aligned with
the *ordo amorum*" (2014, 195). The existence of this hierarchy is key
not only to Augustine's love-ethic but also to his closely related doctrine of sin.

DISORDERED LOVES

The misalignment of loves is at the heart of Augustine's notion of evil and of his hamartiological teaching as a whole. All sin is fundamentally a matter of misdirected or inordinate desire acted upon by the will—that is, by love. For love, in the Augustinian sense, can be defined as the direction of the will toward an object of desire. As Harvey puts it, "Morality consists in directing our liberty towards God" (1951, 8). When people love created things as if they were eternal things, when they direct their will inappropriately toward creatures instead of toward God, when they allow themselves to be captivated by the things of the world rather than letting their restless hearts find rest in God, their true end, the result is sin, evil, judgment, and death.

This basic principle lies at the heart of all Augustinian theology, but it is perhaps most famously expressed in his aforementioned *uti/frui* distinction from *On Christian Doctrine*. There he writes that God alone is to be enjoyed (*frui*), and all else is to be used (*uti*): "Among all the things there are, therefore, those alone are to be enjoyed which we have noted as being eternal and unchanging, while the rest are to be used, in order that we may come at last to the enjoyment of the former sort" (Augustine, *On Christian Doctrine*, 1.20/22).

It is important to note, however, that Augustine does not use "enjoy" (*frui*) as a synonym for "love" (*delectionis*) in this passage. The question is not, "Ought we to love other people or love ourselves?" Scripture provides him with an obvious answer. The question, for Augustine, is, "*How* ought we to love ourselves and others?" or "We ought to love ourselves and others *to what end*?" And the answer he gives is that we ought to love others as a means to enjoying, resting, and finding our ultimate end in God.[7] The metaphysical hierarchy represented in Augustine's *uti/frui* distinction therefore runs parallel to, but is not identical to, the *ordo amorum*. Yet both doctrines manifest the underlying Augustinian principle that sin is rooted in the misdirected will of the individual who is led astray by his or her desire for that which is not or does not lead to God. In this, Augustine is thoroughly Johannine: "Do not love the world or the things in the world. If anyone loves the world, the love of the Father is not in him. For all that is in the world—the desires of the flesh and the desires of the eyes and pride of life—is not from the Father but is from the world. And the world is passing away along with its desires, but whoever does the will of God abides forever" (1 John 2:15–17 ESV).

In a homily on this passage delivered around twenty years after his composition of *De Doctrina*, Augustine writes, "Why wouldn't I love what God has made? Maybe the Spirit of God be in you, so that you may see that all these things are good, but woe to you if you love created things and abandon the creator. They are beautiful as far as you are concerned, but how much more beautiful is he who formed them? . . . God doesn't forbid you to love those things, but you mustn't love them in the expectation of blessedness. Rather, you must favor and praise them *in such a way* that you love the creator" (2008, 2.11; emphasis mine).

Augustine goes on to address the issue metaphorically with a parable in which a bride loves the wedding ring given to her by her bridegroom more than she loves the man himself. Clearly, says Augustine, such a woman possesses an adulterous heart insofar as she loves the gift more than she loves the one who made and gave the gift to her. He emphasizes that the world and the things in it are to be loved in appropriate ways, by which he simply means that they are not to be loved instead of or above God. Rather, it is in loving God that we see how to appropriately love the world.[8]

> Not surely, that there is no allowed measure in these things [food, drink, and sex], or that when it is said, "Love not these things," it means that you are not to eat, or not to drink, or not to beget children? This is not the thing said. Only, let there be measure, because of the Creator, that these things may not bind you by your loving of them: lest you love that for enjoyment which you ought to have for use. But you are not put to the proof except when two things are propounded to you, this or that: Will you [choose] righteousness or gain? (Augustine 2008, 2.12)

Here in the homilies Augustine's *uti/frui* distinction achieves its practical form—when faced with the choice, will you choose the things of the world over God? Will you direct your liberty toward them instead of toward God? Will you love God or something else? All ethics reduces to this one question for Augustine.

God Is Love: Trinity and Pneumatology

GOD IS LOVE; THE SPIRIT IS LOVE

In *De Trinitate*, Augustine proposes a number of metaphors for the triune nature of God, but few are as consequential for his theology and his ethics as this one. "You see a trinity if you see love" (Augustine, *De Trinitate*, 8.12). Indeed, while he says early on that love is *a* trinity, by the end of the work he has come to conclude that love is *the* Trinity and that all true loving (and if it is not true, he writes, it is not worthy of the name Love) is a participation in the triune life of God made possible by the gift of the Holy Spirit (15.4).[9] Thus, he ends the first major section of *De Trinitate* with this observation: "Now love means someone loving and something loved with love. There you are with three, the lover, what is being loved, and love. And what is love but a kind of life coupling or trying to couple together two things, namely lover and what is being loved" (8.13). And in the last book of the work, he writes,

> So God is charity. But the question is whether it is the Father or the Son or the Holy Spirit or the triad, because this triad is not three Gods but one God. . . . I do not know why Father, Son, and Holy Spirit should not all be called charity and all together be one charity. . . . In the same way the Father is God and the Son is God and the Holy Spirit is God, and they are all together one God. And yet it is not without point that in this triad only the Son is called the Word of God, and only the Holy Spirit is called the gift of God. . . . If therefore any of these three can be distinctly named charity, which could it more suitably be than the Holy Spirit. (15.28, 31)

In his metaphor from book 8, the Father is the lover, the Son is the beloved, and the Spirit is the love that binds them together. We see here, even in the very nature of God, an *ordo amorum* at work. The Father is the originating principle and the Son the begotten one, but the Spirit proceeds from and is directed toward both such that not only is the Son bound to the Father but the Father is also bound to the Son. So real equality and mutuality exist within the trinity without the loss of a discernable order of loves—"a truly self-giving reciprocal communion, not a hierarchy of powers" (Ayres 1996, 484).

Joseph Ratzinger points out that the Spirit is this reciprocity—the *communio* between the Father and the Son. The Spirit's particular distinction is that he is that which the Father and the Son have in common, and this, Augustine argues, is evident even in the generic name "Holy Spirit," which he bears (Ratzinger 1998, 326). The words "holy" and "spirit" are both applied to God generically and to the Father and the Son individually. These descriptors, "holy" and "spirit," are "the essential descriptions of God." Thus, Ratzinger argues, the Spirit for Augustine is the paradoxical mutuality of the Godhead (326). Such a view of the Spirit is tied up in the most controversial aspect of Augustinian trinitarian theology—the dual procession of the Spirit. While the Bishop of Hippo acknowledges that the Spirit precedes "principally" from the Father, it is vital to his doctrine of God that the Son also has "life in himself" (Jn. 5:26) from before all worlds and that this life that he receives from the Father by his eternal begetting is the Spirit, which also proceeds from the Son back to the Father (Augustine, *De Trinitate*, 15.47–48).[10] It is this insight along with the identification of the Spirit with the divine gift that led Augustine to identify the Spirit as the love that unites the Father and the Son.

THE SPIRIT AS GIFT

St. Hilary of Poitiers was the first to identify the Spirit as the *Donum Dei*, but Augustine expanded and improved upon Hilary's teaching (see Hilary's *De Trinitate* 2.1 and 2.3).[11] As is typical for most of Augustine's thinking about the Spirit, the Apostle John provided him with the key texts from scripture. The story of the woman at the well in John 4 served as the primary reference for Augustine's Pneumatology. There Jesus tells the woman that his gift is greater than what he asked her to give, for the water he gives is living water, an expression that the Evangelist later explicitly identifies with the Spirit (John 7:37; Ratzinger 1998, 330).[12] This identification of the Spirit with the gift of God allows Augustine to distinguish the Spirit from the Son while maintaining that both are "of God."[13] He makes the distinction most clearly in the following passage:

> He [The Spirit] comes forth, you see, not as being born but as being given, and so he is not called Son because he was not born like the only begotten Son, nor made and born adoptively by grace like us. What was born of the Father is referred to the Father alone when he is called, and therefore he is the Father's Son and not ours too. But what has been given is referred both to him who gave and to those it was given to; and so the Holy Spirit is not only called the Spirit of the Father and the Son who gave him, but also our Spirit who received him. (Augustine, *De Trinitate*, 5.14)

Thus, Augustine lays out three ways that persons have their origin in God (the Father): being begotten, being given, and being created. Of these, the first two are strictly the properties of divine persons and sharply distinguished from the broader category of created things. The two divine modes of origination are similar in that they are both rooted in eternity. The Son is eternally begotten of the Father and the Spirit is always given. God as Son and God as Gift are still fully God and remain fully unified with the Father, but both their mode or origination and their relationship to the Father are distinct. Just as the Son was begotten of the Father independent of his entry into human history via the virgin's womb, so also is the Spirit the Gift of God even before he brooded over the waters or moved the prophets to speak. For the Spirit is the Gift of the Father and the Son not only to creation but also to each other. This mutual giving is foundational for Augustine's argument that the Spirit is the love of God.

THE WORK OF THE SPIRIT: BINDING, TEACHING, DEIFYING

What then does the Love of God poured out into our hearts do? A full answer is beyond the scope of this paper, but there are at least three elements of the Spirit's work that have a direct bearing on the Augustinian love ethic we are examining. First, the Spirit unites the Christian to God. Aquinas said, "Charity signifies not only the love of God, but also a certain friendship with Him" (*Summa Theologiae*, 2A.65.5). "If God is love, then we can be sure that he desires fellowship, friendship, and *communion* for their own sakes and that he implants that desire within his creatures. The Spirit unites both divine and human persons rendering the Christian one with God and with God's people" (Menconi 2014, 222).

Ratzinger characterizes this work of forming deep communal bonds as "abiding." The Spirit abides with us and forms a stable relationship, one that mirrors the Spirit's presence in the life of Christ rather than in the figures of the Old Testament upon whom the Spirit would rush and empower only to depart until needed.[14] Ratzinger identifies "abiding" as the basic criterion of love: "Love proves itself in constancy. [It] abides, overcomes vacillation, and bears eternity within itself" (Ratzinger 1998, 328–29). And because love is characterized by abiding, it cannot take place anywhere except where there is eternity—that is, in God. Here we see the ultimate grounding for the *ordo amorum*. While contemporary notions of both love and the Spirit emphasize unpredictability and the tendency to break out of rules and institutions, Ratzinger points to constancy, loyalty, even the immutability as the fundamental characteristics of love, and he connects these characteristics to the church.

> The word *caritas* receives here [in Augustine's Pneumatology] a very concrete, ecclesiological meaning, and in fact, in Augustine's language it completely penetrates the concepts for he says that the Church is love. . . . As a creation of the Spirit, the Church is the body of the Lord built up by the *pneuma*, and thus also becomes

the body of Christ when the *pneuma* forms men and women for
"*communion*." . . . The dogmatic statement "The Church is love"
is not merely a dogmatic statement for the manuals, but refers
to the dynamism that forms unity, a dynamism that is the force
holding the Church together. (332–33)[15]

The notion of Spirit's work of binding Christians to God and to
each other in an abiding fellowship of love is key for Augustine's Pneumatology and his ecclesiology, but it is also important for his ethics.

Second, as Jesus promised in John 14:26, the Spirit acts as teacher
and guide for the Christian.[16] Drawing on the *Confessions*, Harvey
points to the importance of moral vision for Augustinian ethics
and connects the development of this skill with the work of the Spirit.
Conversion (itself a work of the Spirit and deeply associated with
teaching), he reminds us, is typically the result of the gradual process
of gaining self-knowledge under the light of grace. And this is true
for moral vision as well.

St. Augustine's concept of conscience is not purely philosophic
but theocentric and dynamic. For him the judgments of conscience
are not isolated phenomena, but complicated operations of the
whole person in the varying situations of life—operations done under
the influence of Divine Grace (Harvey 1951, 19–22).[17] This "theocentric dynamism" is the mark of the Spirit's activity. The knowledge of
God and self does not come from a "dead letter" carved in stone for
all ages, but from a living and intimately present tutor who instructs
and corrects over time. Thus, Augustine writes, "That which I know
of myself, I know by thy light shining upon me" (2012, 10.5.7). For
this father of the church, spiritual growth, including moral growth,
is directly tied to self-knowledge, and self-knowledge comes exclusively from Divine illumination, a work explicitly associated with the
Spirit's teaching role.[18]

Finally, the work of the Spirit is tied to Christian eschatology
and the perfecting of God's people. Deification and its attendant
themes of individual moral progress, the formation of a redeemed

community, and the efficacy of the sacraments play a major role in Augustine's thought though it is one that has often been overlooked or denied outright (Menconi 2014, 222–25). The work of *theosis*, the sanctifying deification of the Christian, begins in the present by the indwelling of the Spirit. We are "being transformed from one degree of glory to another for this comes from the Lord who is the Spirit" (2 Cor. 3:18) and are made "partakers of the divine nature" (2 Peter 1:4). But Ratzinger notes that given that this is the work of the Spirit, we ought not to think of the divine nature or the increasing degrees of glory in terms of power and authority but in terms of love and fellowship with God and his people: "Becoming a Christian means *becoming communion* and thereby *entering into the mode of being of the Holy Spirit*. But it can also only happen through the Holy Spirit, who is the power of communication and is himself a Person" (1998, 327; italics mine).

In all three of these major works associated with the Spirit, uniting, teaching, and perfecting, we see the tight connections with Augustine's *ethica caritatis*. In his commentary on 1 John 4:8, "God is love" (ὁ Θεὸς ἀγάπη ἐστίν), Augustine makes the unusual move of flipping John's formulation "God is love" to its inverse "Love is God," a step too far for most commentators and theologians. But this move is a necessary one given Augustine's trinitarian doctrine and his Pneumatology. He offers three arguments in defense of the unusual formulation "Love is God": (1) Verse 7 says that we are "of God" because of the love within us. (2) We know that to act contrary to love is to disobey God. (3) If those who love are indwelt by the Spirit, then love must necessarily be the presence of God (Ayres 1996, 483). He strengthens this last claim by an appeal to Romans 5:5, "Hope does not fail because *God's love has been poured into our hearts by the Holy Spirit*." The love of God that is the Spirit is poured into our hearts by God who is the Spirit—the gift of God who is God himself. It is in this context that we find Augustine's maxim "Love and do what you want": "Once for all, then, a brief precept is given to you: Love, and do what you want. If you are silent, be silent with love; if you cry out, cry out with love; if you chastise, chastise with love; if you spare, spare with love.

The root of love must be within; nothing but good can come forth from this root" (2008, 7.8).

And now we begin to see how human love, which is so easily disordered and which is trapped within a fallen body, wretched and given to all kinds of lusts, can nevertheless function as the exclusive imperative that embodied all of moral theology. The love that Augustine has in mind is not fleshly or natural human affection but the eternal love of God, the source and principle of the *ordo amorum*, the gift of God that is God himself, who has been poured into the Christian's heart and who wars against the flesh and its desires. We might paraphrase Augustine to say, "Be filled with the Spirit and do what you want." Or perhaps, as Paul puts it, "Work out your own salvation with fear and trembling, for it is God who works in you, both to will and to work for his good pleasure" (Philippians 2:12–13 ESV).[19] Augustine's ethics, like his soteriology, is therefore radically God-centered and utterly dependent on grace.

Pneumatological Love Ethics

Ayres writes, "We cannot understand what it means for Augustine to call God love, and to call love God, without beginning to get an overall picture of the interrelationship between his theology of the Trinity, his theology of the incarnation, and his ecclesiology" (1996, 487).

But we should add that his ethics are also deeply embedded in this interrelationship, and understanding what it means for Augustine to call God love, and to call love God carries with it a distinctive approach to ethics both in theory and in practice.

Once we understand that love for Augustine is both the name and the fruit of the Spirit who indwells the Christian, what he means by "Love and do what you want" is suddenly much easier to understand. Indeed, Augustine goes further. For the one who loves (i.e., the one who has the Spirit and is led by him), evil character becomes impossible. "The light shines in the darkness, and the darkness has not overcome it" (John 1:5).

To have baptism is possible even for a bad man; to have prophecy is possible even for a bad man. To receive the sacrament of the body and blood of the Lord is possible even for a bad man. To have the name of Christ is possible even for a bad man. I say, to have all these sacraments is possible even for a bad man, but to have charity and to be a bad man is not possible. This then is the peculiar gift, this the Fountain that is singly one's own. To drink of this the Spirit of God exhorts you, to drink of Himself the Spirit of God exhorts you. (Augustine 2008, 7.6)

We see in this quotation traces of a wide range of Augustine's thoughts on the topic. The reference to fountains and drink along with the language of "peculiar gift" recalls his commentary on John 4 and 7. We see also his ethical emphasis on the internal life of the Christian as the only true locus of good and evil. Both Ratzinger and Ayres have explored the connections between Augustine's Pneumatology and the church, the sacraments, and Christian spirituality, but such connections with his ethical thought are sometimes overlooked. Therefore, I will close with a few brief observations about Augustine's Pneumatological ethics and some suggestions for further research.

First, the identification of the indwelling Holy Spirit with the ethical principle of love helps explain some of Augustine's more complex and controversial positions—for example, his willingness to see Christians mete out punishment of evil, a key element of his teaching on war. Augustine points out that the loving God of scripture is not afraid to rebuke, discipline, and destroy the evil in this world, and the Christian in whom God dwells by the Spirit will be called upon at times to express his love in just the same manner.

If any of you perchance wish to keep charity, brethren, above all things do not imagine it to be an abject and sluggish thing; nor that charity is to be preserved by a sort of gentleness, nay not gentleness, but tameness and listlessness. Not so is it preserved. Do not imagine that you then love your servant when you do not beat him, or that you then love your son when you give him not discipline, or that you then love your neighbor when you do not rebuke him: this is not charity, but mere feebleness. (Augustine 2008, 7.11)

Augustine goes on to describe the "charity betokened by a dove," which descended at Christ's baptism. "Why a dove?" he asks. "The dove has no gall: yet with beak and wings she fights for her young; hers is a fierceness without bitterness" (Augustine 2008, 7.11). This "fierceness without gall" is the charity that the doctor of the church commends to his audience.

Second, Augustine's Pneumatological love ethics have an important role to play in contemporary virtue theory. Though he is not a systematic virtue theorist in the mold of Aquinas, his *ad hoc* approach to ethical questions, his deep commitment to moral principles along with his tendency to find unpredictable exceptions to those principles that can nevertheless be reasonably justified and compellingly presented, and his emphasis on becoming a new sort of person rather than simply making the right decision all run parallel to the themes of modern virtue ethics. While ethicists like Alasdair MacIntyre and Stanley Hauerwas have helped to reinvigorate interest in virtue theory and have connected it with the person of Jesus, both have an underdeveloped Pneumatology.[20] But the ascendency of virtue ethics in contemporary moral theology demands a parallel increase in attention given to the Holy Spirit. Here Augustine has important insights to share, not least of which is his abiding claim that genuine moral transformation is dependent on the prevenient work of the Spirit as well as his indwelling and sanctifying activities that come later.

Finally, it would benefit us to ask about the ways in which Augustine's *ethica caritatis* helps inform our theology, in particular our doctrine of the Spirit. Ayres writes, "The temporal and bodily practice of love of neighbor is the process at the core of all our attempts to come to terms with the mystery of God's presence" (1996, 481). That is, if we want to understand the person and work of the Spirit more fully, our best path may lie in caring for the poor, working for peace and the preservation of life in our communities, and disciplining our appetites so that they conform to Christian principles. These ethical practices may appear trite to those seeking to delve deeply into the study of esoteric realms of academic theology, but Augustine's collapsing of ethics and Pneumatology into a single category demonstrates that knowledge of God is impossible outside of love for God and love for neighbor. Here, as always, Augustine's invaluable contribution is to challenge our pride and humble our hearts so that they can become open to the work of the Spirit who seeks to make a home for God there.

Notes

1 For more on the significance of weeping in Augustine's theology see Werpehowski (1991, 175–91); and Griffiths (2011, 19–28).

2 Nowhere is this more clear than in the famous story from *Confessions* (2, 9–14) in which he describes stealing pears. The allusions to the Garden of Eden are meant to show not that he was especially wicked, but that he was typical of humanity—that Adam's story is the story of us all.

3 For examples of how this "use" vs. "enjoy" polarity plays out in Augustinian ethics see McGowan (2010, 89–99); Dupont (2006, 89–93); and Dodaro (2015, 511–26).

4 Of course, this in no way implies that the Sermon on the Mount was irrelevant for Augustine.

5 This is a theme explored in a variety of Augustine's works but is most clearly and concisely presented in his *Enchiridion on Faith, Hope, and Love* 3.9–11 and 4.12–15. See also *Confessions* 7.7; 16.22; *City of God*, 11.9; and so on. For a robust discussion of the Augustinian view of evil and the will, see Burns (1988, 9–28); Evans (1990); and especially Willows (2014, 255–69).

6 "It is the will, therefore, and the will alone, that is essentially evil [for Augustine]. The thing toward which the evil will turns is neither evil nor good. Nothing is evil but the evil will" (Augustine 1925, 52).

7 Thus, the *uti/frui* distinction is primarily about the transcendent nature of God and not about any comprehensive ethical system. When Augustine says that people are to be "used," he means by this something radically different than what Kant has in mind in his categorical imperative

prohibiting treating people as means rather than ends. For a fuller treatment of this difference and of the *uti/frui* distinction in general see Naldini and Hill (1990, 17–19).

8 In both *De Doctrina* and *Homilies on First John*, Augustine identifies temporality as the key failing of the world. God is to be enjoyed because he is the eternal one. In *Homilies*, Augustine makes this point powerfully in his discussion of the Incarnation: "Will you love the things of time, and pass away with time; or not love the world, and live to eternity with God? The river of temporal things hurries one along; but like a tree sprung up beside the river is our Lord Jesus Christ. He assumed flesh, died, rose again, ascended into heaven. It was his will to plant himself, in a manner, beside the river of the things of time. Are you rushing down the stream to the headlong deep? Hold fast the tree. Is love of the world whirling you on? Hold fast Christ. For you he became temporal, that you might become eternal" (Augustine 2008, 2.10).

9 The comment about "true love" comes in the opening lines of book 8.

10 For an excellent description of the filioque in Christian theology and history see Siecienski (2010).

11 For an extended treatment of this important element of Augustinian Pneumatology, see Smith (2011, 121).

12 Ratzinger points out that these passages join Augustine's Christology with his Pneumatology; Christ is the well or spring and the Spirit is the water. "The well of the Spirit is the crucified Christ. From him each Christian becomes a well of the Spirit." For an excellent exegetical treatment of the passages in question and their attendant Pneumatology, see Allison (1986, 143–57).

13 This distinction is vital for Augustinians like Ratzinger who wish to rebut accusations that Augustine's trinitarian doctrine smacks of modalism. For an example of one such critique see Myendorff (1979, 186–87).

14 Samson is the chief example of such a pattern (Judges 13–16). But the same can be said of all the judges of Israel and her first king.

15 It should be noted that much of the primary source material Ratzinger draws on, including the *Homilies on First John*, was produced during the conflict with the Donatists and therefore has particularly strong ecclesiological emphases.

16 "But the Helper, the Holy Spirit, whom the Father will send in my name, he will teach you all things . . ."

17 The divine grace in question can be identified as the gift of the Holy Spirit.

18 This illuminationist view of knowledge is present in early works such as *De Magistro*, but deepened and became more sophisticated over the course of Augustine's career.

19 Paul's language here of "will" and "good pleasure" have direct connections to Augustine's concept of love as "the free will directed toward a desire."

20 MacIntyre writes as a philosopher and tends to eschew theological questions, and Hauerwas has long been hesitant to talk about the Spirit too much because, he says, "I do not want to give the impression that the Holy Spirit is on my side" (Hauerwas 2015, 36–37). Hauerwas has, in recent years, sought to fill the Pneumatological lacuna in his work, and this essay represents an important step in that direction.

References

Allison, Dale C. 1986. "The Living Water: John 4:10–14, 6:35c, and 7:37–39." *St. Vladamir's Theological Quarterly* 30 (2): 143–57.

Augustine. 1925. *On the Spirit and the Letter*. Translated by William John Sparrow-Simpson. New York: Society for Promoting Christian Knowledge.

———. 1990. *The Catholic Way of Life and the Manichean Way of Life (De Moribus ecclesiae Catholicae et De Moribus Manichaeorum)*. In *The Manichean Debate*, vol. 19 of *The Works of St. Augustine*, translated by Roland Teske and edited by Boniface Ramsey. Hyde Park, NY: New City.

———. 1996. *Teaching Christianity/De Doctrina Christiana*. Translated by Edmund Hill, OP. New York: New City.

———. 2008. *Homilies on the First Epistle of John*. In *Works of St. Augustine*, vol. 3/14, edited by Boniface Ramsey. Translated by Edmund Hill, OP. New York: New City.

———. 2012. *The Confessions*. In *Works of Saint Augustine*, vol. 1, edited by John E. Rotelle and translated by Maria Boulding. 2nd ed. New York: New City.

———. 2013. *City of God (De Civitate Dei)*. Translated by William Babcock. Hyde Park, NY: New City.

Ayres, Lewis. 1996. "Augustine on God as Love and Love as God." *Pro Ecclesia* 5 (4): 470–87.

Brown, Peter. 1960. *Augustine of Hippo: A Biography*. Los Angeles: University of California Press.

Burns, J. Patout. 1988. "Augustine on the Origin and Progress of Evil." *Journal of Religious Ethics* 16:9–28.

Cary, Phillip. 2013. "Evil, Free Will, Original Sin, and Predestination." Lecture 8 in *Augustine, Philosopher and Saint*. Chantilly, VA: Great Courses.

Chappell, Timothy. 2014. "Augustine's Ethics." In *The Cambridge Companion to Augustine*, edited by David Vincent Menconi, SJ, and Eleonore Stump. 2nd ed. Cambridge: Cambridge University Press.

Dodaro, Robert. 2015. "Augustine on Enjoying One's Neighbor: Uti-Frui Once Again." *Lateranum* 80:511–26.

Dupont, Anthony. 2006. "To Use or Enjoy Humans? Uti and Frui in Augustine." Paper presented at 14th International Conference on Patristic Studies, Oxford, August 8.

Evans, Gillian R. 1990. *Augustine on Evil*. Cambridge: Cambridge University Press.

Greenman, Jeffrey P., Timothy Larsen, and Stephen R. Spencer, eds. 2007. *The Sermon on the Mount through the Centuries*. Grand Rapids, MI: Brazos.

Griffiths, Paul J. 2011. "Tears and Weeping: An Augustinian View." *Faith and Philosophy* 28:19–28.

Harvey, John F. 1951. *Moral Theology of the Confessions of Saint Augustine*. Washington, DC: Catholic University of America Press.

Hauerwas, Stanley. 2015. "How the Spirit Works." In *The Work of Theology*, 36–37. Grand Rapids, MI: William B. Eerdmans.

Johnson, Luke Timothy. 2000. "The Sermon on the Mount." In *The Oxford Companion to Christian Thought*, edited by Adrian Hastings. Oxford: Oxford University Press.

McGowan, Andrew. 2010. "To Use and to Enjoy: Augustine and Ecology." *St. Mark's Review* 212:88–99.

Menconi, David Vincent. 2014. "Augustine's Doctrine of Deification." In *The Cambridge Companion to Augustine*. Cambridge: Cambridge University Press.

Myendorff, John. 1979. *Byzantine Theology: Historical Trends and Doctrinal Themes*. New York: Fordham University Press.

Naldini, Mario, and Edmund Hill, OP. 1990. "Structure and Pastoral Theology of *Teaching Christianity*." Introduction to *Teaching Christianity*, translated by Edmund Hill, OP. Hyde Park, NY: New City.

O'Donovan, Oliver. 2006. *The Problem of Self-Love in St. Augustine*. Eugene, OR: Wipf and Stock.

Pratt, James Bissett. 1903. "The Ethics of St. Augustine." *International Journal of Ethics* 13 (2): 222–35.

Ratzinger, Cardinal Joseph. 1998. "The Holy Spirit as Communio: Concerning the Relationship of Pneumatology and Spirituality in Augustine." *Communio* 25 (2): 324–37.

Siecienski, A. E. 2010. *The Filioque: History of a Doctrinal Controversy*. Oxford: Oxford University Press.

Smith, J. Warren. 2011. "The Trinity in the Fourth-Century Fathers." In *The Oxford Handbook of the Trinity*, edited by O. P. Gilles Meery and Matthew Levering. Oxford: Oxford University Press.

Werpehowski, William. 1991. "Weeping at the Death of Dido: Sorrow, Virtue, and Augustine's 'Confessions.'" *Journal of Religious Ethics* 19:175–91.

Willows, Adam M. 2014. "Augustine, the Origin of Evil, and the Mystery of Free Will." *Religious Studies* 50:255–69.

CHAPTER 10

Militant Liturgies

Practicing Christianity with Kierkegaard, Bonhoeffer, and Weil

J. Aaron Simmons

ABSTRACT: Traditional philosophy of religion has tended to focus on the doxastic dimension of religious life, which although a vitally important area of research, has often come at the cost of philosophical engagements with religious practice. Focusing particularly on Christian traditions, this essay offers a sustained reflection on one particular model of embodied Christian practice as presented in the work of Søren Kierkegaard. After a discussion of different notions of practice and perfection, the paper turns to Kierkegaard's conception of the two Churches: the Church Triumphant and the Church Militant. Then in light of Kierkegaard's defense of the latter and critique of the former, it is shown that Kierkegaard's specific account gets appropriated and expanded in Dietrich Bonhoeffer's account of "costly grace" and "religionless Christianity," and Simone Weil's conception of "afflicted love." Ultimately, it is suggested that these three thinkers jointly present a notion of "militant liturgies" that offers critical and constructive resources for contemporary philosophy of religion.

Introduction

It is often the case that philosophical discussions of Christianity overstate the unity by which the Christian traditions operate. In the name of referential precision, perhaps we should only ever speak of "Christianities" or, as this [volume] admirably does, "Christian traditions." The task is to acknowledge such diverse approaches as those of not only Aquinas, Anselm, and Augustine but also Marguerite Porete, Meister Eckhart, and John of the Cross and those of not only Richard Swinburne, Alvin Plantinga, and Marilyn Adams but also James Cone's Black Liberation Theology, Emile Townes's Womanist Theology, Pope Francis's preferential option for the poor, and Marcella Althaus-Reid's defense of Queer Theology. When it comes to thinking well about Christianity, philosophers should appropriate Alasdair MacIntyre's (1988) contextual awareness and ask, Whose Christianity? Which God? Or following MacIntyre, ask with Merold Westphal (2009), in recognition of the complicated hermeneutic realities that attend Christian identity, "Whose Community? Which Interpretation?"

In light of such diversity in the traditions that operate under the name of "Christianity," philosophers of religion have recently begun to be more sensitive to the ways in which different strands of Christianity might yield contrasting conceptions of Christian life.[1] Although this awareness can certainly play out at the level of propositional assertions about the existence and nature of God, it is also important to attend to the ways in which such diversity is reflected in the varieties of Christian practice. While recognizing the importance of thinking carefully about the cognitivist dimensions of Christian traditions, such a focus can often come at the cost of minimizing, or simply not attending to, the role of embodied practice in such traditions. In this vein, Kevin Schilbrack (2014) has recently argued that "traditional" philosophy of religion (whether Continental or analytic) has been remiss in not giving more attention to the idea of ritual, liturgy, and the embodied enactment of such doxastic commitments. Importantly, in recent years, there has emerged a greater philosophical interest in embodied religious practice,[2] but there remains important work to be done on exploring the ways in which key texts and thinkers in Christian traditions can stand as resources for such work.

One thinker who offers important potential contributions to such debates is Søren Kierkegaard. Given Kierkegaard's complicated conception of the relationship of faith and reason, many have assumed that his thought is simply a concern for such doxastic dynamics, but (as is often suggested) without rational support.[3] Even though there has been good work done demonstrating that the charges of irrationalist fideism are misapplied to Kierkegaard,[4] I do not intend to take that question up here. Instead, my focus will be on the way that Kierkegaard stresses the importance of practice as key to Christian living.[5] His important text, *Practice in Christianity*, is something of a clarion call for Christianity to be a matter of critical awareness and constructive enactment. Of particular note in that text is the way that Kierkegaard understands two different models of Christianity, which he identifies with two conceptions of the Church's role in the world: the Church Triumphant and the Church Militant. In this distinction, Kierkegaard argues compellingly that Christian practice should invite a deeply critical awareness of the ways in which Christianity can fail to live up to the example of Christ in a variety of ways. In the attempt to contribute to the emerging debates on the role of practice in Christian traditions, in this essay I will turn to Kierkegaard's *Practice in Christianity* as providing a model well worth serious consideration. I will begin by offering a hermeneutic consideration of different ways to conceive of practice and perfection, then I will move on to Kierkegaard's presentation of the two different "Churches," and finally turn to Dietrich Bonhoeffer and Simone Weil as contemporary examples of how Kierkegaard's notion of Christian practice might be appropriated in relation to the ideas of grace and liturgy, respectively. I will conclude by suggesting a couple of ways in which this generally Kierkegaardian notion of Christian practice as a devotion to "militant liturgies" can be engaged both critically and constructively by contemporary philosophy of religion.

Before diving in, let me note that this essay is not meant to be normative regarding what Christianity should be—such a normative proclamation would require a different essay. Instead, this essay is simply an attempt to think with Kierkegaard, Bonhoeffer, and Weil about what Christian practice might involve, while still remaining cognizant that the diversity of Christian traditions will likely yield other rival accounts worthy of serious engagement.

Practice Makes "Perfect"

In order to situate Kierkegaard's account of Christian practice, let's get some general distinctions in place that then can serve as hermeneutical frameworks for considering the alternatives that he provides. We often hear that practice makes perfect, but it is important to realize that there are two different notions of perfection toward which our practices might aim. In the first place, and this is by far the more common notion in popular parlance, there is the idea of perfection as a state of *being accomplished*. This conception of perfection is about the elimination of any continued need to practice. It is a matter of ultimacy and finality. Let's call this model of perfection *the success orientation*. There is another option, however, whereby perfection is about not being accomplished but *continually striving to be better*. Rather than perfection ending the need to practice, on this second version, perfection deepens the commitment to practice as essential to who one is and who one hopes to become. Let's term this model of perfection *the faithfulness orientation*. The success orientation is widespread within our cultural logic because it is a matter of economic achievement: do this and get that in return. The faithfulness orientation of perfection, alternatively, is much rarer because it operates according to a kenotic logic of dispossession: no matter how good we are, we recognize the importance of humbly admitting that we are still "on the way" instead of thinking that we have "already arrived." The success orientation is a matter of perfected *results*. The faithfulness orientation is a matter of *the way* of perfectibility.

Keeping in mind these two different notions of perfection is important as we think about the idea of Christian *practice* and the *perfection* toward which it aims. As we will see, for Kierkegaard, what it means to practice Christianity is always to be invested in the faithfulness orientation of perfection. The task is ever to move closer to the lived example of Christ, while recognizing the infinite distance that still remains, as opposed to believing that one has achieved the higher calling and now stands in distinction from those still on the way. For all the thinkers that we will be considering here, it is important to remember that the idea of Christian practice is never about being better than others, or resting on one's laurels, but instead about ever pressing forward. As we will see, for Kierkegaard, Bonhoeffer, and Weil, the logic by which Christian practice functions is decidedly kenotic and stands critically of any time when we think we have got it all figured out—for example, as displayed in the "Rich Young Ruler" who claims that he is justified because of his external activities: I have kept the commandments since my youth (Matthew 19:16–22). Indeed, Kierkegaard suggests that it is an "upbuilding thought" to realize that in relation to God we are "always in the wrong" (1987, 339–54). Rather than *being perfected*, Kierkegaard's entire approach to Christian practice is a matter of *becoming perfectible*. The two notions of perfection that yield two different approaches to practice underwrite the two different models of the Church that Kierkegaard will deploy as his guiding framework for calling for individuals to "become" Christians by following the way of Christ, rather than falling into the potential complacency that attends thinking that they have perfected "being" Christian and achieved the results guaranteed by such a status.

Kierkegaard on the Two Churches

Kierkegaard's distinction between the Church Militant and the Church Triumphant maps directly onto the distinction between the success orientation and faithfulness orientation of perfection. Read the way that Kierkegaard frames the options: "If one wants to maintain . . . that the truth is the way, one will more and more clearly perceive that a Church triumphant in this world is an illusion, that in this world we can truthfully speak only of a militant Church. But the Church militant is related, feels itself drawn, to Christ in lowliness; the Church triumphant has taken the Church of Christ in vain" (1991, 209).

Kierkegaard does not pull his punches here. He is not interested in softening the critical bite of his words, but instead seeks to have his words cut through the cultural calcification that often prevents people from practicing Christianity faithfully (rather than successfully). Understanding Christianity as a "way," rather than an outcome, Kierkegaard presents the Church Triumphant as ultimately nothing more than an "illusion" of our own social making. As such, Kierkegaard accuses the Church Triumphant of idolatry when he contends that it has "taken the Church of Christ in vain."

Idolatry of this form is difficult to see in society due to the fact that so many cultural ideals are grounded in, and oriented toward, an economic logic of results-based justification. "What has completely confused Christianity and what has to a large extent occasioned the illusion of a Church triumphant is this," Kierkegaard explains, "that Christianity has been regarded as truth in the sense of results instead of its being truth in the sense of the way" (1991, 207). Here he is clear that the difference between a results-based success orientation and an along-the-way faithfulness orientation is quite stark. Firmly rejecting any compromise between Christianity and worldly power, Kierkegaard solidly situates the Church Triumphant as opposed to Christ's kingdom—a kingdom represented by militancy toward worldly status: "As soon as Christ's kingdom makes a compromise with this world and becomes a kingdom of this world, Christianity is abolished. But if Christianity is in the truth, it is certainly a kingdom in this world, but not of this world, that is, it is militant" (1991, 211).

Standing opposed to this triumphalist narrative of Christian greatness—anchored in a results-based perfection that views worldly success as the goal of "Christian" practice—we find Kierkegaard's conception of the Church Militant. In contrast to triumphalist privilege, militancy is enacted by imitating Christ's example of humility and abasement. As Kierkegaard says of Jesus, "You yourself were the Way and the Life—and you have asked only for imitators" (1991, 233). Christian truth is, thus, not a matter of external manifestation, but of internal transformation whereby humility is the ground of greatness, and fallibility is the condition of perfectibility. "Only the Church militant," Kierkegaard explains, "is truth, or the truth is that as long as the Church endures in this world it is the militant Church that is related to Christ in his abasement even if drawn to him from on high" (232). Here we see the kenotic logic in high relief: the weak will be made strong, the low will be elevated, the poor will be made rich, the sick will be made well. Pay attention, though, to the conditional access point that Kierkegaard highlights: being related to Christ "in his abasement." There is no way to follow the way of Christ, Kierkegaard suggests, unless one embraces radical self-dispossession. "Humanly speaking," Kierkegaard explains in an expansion of the account of the kenotic logic that underwrites Christian militancy, "it is indeed the most utter crazy contradiction that the one who has no place where he can lay his head—that the man about whom it so accurately (humanly speaking) was said, 'See what a man'—that he says: Come here to me all you who suffer—I will help!" (239).

The invitation/requirement of such humility, such suffering, is strikingly at odds with the worldly/triumphalist conception that wealth, power, and strength are tantamount to righteousness. Instead, Kierkegaard's contention is that those who would associate with the Church Militant, and imitate a Jesus who divests himself of divine power in order to model incarnational relational love would likely be dismissed as irrelevant by those seeing triumphalism as an appropriate mode of Christian life.

On this point, Kierkegaard almost anticipates the distinction drawn by John Sanders (2020) between "authoritative" and "nurturant" Christians. Whereas authoritatives are invested in an objectivist conception of divine retributive justice, nurturants are committed to a radically relational idea of divine restorative justice. The former is a matter of what Kierkegaard terms the finality of being, and alternatively the latter is a matter of Kierkegaard's emphasis on the constancy of becoming. Challenging authoritative approaches and conceptions, Kierkegaard views Christian militancy to yield a radical social inversion of the success orientation. Indeed, Kierkegaard admits that for those who defend a triumphalist approach it will seem that "it is only the idle and the unemployed who run after him [Christ]" (1991, 51).

In an amazing inversion of common cultural assessments of what is practical, important, and valuable, Kierkegaard is unflinching in his rejection of the idea that it is due to our material success that we are now in the right position with each other and God: "The deification of the established order . . . is the smug invention of the lazy, secular human mentality that wants to settle down and fancy that now there is total peace and security, now we have achieved the highest" (1991, 88). In contrast to the smug, self-aggrandizing, other-dismissing, and result-based understanding of triumphalism, "there stands Christianity with its requirements for self-denial: Deny yourself—and then suffer because you deny yourself" (Kierkegaard 1991, 213). Suffering, self-denial, humility—these are hardly inviting ideas, and yet this is precisely that to which Kierkegaard understands Christ to beckon all those who would seek to follow the "way" to come. But outside of the economic logic of worldly success, Kierkegaard implores us to ask why we have thought that grace would ever have been anything other than costly to our own narratives of self-sufficiency. Grace, as Kierkegaard makes very clear, is always "costly."

Costly Grace and Religionless Christianity: Kierkegaard and Bonhoeffer

Although the idea of "costly grace" is perhaps most commonly associated with Bonhoeffer's *Cost of Discipleship*, the ideas presented therein are rightly viewed as developing out of a framework that Kierkegaard had already mapped out in *Practice in Christianity*. In the context of nineteenth-century Danish Lutheranism in which being a Christian was largely a matter of social identity,[6] "Christ's teaching [is] taken, turned, and scaled down," Kierkegaard notes, such that "everything [becomes] as simple as pulling on one's socks—naturally, for in that way Christianity has become paganism" (1991, 35). It is indisputable that the creature comforts of modern technology had significant impacts on the way that one might relate to Christian living. But what about the virtues of self-denial and humility? Does Kierkegaard now just see such virtues as entirely rejected within the Church Triumphant? Well, although it might seem so on first glance, Kierkegaard's assessment is a bit more nuanced than that. Rather than owning up to the abandonment of the way of Christ, and the virtues that characterize that way, triumphalists "do not wish to do away with all these glorious virtues; on the contrary, they want—at a cheap price—to have as comfortably as possible the appearance of and the reputation for practicing them" (60). This is a striking acknowledgment on Kierkegaard's part that speaks directly to the possibility of excusing the abandonment of Christ in the very name of "Christianity." To those who would claim that Christianity is a matter of external achievement—again, think of the Rich Young Ruler—Kierkegaard boldly declares, "No, one does not manage to become a Christian at such a cheap price!" (136).

Even if Bonhoeffer did get his basic idea of cheap grace from broadly Kierkegaardian notions, he is certainly the thinker who has done the most to work through the details of what cheap vs. costly grace is all about as concerns Christian practice.[7] Like Kierkegaard, Bonhoeffer is not one to mince words: "Cheap grace is the deadly enemy of our church. We are fighting today for costly grace" (1991, 157). Given how dramatic Bonhoeffer's critique of cheap grace is, what, exactly, is the difference between it and the costly version that he claims to be in line with the way of Christ? "Cheap grace," he explains, "means grace as a doctrine, a principle, a system," but alternatively, "costly grace is the gospel which must be sought again and again, the gift which must be asked for, the door at which a man must knock" (158). Notice the ways in which this description resonates with Kierkegaard's two Churches and the two ideas of perfection that we discussed earlier. Cheap grace, like the Church Triumphant and success-oriented perfection, is about achievement, finality, and being. In stark contrast, costly grace, like the Church Militant and faithful-ness oriented perfectibility, is about striving, continued commitment, and becoming. Cheap grace is *cheap* because it is not something that humbles us in a continued demand. Costly grace is *costly* because it never allows us to escape the call of self-denial.

Famously, toward the end of his short life, Kierkegaard (1968) waged what he termed the "attack on Christendom." This attack should never have been understood as a critique of Christianity as undertaken by those who would strive to imitate Christ, to follow along the way, and to militantly position themselves in opposition to the worldly logic of success oriented perfection. Kierkegaard's critical ire was, instead, always directed toward those who would waive the banner of Christ over their own self-seeking interests. His challenge was not to Christians, *tout court*, but those who refused to commit to the difficult task of becoming Christians while presenting themselves as Christians wrapped in "peace," "security," and already having "achieved the highest." Similarly, toward the end of his own short life, Bonhoeffer increasingly explicit about a significant chal-lenge to Christian living: far too many who claimed to be "Christian." In unison with Kierkegaard's challenge to those who would seek the easy way out, Bonhoeffer suggests that genuine Christianity will "bar the way to any escapism disguised as piety" (1967, 142). Calling for a "religionless Christianity" (78–79, 138–45, 166), Bonhoeffer notes that his "fear and distrust of 'religiosity' have become greater" during his time in prison and then later admits that he no longer thinks he can use the term *God* around "religious" people because what they mean by it bears no relation to the way of Christ: "While I am often reluctant to mention God by name to religious people—because that name somehow seems to me here not to ring true, and I feel myself to be slightly dishonest (it is particularly bad when others start to talk in religious jargon; I then dry up almost completely and feel awkward and uncomfortable)—to people with no religion I can on occasion mention him by name quite calmly and as a matter of course"

(141–42). Kierkegaard's "attack" and Bonhoeffer's rejection of "religiosity" are two modes of the same commitment: a refusal to allow the way of Christ to be reducible to a focus on one's own status, rather than a tireless devotion to neighbor-love. As Bonhoeffer so beautifully writes, it is only by turning away from the individualism that infects our self-oriented social logic that we can begin to live into the other-oriented love modeled in Christ: "Does the question about saving one's soul appear in the Old Testament at all? Are not righteousness and the Kingdom of God on earth the focus of everything, and is it not true that Rom. 3.24ff. is not an individualistic doctrine of salvation, but the culmination of the view that God alone is righteous? It is not with the beyond that we are concerned, but with this world as created and preserved, subjected to laws, reconciled, and restored" (1967, 144). Kierkegaard and Bonhoeffer both suggest that costly grace turns one's attention from themselves to others, and from escaping to heaven to being invested in the Kingdom of God here and now. The task is to *practice* Christianity, not to narrate one's social position as having *perfected* it.

For Kierkegaard and Bonhoeffer, it is here, aware of human brokenness, fully cognizant of the requisite self-denial that attends neighbor-love, humbly taking up the cross daily, that one follows "along the way." As such, for both thinkers, embodied Christian practice is a matter of militant liturgies, not triumphalist applause.

Militant Liturgies and Afflicted Love: Kierkegaard and Weil

There are a variety of ways to conceive of liturgy. Nicholas Wolterstorff (2015, 2018) suggests that liturgy is a scripted practice enacted by a religious community. Jean-Yves Lacoste (2004) offers a view that expands liturgy to include the very condition of being constituted before God. Bruce Ellis Benson (2013) suggests that it is a way of life that attempts to cultivate beauty and excellence.[8] Regardless of one's approach to liturgy, what cuts across all the various accounts is the idea of an investment in embodied relational becoming. Liturgical practice is a matter of shaping one's identity in relation to that which one lives toward. Whether understood as specific rituals, theological constitutions, or aesthetic narrative, liturgy concerns the embodied act of living. Kierkegaard appreciates this broadly liturgical conception of Christian truth when he distinguishes between truth as something lived and truth as something affirmed: "Truth in the sense in which Christ is the truth is not a sum of statements, not a definition etc., but a life. . . . The being of truth is the redoubling of truth within yourself, within me, within him, that your life, my life, his life expresses the truth approximately in the striving for it, that your life, my life, his life is approximately the being of the truth in the striving for it, just as the truth was in Christ a life, for he was the truth" (1991, 205). Kierkegaardian faith is about passionate becoming, not simply about propositional assent. Embodied practice, then, becomes, for Kierkegaard, the lived site of religious knowledge because what it concerns is one's own living after Christ's example, not simply affirming facts about Christ's having lived.[9]

Here Kierkegaard is quite close to Simone Weil's account of the love of God being a matter of embracing the realities of embodied affliction.[10] But pushing a bit further than Kierkegaard's insistence that Christian life is never about social status but about self-denial, Weil's account is more enfleshed; more affectively impacted as concerns historical social identity. "The social factor is essential," she notes, because "there is not really affliction unless there is social degradation or the fear of it in some form or another" (Weil 1951, 119). Stressing the social, psychological, and physical dimensions of affliction, Weil, Kierkegaard, and Bonhoeffer all focus their attention on what we might term the *Liturgical Trinity*: God, Self, and Society. It is that last aspect that often gets lost in philosophical considerations of Christianity. By focusing so heavily on the cognitivist, and especially doxastic, dimensions of Christianity, philosophers sometimes not only miss the importance of practice but sidestep the social context in which such practices are enacted and beliefs are held (see Schilbrack

2014). Indeed, even the majority of discussions of the philosophy of liturgy commonly act like religious life is a matter purely of what happens within the walls of the Church, rather than being concerned with such church practice as a broader question of Christianity's social witness and activism.[11] Weil excellently intervenes as a reminder that liturgy can never simply be a matter of one's relation to God, or one's relation to other Christians, but instead must concern society itself as a context in which one bear's witness to the lived truth of Christ: "The present period is one of those when everything that seems normally to constitute a reason for living dwindles away, when one must, on pain of sinking into confusion or apathy, call everything in question again. That the triumph of authoritarian and nationalist movements should blast almost everywhere the hopes that well-meaning people had placed in democracy and in pacifism is only a part of the evil from which we are suffering; it is far deeper and far more widespread" (1973, 37).[12]

Militant Liturgies are perhaps obviously necessary in a time when the Church becomes wedded to authoritarian and nationalist movements (as was the case for Bonhoeffer and Weil). However, Weil's critique is subtler than that. She also realizes that even democratic commitments and pacifist tendencies could override the commitment to the lived truth of Christ's example whenever one confuses political strategy with imitating Christ. Indeed, Kierkegaard's own opposition to the cultural erasure of the way of Christ by the tendency to confuse Danish citizenship with Christian faith nicely anticipates her point here.[13] It is important that Bonhoeffer warned about the moral bankruptcy of the German Lutheran Church in the face of Hitler's political emergence, but Weil worries that sometimes we can fail to recognize the devil in our midst: complacency, acquiescence, and abstraction are temptations regardless of one's political association. For Weil, a social manifestation of the embodied truth of Christ's example is an opposition to not just obvious moral evils but even those sins of apathy that emerge from a life that confuses external success with Christian righteousness. Weil is not optimistic about how to pull back from the brink. "We are living through a period bereft of a future," she fears, and concludes that "waiting for that which is to come is no longer a matter of hope, but of anguish" (1973, 38).

Conclusions: Critique and Construction

The ideas of costly grace and militant liturgies clearly are not for the faint of heart. However, the idea of Christian practice has rarely been presented as easygoing—the idea of "taking up one's cross" is not exactly a joyful recommendation toward a life of leisure. As an example from the biblical archive upon which Christian traditions draw, consider that in Paul's letter to the Ephesians, he speaks precisely to the need for fortitude in Christian community:

> Be prepared. You're up against far more than you can handle on your own. Take all the help you can get, every weapon God has issued, so that when it's all over but the shouting you'll still be on your feet. Truth, righteousness, peace, faith, and salvation are more than words. Learn how to apply them. You'll need them throughout your life. God's Word is an *indispensable* weapon. In the same way, prayer is essential in this ongoing warfare. Pray hard and long. Pray for your brothers and sisters. Keep your eyes open. Keep each other's spirits up so that no one falls behind or drops out. (Ephesians 6:13 *The Message*)

In light of Paul's encouragement, how might philosophers of religion appropriate the account of Christian practice presented by Kierkegaard, Bonhoeffer, and Weil?[14] I think that in the context of philosophical consideration of Christian traditions, these three voices speak in harmony about the importance of the joint virtues of critical awareness and constructive enactment. Regarding critical awareness, consider Kierkegaard's warning about "the established order"—which we might hear as applying both to Christian communities and also to philosophical communities: "But the established order will not put up with consisting of something as loose as a collection of millions of individuals, each of whom has his relationship with God. The established order wants to be a totality that recognizes nothing above itself but has every individual under it and judges every individual who subordinates himself to the established order" (1991, 91). Additionally, and again in a critique that speaks to both Christian life and philosophical engagement, Kierkegaard, Bonhoeffer, and Weil all warn against confusing traditionalism with responsible living. Although there are surely going to be scripted aspects of Christian practice handed down in community (indeed, Wolterstorff's notion of liturgy depends on this), these thinkers jointly caution against replacing the "way" of imitating Christ with the "results" of an inherited history of how others have done so. Accordingly, they call for critical awareness such that we avoid a situation where "finally custom and usage become articles of faith; everything becomes equally important, or ordinances, usage, and custom become what is important" (Kierkegaard 1991, 92).[15]

However, the account of Christian practice that they articulate must be understood as not purely critical. It is also constructive. They jointly encourage constructive approaches to thinking and living together as "neighbors." Although it would be too far afield here to explore the sociopolitical, ecclesial, and philosophical results of such a notion, it is still important to appreciate that their account is not one that simply stands *against something*, but instead stands *for others*. For Kierkegaard, Bonhoeffer, and Weil, following the way of Christ as a work of embodied love requires us to realize that Christ does not allow for favoritism to be shown according to the economic logic of worldly status. Indeed, "He who opens his arms and invites all—ah, if all, all you who labor and are burdened, were to come to him, he would embrace them all and say: Now remain with me, for to remain with me is rest" (Kierkegaard 1991, 15). Kierkegaard is clear that neighbor love is not simply an option but is commanded: "You *shall* love your neighbor as yourself" (1995, 17–43). Philosophically, we might say that they call for dialogical charity to be a mode of embodied practice.

Let's conclude, then, by again turning to the biblical archive as an important resource for philosophical reflection (even if it should not stand as authoritative within philosophical discourse in the way that it does in theology). Listen to the words of Micah, who, like Kierkegaard, Bonhoeffer, and Weil, does not mince words, but instead presents the simple kenotic wisdom that calls for Christian practice to be a daily task:

> But he's already made it plain how to live, what to do,
> what God is looking for in men and women.
> It's quite simple: Do what is fair and just to your neighbor,
> be compassionate and loyal in your love,
> And don't take yourself too seriously—
> take God seriously. (Micah 6:8 *The Message*)

Hospitality, humility, and reverence—these are philosophical virtues for sure, but also, if Kierkegaard, Bonhoeffer, and Weil are right, they are tasks for embodied Christian practice. As philosophers increasingly attend to the importance of practice for religious life, I hope that these three thinkers become more common resources upon which they might draw and interlocutors with whom they might engage.[16]

Notes

1 For an example of recent philosophical considerations of such diversity within Christian traditions, see Simmons (2019).

2 This has especially been manifest in a sustained interest in liturgy, as will be considered in what follows.

3 This misguided critique has been frequently been articulated regarding Kierkegaard. As just a few influential examples, see Blanshard (1969, 118–20; 1975); MacIntyre (1984, 42); Schaeffer (1976, 174).

4 As just one example, see Evans (2008).

5 For a good general consideration of Kierkegaard and religion, see Walsh (2018).

6 See Coe (2020); Holm (2013).

7 For more on the relationship of Kierkegaard and Bonhoeffer, see Kelly (1974); Law (2011); Kirkpatrick (2011).

8 There is an emerging literature on the philosophy of liturgy that is relevant to the framework that I am developing here. See especially Cuneo (2016); Gschwandtner (2019); and Butcher (2018).

9 Indeed, Kierkegaard (1985), under the name of Johannes Climacus, spends a great deal of time thinking about the relation of historical truth to Christian theology.

10 For considerations of Kierkegaard and Weil, see Allen (2006) and Andic (1985). For Bonhoeffer's take on the relationship between love and suffering, see Bonhoeffer (1995, 194–98).

11 As a good counterexample to this trend, see Farley (forthcoming) and the excellent essays in Hereth and Timpe (2020).

12 For more on Weil's integration of Christianity and political life, see Weil (1977, part 2).

13 For more on Kierkegaard's specific religious inheritance and its roots in pietistic movements, see Barnett (2011).

14 See also Polk (1997) and Martens (2013) who both consider the way in which Kierkegaard approaches biblical interpretation.

15 For an excellent Kierkegaardian consideration of the ways in which such traditionalism can lead to dangerous tendencies toward Christian nationalism, see Backhouse (2011). See also Westphal (1991, 2013) for a substantive consideration of Kierkegaard's approach to social theory, as well as Bukdahl (2001) and Garff (2013).

16 I would like to thank John Sanders, Kevin Carnahan, and the editors of [this volume] for their helpful feedback. Additionally, a very early version of this essay was presented as a guest lecture for the Hong Kierkegaard Library at St. Olaf College and I would like to thank the audience at that event for their questions and suggestions.

References

Allen, Diogenes. 2006. *Three Outsiders: Pascal, Kierkegaard and Simone Weil.* Eugene, OR: Wipf and Stock.

Andic, Martin. 1985. "Simone Weil and Kierkegaard." *Modern Theology* 2:21–41.

Backhouse, Stephen. 2011. *Kierkegaard's Critique of Christian Nationalism.* Oxford: Oxford University Press.

Barnett, Christopher B. 2011. *Kierkegaard, Pietism, and Holiness*. New York: Routledge.

Benson, Bruce Ellis. 2013. *Liturgy as a Way of Life: Embodying the Arts in Christian Worship*. Grand Rapids, MI: Baker.

Blanshard, Brand. 1969. "Kierkegaard on Faith." In *Essays on Kierkegaard*, edited by Jerry H. Gill, 113–26. Minneapolis: Burgess.

——. 1975. *Reason and Belief*. New Haven, CT: Yale University Press.

Bonhoeffer, Dietrich. 1967. *Letters and Papers from Prison*. Edited by Eberhard Bethge. New York: Macmillan.

——. 1991. *Dietrich Bonhoeffer: Witness to Jesus Christ*. Edited by John de Gruchy. Minneapolis: Fortress.

——. 1995. *A Testament to Freedom*. Edited by Geffrey B. Kelly and F. Burton Nelson. San Francisco: Harper San Francisco.

Bukdahl, Jørgen. 2001. *Søren Kierkegaard and the Common Man*. Translated and edited by Bruce H. Kirmmse. Grand Rapids, MI: William B. Eerdmans.

Butcher, Brian A. 2018. *Liturgical Theology after Schmemann: An Orthodox Reading of Paul Ricoeur*. New York: Fordham University Press.

Coe, David Lawrence. 2020. *Kierkegaard and Luther*. Lanham: Lexington Books.

Cuneo, Terence. 2016. *Ritualized Faith: Essays on the Philosophy of Liturgy*. Oxford: Oxford University Press.

Evans, C. Stephen. 2008. "Kierkegaard and the Limits of Reason: Can There Be a Responsible Fideism?" *Revista Portuguesa De Filosofia* 64:1021–35.

Farley, Wendy. Forthcoming. "Dark Times and Liturgies of Truth: The Uses and Abuses of Reason." Unpublished manuscript.

Garff, Joakim. 2013. "Formation and the Critique of Culture." In *The Oxford Handbook to Kierkegaard*, edited by John Lippitt and George Pattison, 252–72. Oxford: Oxford University Press.

Gschwandtner, Christina M. 2019. *Welcoming Finitude: Toward a Phenomenology of Orthodox Liturgy*. New York: Fordham University Press.

Hereth, Blake, and Kevin Timpe. 2020. *The Lost Sheep in Philosophy of Religion: New Perspectives on Disability, Gender, Race, and Animals*. New York: Routledge.

Holm, Anders. 2013. "Kierkegaard and the Church." In *The Oxford Handbook to Kierkegaard*, edited by John Lippitt and George Pattison, 112–28. Oxford: Oxford University Press.

Kelly, Geffrey B. 1974. "The Influence of Kierkegaard on Bonhoeffer's Concept of Discipleship." *Irish Theological Quarterly* 42:148–54.

Kierkegaard, Søren. 1968. *Kierkegaard's Attack upon "Christendom": 1854–55*. Translated by Walter Lowrie. Princeton: Princeton University Press.

———. 1985. *Philosophical Fragments* and *Johannes Climacus*. Edited and translated by Howard V. Hong and Edna H. Hong. Princeton: Princeton University Press.

———. 1987. *Either/Or Part II*. Edited and translated by Howard V. Hong and Edna H. Hong. Princeton: Princeton University Press.

———. 1991. *Practice in Christianity*. Edited and translated by Howard V. Hong and Edna H. Hong. Princeton: Princeton University Press.

———. 1995. *Works of Love*. Edited and translated by Howard V. Hong and Edna H. Hong. Princeton: Princeton University Press.

Kirkpatrick, Matthew D. 2011. *Attacks on Christendom in a World Come of Age: Kierkegaard, Bonhoeffer, and the Question of "Religionless Christianity."* Eugene, OR: Pickwick.

Lacoste, Jean-Yves. 2004. *Experience and the Absolute: Disputed Questions on the Humanity of Man*. Translated by Mark Raftery-Skehan. New York: Fordham University Press.

Law, David R. 2011. "Redeeming the Penultimate: Discipleship and Church in the Thought of Søren Kierkegaard and Dietrich Bonhoeffer." *International Journal for the Study of the Christian Church* 11:14–26.

MacIntyre, Alasdair. 1984. *After Virtue: A Study in Moral Theory*. 2nd ed. Notre Dame, IN: University of Notre Dame Press.

———. 1988. *Whose Justice? Which Rationality?* Notre Dame, IN: University of Notre Dame Press.

Martens, Paul. 2013. "Kierkegaard and the Bible." In *The Oxford Handbook to Kierkegaard*, edited by John Lippitt and George Pattison, 150–65. Oxford: Oxford University Press.

Polk, Timothy Houston. 1997. *The Biblical Kierkegaard: Reading by the Rule of Faith*. Macon, GA: Mercer University Press.

Sanders, John. 2020. *Embracing Prodigals: Overcoming Authoritative Religion by Embodying Jesus' Nurturing Grace*. Eugene, OR: Cascade.

Schaeffer, Francis A. 1976. *How Should We Then Live? The Rise and Decline of Western Thought and Culture*. Old Tappan, NJ: Fleming H. Revell.

Schilbrack, Kevin. 2014. *Philosophy and the Study of Religions: A Manifesto*. Malden, MA: Wiley-Blackwell.

Simmons, J. Aaron, ed. 2019. *Christian Philosophy: Conceptions, Continuations, and Challenges*. Oxford: Oxford University Press.

Walsh, Silvia. 2018. *Kierkegaard and Religion: Personality, Character, and Virtue*. Cambridge: Cambridge University Press.

Weil, Simone. 1951. *Waiting for God*. New York: Harper and Row.

———. 1973. *Oppression and Liberty*. Translated by Arthur Wills and John Petrie. Amherst: University of Massachusetts Press.

———. 1977. *The Simone Weil Reader*. Edited by George A. Panichas. New York: David McKay.

Westphal, Merold. 1991. *Kierkegaard's Critique of Reason and Society*. University Park: Pennsylvania State University Press.

———. 2009. *Whose Community? Which Interpretation? Philosophical Hermeneutics for the Church*. Grand Rapids, MI: Baker.

———. 2013. "Society, Politics, Modernity." In *The Oxford Handbook to Kierkegaard*, edited by John Lippitt and George Pattison, 309–27. Oxford: Oxford University Press.

Wolterstorff, Nicholas. 2015. *The God We Worship: An Exploration of Liturgical Theology*. Grand Rapids, MI: William B. Eerdmans.

———. 2018. *Acting Liturgically: Philosophical Reflections on Religious Practice*. Oxford: Oxford University Press.

 CHAPTER 11

Correcting Acedia through Wonder and Gratitude

Brandon Dahm

ABSTRACT: In the capital vices tradition, acedia was fought through perseverance and manual labor. In this paper, I argue that we can also fight acedia through practicing wonder and gratitude. I show this through an account of moral formation developed out of the insight of the virtues and vices traditions that character traits affect how we see things. In the first section, I use Robert Roberts's account of emotions to explain a mechanism by which virtues and vices affect vision and thus moral formation. Then by looking at the capital vices tradition, I argue that restless boredom is a primary construal of the vice of acedia. Third, I explain wonder and gratitude through the work of G. K. Chesterton and Roberts, respectively. In light of their accounts, I explain how the construals of wonder and gratitude are contrary to the construal of acedia. Finally, I offer some practices that encourage gratitude and wonder.

Introduction

O utside of traditional Christian ethics, the vice of acedia, usually translated as "sloth," is not on standard lists of bad character traits. Acedia is a deeper vice than sloth, though, which is just a form of laziness. Instead, acedia is an avoidance of the demands made on our life by the spiritual or higher goods in our life. As many have recently argued (DeYoung 2009; Nault 2015; Snell 2015; Waugh 1962) and as should become clear once a person reads the classic descriptions of acedia,[1] acedia is a vice we clearly see in our lives and in our times. We avoid the demands of the deeper goods in our lives—the demands of friendship, family, faith, fairness, and so on—through both inactivity or sloth (Netflix, Instagram, favorite avoidance reading, etc.) and busyness (extra hours at work, packing our calendars, correcting people on the internet, etc.). A survey of self-help books shows such avoidance is a standard feature of human experience (and reading such self-help books is one of the ways some of us avoid the things we should be doing). So as I hope becomes clear through the treatment of acedia, most of us need to correct for this vice.

In the capital vices tradition, the vice of acedia was fought through perseverance and manual labor. In this paper, I argue that we can also fight acedia through practicing wonder and gratitude. I show this through an account of moral formation developed out of the insight of the virtues and vices traditions that character traits affect how we see things. In the first section, I use Robert Roberts's account of emotions to explain a mechanism by which virtues and vices affect vision and thus moral formation. Then by looking at the capital vices tradition, I argue that restless boredom is a primary construal of the vice of acedia. Third, I explain wonder and gratitude through the work of G. K. Chesterton and Roberts, respectively. In light of their accounts, I explain how the construals of wonder and gratitude are contrary to the construal of acedia. Finally, I offer some practices that encourage gratitude and wonder. As Roberts and MacIntyre have made clear, virtues must be understood within some moral framework or tradition (Roberts 2013, 13–18; MacIntyre 1981). If we are working within a Humean tradition, gratitude will be one thing, and if we are working within an Aristotelian tradition, gratitude will be another, similar but different, thing. In this paper, I work within a

Christian moral framework, which affects how I understand acedia, wonder, and gratitude.

Virtue and Vice Affect Vision

Our character affects how we see things. The gracious person perceives favors differently from the ingrate; the cruel person experiences the suffering of others differently than the kind person. That virtue comes with a change in vision is a standard insight of the virtue tradition. For example, Seneca explains this insight in terms of what virtue and vice fix our mind on: "Vices assail and surround us on all sides, and they don't allow us to rise again and lift our eyes to the clear discernment of truth; but they press down on them, keeping them lowered and fixed on mere desire" (2014, 111). More recently, John McDowell (1979) argues that virtues are specialized sensitivities or perceptual capacities for virtue salient features. Virtues affecting sight have also recently been important in replying to an objection to virtue theory.[2]

In the vices tradition, we find the corresponding insight that vices affect sight. Writing from his ascetic experience in the desert in the fourth century, Evagrius Ponticus explains, "Both the virtues and vices make the man blind. The one so that it may not see the vices; the other, in turn, so that it might not see the virtues" (1972, chap. 62). This affected sight is one of the reasons Evagrius notes for why we need to rely on others in our battle for virtue: "The spirit that is engaged in the war against the passions does not see clearly the basic meaning of the war for it is something like a man fighting in the darkness of night. Once it has attained purity of heart though, it distinctly makes out the designs of the enemy" (chap. 83). Anger and sadness, for example, hinder our ability to see or experience things as they are:

A passing cloud darkens the sun; a thought of resentment darkens the mind. (Evagrius 2003, sect. 4.6)

A monk afflicted by sadness knows no spiritual pleasure, nor can someone with a very high fever taste honey. (sect. 5.5)

Evagrius and John Cassian, who was deeply influenced by Evagrius despite not mentioning him (Stewart 1998, 11–12), thought the mechanics of temptation involve a mental representation of something being introduced to the soul and described the vices through persuasive personifications causing these representations. The vices move us to focus on certain things—the limitations of our community, the offenses of this or that brother—and then bring us to imagine other things—that I could be holy even if I leave the community, or that I would be holier if I were just free of this brother. These ways of seeing the world are part of what it is to have the vices. We will see this in detail in the next section in the classic description of the monk suffering from acedia.

Recently, Robert Roberts has developed an account of the emotions as concern-based construals.[3] Emotions are quasi-perceptual states arising in connection to a care for something. To exemplify how construals work, Roberts provides the image of the duck-rabbit. Construed in one way, the lines make a rabbit; construed in another way, the lines make a duck. The thing in front of our eyes remains the same in both construals, but we experience it differently by emphasizing different features. An emotion is a way of construing something, whether it be a person, object, event, or state of affairs. The construal that is the emotion arises from some care, aversion, or attachment of the person. Imagine that my wife and I take along our three-year-old to a dinner party hosted by Important Person. As we are eating, we hear a crash from the other room and rush to see what has happened. There sits our daughter, surrounded by a shattered vase. The good parent she is, my wife has fear arising from her concern for our daughter and construes the situation as dangerous. What is salient to her in the situation is the shattered glass around my daughter. I, on the other hand, perceive the situation as embarrassing arising from my concern about the host's opinion of me. What stands out to me is the potential harm this could do to my reputation. Finally, Important

Person is angry and perceives the situation as a kind of offense due to his care for the vase. Each of us has a different quasi-perceptual experience—we experience the situation in various ways—connected to our concerns. Such concerned-based construals are what Roberts considers emotions.

Aristotle thought we could find different virtues and vices for different realms of feeling (2000, books II–IV). For example, there are different virtues and vices for the realms of anger and fear. If Aristotle helps us see the need for virtues to moderate emotion, then Roberts helps us understand how emotions follow from virtues and vices. Virtues, according to Roberts, enable a set of functions, including "perceiving, feeling, judging, deliberating, acting" (2013, 191). In a variety of ways, virtues (and the same goes for vices), which include some set of concerns, dispose us to feel some range of emotions in some range of situations. For example, the virtue of justice is a concern for justice and disposes the just person to a range of emotions depending on the justice or injustice of a situation, such as "joy, hope, gratitude, anger, indignation, guilt, sorrow, admiration, emulation."[4] So virtues and vices are caused by the activities of their type but are also causes of the activities of their type. We become generous through acts, desires, thoughts, and feelings of generosity, which then become the expression (and sustaining nourishment) of generosity. As I hope will become clear, Roberts's account provides a way for us to analyze a vice and identify how exactly a virtue will correct it.

As a vice, acedia generates construals, but it also needs them. We are historical beings and are continuously changing. A standard thesis of virtue theory is that virtues and vices are formed by habituation. Extending what we usually think of as habituation, Aquinas argues that traits degenerate over time through a kind of erosion if they are not sustained by acts of their kind (1981, *Summa Theologiae*, I–II.53.3). If temperance is not strengthened through temperate actions, desires, patterns of thought, and construals, then actions of other kinds (both nontemperate and intemperate) disrupt it little by little. Over time, such unnourished traits erode away. For virtues, this is worrisome and encourages moral upkeep; for vices, it gives us a point of attack:

starvation. If we can keep a vice from the nourishment it needs by performing activities of contrary traits, including the construals of the trait, then the vice will diminish until it erodes away. Like weeds and crops, vices and virtues compete for the same nutrients, which are our varied activities. If we cannot directly pull the weeds, then we can nourish the crops and starve the weeds out. I propose this strategy for fighting acedia. To do this, I turn to acedia and its construal.

The Vice of Acedia and Its Construal

Acedia and its experience could be described in many ways, as we will see, but I argue that the common construal of the vice is rest-less boredom. I develop this by looking at treatments of acedia in the capital vices tradition and Roberts's account of boredom. I start at the beginning with Evagrius. In Evagrius's classic description of the monk suffering from acedia, which Cassian uses, we see that the experience of acedia involves a loss of interest with one's life and a distaste for its demands:

> The demon of *acedia*—also called the noonday demon—is the one that causes the most serious trouble of all. He presses his attack upon the monk about the fourth hour and besieges the soul until the eighth hour. First of all he makes it seem that the sun barely moves, if at all, and that the day is fifty hours long. Then he con-strains the monk to look constantly out the windows, to walk outside the cell, to gaze carefully at the sun to determine how far it stands from the ninth hour, to look now this way and now that to see if perhaps [one of the brethren appears from his cell]. Then too he instills in the heart of the monk a hatred for the place, a hatred for his very life itself, a hatred for manual labor. He leads him to reflect that charity has departed from among the brethren, that there is no one to give encouragement. Should there be someone at this period who happens to offend him in some way or other, this too the demon uses to contribute further to his hatred. This

demon drives him along to desire other sites where he can more easily procure life's necessities, more readily find work and make a real success of himself. He goes on to suggest that, after all, it is not the place that is the basis of pleasing the Lord. God is to be adored everywhere. He joins to these reflections the memory of his dear ones and of his former way of life. He depicts life stretching out for a long period of time, and brings before the mind's eye the toil of the ascetic struggle and, as the saying has it, leaves no leaf unturned to induce the monk to forsake his cell and drop out of the fight. No other demon follows close upon the heels of this one (when he is defeated) but only a state of deep peace and inexpressible joy arise out of this struggle. (1972, chap. 12)

The monk's acedia makes him see his life as repressive and other modes of life as desirable. Cassian expands on Evagrius's account, describing the monk under the attack of acedia as having a "wearied" or "anxious" heart (2000, book 10, chap. 1). Being in this state renders the monk slothful and immobile in the face of all prescribed work, but because acedia is not merely sloth, it does not let him stay still (chaps. 2, 6). Acedia also manifests as busyness, which is why "sloth" only captures some of what acedia is. The restlessness of the monk impels him from one activity to another, avoiding what he is supposed to be doing. So acedia wields both the sword of sleep that fells the couch potato and the sword of busyness that dispatches the workaholic.

In the early capital vices tradition of Cassian and Evagrius, acedia and sadness are distinct vices. It is important to clarify that sadness the emotion is not identical to sadness the vice. Most generally, sadness the vice is a kind of despairing sadness that should be distinguished both from being sad about some circumstance, which can be healthy and good to feel, and clinical depression, which is not a moral fault.[5] Cassian's treatment of the vice of sadness is fairly thin, and the later tradition combines sadness with acedia in different ways—Gregory the Great incorporates acedia under sadness and Aquinas incorporates sadness within acedia (St. Gregory the Great 1844, XIII). I am going to follow Aquinas's account of thinking of acedia as a form of sadness. The account is complicated, but he argues that acedia is "a sadness and abhorrence or boredom" regarding a spiritual and divine good within.[6] The spiritual good within causes sadness because it conflicts with the desires of the flesh. "And so when desire of the flesh is dominant in human beings, they have distaste for spiritual good as contrary to their good. Just so, human beings with infected taste buds have distaste for healthy food and grieve over it whenever they need to consume such food" (Aquinas 2003).

On Aquinas's account, the "divine good within" primarily means charity or the infused grace of friendship with God that demands a certain way of life. Extending Aquinas's explicit claims, the spiritual or divine good can also be our friendships, family, vocations, and the general call of all humans to virtue and holiness. Any deep good connected to our flourishing can be a cause of acedia. As Heather Hughes Huff explains, "Here is why *acedia* is so difficult to identify: this vice does not attempt to replace our human *telos*, which is to love and serve God, with some secondary good like sex, possessions, or food. It does not inordinately prefer a particular good at all; rather, it says 'no' to a difficult and demanding good" (2013, 46). So acedia is a sadness or aversion to some spiritual good that makes demands on our life.

Rebecca Konyndyk DeYoung insightfully interprets this distaste for spiritual good as a "resistance to the demands of love."[7] In Aquinas this resistance arises partly from one's apprehension being bent by her concerns.[8] Spiritual goods make demands on us that interfere with our lower desires, loves, and projects. We thus construe the spiritual goods as evil and are saddened by their presence. Avoiding the pain of this sorrow gives rise to many actions "that we may avoid it, or through being exasperated into doing something under pressure thereof" (Aquinas 1981, ST II–II.35.4). We then give up, exemplifying slothful acedia, or look for distractions, exemplifying the acedia of busyness.

With acedia and sadness connected, we can incorporate some of Cassian's treatment of sadness into our understanding of acedia. In the desert account of the vices, there is a kind of overflow or concatenation model of their connection.[9] When one gives into gluttony, the first of the evil thoughts, one becomes accustomed to being sated and satisfying desire whenever it arises. This overflows into lust, which similarly overflows into greed. In Cassian's treatment, acedia follows sadness, and we can see a helpful connection between them. A significant portion of his treatment of sadness involves a reading of Proverbs 25:20: "As a moth with a garment and a worm with wood, so sadness does to a man's heart."[10] Cassian expands on the verse: "For a moth-eaten garment no longer has any value or good use, and likewise worm-eaten wood deserves to be consigned to the flames rather than to be used for furnishing even an insignificant building. In the same way, then, the soul that is eaten away and devoured by sadness is certainly useless for that priestly garment" (2000, book 10, chaps. 3, 9). The vice of sadness, then, empties the person of one's purpose and usefulness for good.

One way of seeing the connection of sadness to acedia is to see this emptiness transition from the person to the person's perception of one's work and purpose. The monk suffering from acedia sees daily work—his prayers, reading, manual labor, and so on—as empty and lacking purpose. The wood and garments are hollowed out by the worms and moths, and they no longer have the solidity and integrity to be useful. Similarly, things like a rule of life and the work of his vocation now lack the solidity and integrity to draw him. Instead, they appear thin, transparent, or hollow. So under the attack of sloth, he either gives up or moves on to the next thing. Unfortunately for him, neither is satisfying: the sleep of sloth is not restful, and the next distraction will soon become hollow as well. Things feeling empty or hollowed-out is one way to express the experience of boredom.

In his treatment of emotions, Roberts offers a defining proposition that expresses the intelligible character of each emotion. The proposition need not be explicitly thought by the subject of the emotion, but it provides the form or structural content of the emotion (Roberts 2003, 106–12). For boredom, Roberts offers the following defining proposition: "It is very important for me to be interested, absorbed, to have my attention engaged, but everything I currently behold, and everything I currently might do, is uninteresting; may I soon be free from this state of mind" (248). On Roberts's account, when something is construed as boring it has lost all interest for us. Remember, an emotion is a *concern-based* construal, and the concern of the bored is to be interested and engaged. The pain of this concern not being realized, which Aquinas describes as a sadness, moves us to avoid those things, situations, and people that no longer engage us. We can see this in Evagrius's monk who has lost interest in the life of the desert and looks anywhere else to avoid the pain of boredom.[11] This is the restlessness of boredom in the face of emptied-out experience.

Following Roberts, I have claimed that virtues and vices cause emotions, and emotions are concern-based construals. On this account, the vice of acedia generates the emotion of boredom.[12] Through the construal of acedia, we see things as moth-eaten, empty, and hollowed out, as boring. Moreover, this way of seeing them arises from a concern or care within us, which is an aversion to the good that is making a demand on our life. The movement away from the thing perceived as boring is a restlessness in the face of the good that manifests as both inactivity and frenetic activity. If we can cultivate construals contrary to boredom, then we can starve acedia of the nourishment it needs.

Wonder and Gratitude Correct Acedia

In this section, I explain how wonder and gratitude both oppose acedia by producing contrary construals. In the next section, I turn to practices that help form these virtues. I understand wonder primarily through two texts of G. K. Chesterton, *Tremendous Trifles* and *Orthodoxy*. In the opening essay of *Tremendous Trifles*, we get a perfectly Chestertonian fairy tale. Two young boys playing in their small front yard are visited by the milkman, who is also a fairy. He offers the boys each a wish, as fairies do. The first boy, Paul, wishes to become a giant so that he can travel about seeing the great wonders of the world.

> He went striding away with his head above the clouds to visit Niagara and the Himalayas. But when he came to the Himalayas, he found they were quite small and silly-looking, like the little cork rockery in the garden; and when he found Niagara it was no bigger than the tap turned on in the bathroom. He wandered round the world for several minutes trying to find something really large and finding everything small, till in sheer boredom he lay down on four or five prairies and fell asleep. Unfortunately his head was just outside the hut of an intellectual backwoodsman who came out of it at that moment with an axe in one hand and a book of Neo-Catholic Philosophy in the other. The man looked at the book and then at the giant, and then at the book again. And in the book it said, "It can be maintained that the evil of pride consists in being out of proportion to the universe." So the backwoodsman put down his book, took his axe and, working eight hours a day for about a week, cut the giant's head off; and there was an end of him. Such is the severe yet salutary history of Paul. (Chesterton 1909, 2–3)

Peter, Paul's more sensible brother, wished the opposite, to become tiny. Their little yard immediately grew to a vast wilderness. Every ordinary and boring feature of the yard transformed into a wonder. Peter "set out on his adventures across that coloured plain; and he has not come to the end of it yet" (Chesterton 1909, 4).

The moral of the tale is fairly obvious: real adventure is all around us in the everyday. Yet we are Pauls that look across the street or world when our yard has become boring. In *Orthodoxy* (1986), Chesterton critiques our tendency to flatten the world from the perspective of his fairy tale philosophy. We do not do this as Paul did, by becoming literal giants, but by seeing things around us as necessarily how they are. Chesterton thinks at least two things contribute to this mindset.

271

We become Pauls by being "scientifically minded." Chesterton's point is not a critique of science or scientists per se, but a critique of those who think necessary "scientific" connections adequately explain the world around them.[13] So the "scientifically minded" person experiences the world as just how it has to be according to scientific law. We also become Pauls by the repetition of experience. Every time I see moving water it is running downhill, making me think this must be the case. The constant conjunction of two things, whether it be water running downhill, the color of grass, or the humps on a camel, obscures the deeper magic of the connection the way Paul's size kept him from seeing the wonder of the world.

To correct our tendency toward giantism, Chesterton instructs us in a deeper magic through the ethics of elfland. He summarizes, "I have explained that the fairy tales founded in me two convictions; first, that this world is a wild and startling place, which might have been quite different, but which is quite delightful; second, that before this wildness and delight one may well be modest and submit to the queerest limitations of so queer a kindness" (1986, 262). Examining these two convictions will show us how wonder can be a corrective to acedia.

The first conviction: The world is a wild and startling place. Instead of being surrounded by necessary connections according to scientific law, the fairy tale school teaches that things could have been radically different. Chesterton explains that we can enjoy the things around us because they do not have to be as they are: "Now, the fairy-tale philosopher is glad that the leaf is green precisely because it might have been scarlet. He feels as if it had turned green an instant before he looked at it. He is pleased that snow is white on the strictly reasonable ground that it might have been black. Every colour has in it a bold quality of choice; the red of garden roses is not only decisive but dramatic, like suddenly spilt blood. He feels that something has been done" (1986, 262). We are worn down by repetition and our sense of mystery is dulled to the fact that things, even the color of leaves, could have been otherwise. Because thinking about nature through words like "law" and "necessity" can empty things of their mystery, Chesterton prefers words like "charm," "spell," and "enchant-ment" to capture the deeper could-have-been-otherwise in the things joined together (256). Consider the experience of watching a nature documentary about unfamiliar animals. The deerlike creatures from different ecosystems look strange and otherworldly by varying just enough from my local white tail deer to reveal that the familiar might have been otherwise.

Unlike world-worn adults, children can remain enchanted by the same thing, over and over. As I was writing this morning, I made a funny face at my daughters after they mentioned going on a walk in the rain. They then wanted to reenact the scene over and over. Agreeing with my children, Aquinas recognizes that each thing has an unconquerable depth to its being.[14] So our perception is mistaken when the things around us seem moth-eaten or hollow from famil-iarity. We need to learn to see things as they are, to recognize with kids that the ordinary is truly extra. Then we might be able to realize, with Chesterton, that we are in a fairy tale. "It was good to be in a fairy tale. The test of all happiness is gratitude; and I felt grateful, though I hardly knew to whom. . . . We thank people for birthday presents of cigars and slippers. Can I thank no one for the birthday present of birth?" (Chesterton 1986, 258).

The second conviction is the doctrine of conditional joy: "In the fairy tale an incomprehensible happiness rests upon an incompre-hensible condition" (Chesterton 1986, 259). The Japanese fairy tale *Tsuru no Ongaeshi* provides an example of this doctrine. In the story a poor man saves an injured crane and releases it. That night a beautiful woman comes to his door and says she is his wife. He worries that he will not be able to support them, but she is able to weave luxurious clothing that makes them wealthy. The only condition is that he must not observe her making the clothing. One day, his curiosity becomes too much and he peeks in to see the crane making the clothing from its feathers. The condition violated, the crane flies away and never returns. For a time, the man had been given happiness, but happi-ness has its conditions. "Happiness is bright but brittle" (Chesterton 1986). Many of us want to rebel against the conditions of happiness.

Acedia is just one such rebellion; we see the wonderful as boring and try to avoid the good instead of pursuing it.

Chesterton argues against such a rebellion: "If I leave a man in my will ten talking elephants and a hundred winged horses, he cannot complain if the conditions partake of the slight eccentricity of the gift. He must not look a winged horse in the mouth. And it seemed to me that existence was itself so very eccentric a legacy that I could not complain of not understanding the limitations of the vision when I did not understand the vision they limited. The frame was no stranger than the picture" (1986, 260).

The world is a wild and startling place, and we should not be surprised that great mysteries like friendship, love, and existence have mysterious conditions. Instead of rebelling against the conditions we find on happiness, Chesterton suggests, "Surely one might pay for extraordinary joy in ordinary morals" (1986, 261). Adjusted for our desert monk: Surely one might pay for holiness by following the community's rule of life.

Chesterton concludes the chapter in *Orthodoxy* on the ethics of elfland again being moved to give thanks in light of living in a fairy tale: "I came to feel as if magic must have a meaning, and meaning must have some one to mean it. There was something personal in the world, as in a work of art; whatever it meant it meant violently. . . . The proper form of thanks to it is some form of humility and restraint: we should thank God for beer and Burgundy by not drinking too much of them" (1986, 268). Wonder, especially Chestertonian wonder, includes a moment of gratitude. To understand gratitude, we turn to Roberts's account.

Roberts summarizes his account in terms of three *benes*: beneficiary, benefactor, and benefit. He explains,

> So the conditions for gratitude are the following: The situation is that of two parties and a good. One of the parties is the beneficiary, one is the benefactor; and the good is a gift from the one to the other. Gratitude is the beneficiary's concern-based construal of the situation in these terms. The concerns involved are the desire

for the gift and a willingness to receive it from the benefactor. Gratitude is correct, as a construal, only if what is given really is a good, and the attitude of the giver really is benevolent toward the recipient. (2007, 143)

Gratitude as a virtue is then the disposition to gratefully construe things at the right times and for the right reasons. So Chesterton (beneficiary) is grateful to God (benefactor) for existence (benefit), and that involves construing it in these terms (although it need not be done explicitly).

Roberts rightly points out that gratitude inflects differently for different moral frameworks or traditions. In an atheistic moral framework, it does not make sense to be grateful to God, but it does make sense to be grateful to other people. In an Aristotelian moral framework, gratitude is a sign of weakness, and the magnanimous man avoids occasions of gratitude because they indicate his dependence on others (Roberts 2007, 137–39; Aristotle 2000, book IV.4). Christian gratitude is different from both of these. Consider the preface to the Mass in the Roman Rite of the Catholic Church: "It is truly right and just, our duty and our salvation, always and everywhere to give you thanks, Lord, holy Father, almighty and eternal God, through Christ our Lord" (*Roman Missal* 2011). Christians, then, should give thanks to God, and should recognize that each moment and situation is an occasion for gratitude. Roberts (2014) calls this gratitude that goes beyond human benefactors "cosmic gratitude" and argues that Christians, always able to be thankful for their creation, preservation, and the work of Christ, can achieve a kind of emotional transcendence in relation to the ebb and flow of life's events. So Christians should always be able to construe things, at least at some level of generality, as a good gift from God.

We can now clarify the way in which wonder and gratitude are contrary to acedia. Remember, acedia typically generates a construal of restless boredom in relation to some object. Consider being forced to read a philosophy paper instead of having an engaging discussion with peers. One might construe this with restless boredom and feel the weight of each page assigned push them toward social media, cleaning, or bed. Seeing the reading this way is incompatible with a construal of wonder or gratitude. If you see the reading with a construal of wonder, you see it as full of meaning, mystery, and desirable depth. The wonderful draws us into itself through awe. If you see the reading with a construal of gratitude, you see it as a good gift from a good giver. Wonder and gratitude are complementary and mutually encouraging construals. As we saw in Chesterton, wonder finds its way to gratitude. And if you have ever really been "bowed over" in gratitude, to quote Roberts quoting Dickens, you know it suggests a humble wonder of the gift and giver (2007, 144).

Thus, as long as one is construing her rule of life or vocation as wonderful or a good gift from a good giver, she is not construing it as boring. Each moment that sees something with eyes of wonder and gratitude, then, is a moment that the acedia in our soul is starved and disrupted. The problem is that the emotions of gratitude and wonder are not directly under our volitional control. We can voluntarily bring ourselves to consider that something is a gift or is full of wonder in an intellectual way, but this alone does not cure acedia. Indeed, such considerations can sometimes even inflame acedia, which is pained by the presence and demands of the good. So we need to also find ways to see wonderfully and graciously. In the next section, I explain some practices that help us construe the world with wonder and gratitude. The more we can construe the world as such, the more wonder and gratitude will take root in our soul, building the virtues of wonder and gratitude and starving out the weed of acedia.

Practicing Wonder and Gratitude

Although Roberts's rigorous and clarifying account of gratitude helps us aim at a clear target, he provides limited advice on developing gratitude: "Given this perceptual character of gratitude, one obvious way to develop it is to *practice* seeing things this way. How does one practice seeing? By *looking*. Looking is active seeing, and as we succeed in seeing what we are looking for, we train our seeing into conformity with our looking" (Roberts 2007, 146).

Over time our gratitude increases because our active, effortful looking becomes habitual, effortless seeing. This is helpful advice, but it remains fairly abstract. One way to approach growing in gratitude is through the three *benes*. We can practice seeing benefits, appreciating benefactors, and recognizing causes for failing to be grateful in the beneficiary. Approaching these one by one, we find guidance in positive psychology, Aquinas, and Seneca.

The positive psychology movement, which developed out of an attempt to correct the focus on abnormal psychology, offers an account of healthy psychology and well-being.[15] Gratitude and gratitude interventions are a centerpiece of positive psychology, which offers a number of practices, or "interventions," to encourage gratitude. Although the evidence for the efficacy of the practices is mixed (Davis et al. 2016, 20–31),[16] the four main interventions have had beneficial results for many. One review summarizes the evidence for these practices: "Gratitude interventions in adults consistently produce positive benefits, many which appear to endure over reasonably lengthy periods of time. Gratitude interventions lead to greater gratitude, life satisfaction, optimism, prosocial behavior, positive affect, and well-being, as well as decreased negative affect, compared with controls, for up to six months" (Lomas et al. 2014, 9).[17] The first two interventions are similar, counting blessings and "three good things," and involve recording things one is grateful for. Each day, one takes the time to identify and record blessings or benefits. This concrete way of practicing seeing, as Roberts recommends, solidifies the things one is grateful for by recording them in a journal or in a brief list. The practice of recording encourages the practice of seeing and remembering seeing in that way. These two practices focus on the benefit part of the construal and thereby train our ability to see gifts.

The next gratitude intervention focuses on the benefactor. Recognized as the most powerful intervention, the "gratitude visit" involves writing a letter of gratitude to someone to whom one is grateful (Lomas et al. 2014, 8–9). This practice emphasizes the deeply interpersonal nature of gratitude (unlike the others in which the *benefactor* feature of the gratitude construal is sometimes left off), and encourages seeing the person we are thankful to in addition to seeing the benefits given. Although beyond the studied intervention, one could extend the "gratitude visit" into a daily practice of expressing gratitude to one's benefactors. Just as the three good things or counting one's blessings interventions encourage seeing benefits, daily intentional expressions of gratitude should encourage one to see benefactors.

The last positive psychology intervention, grateful self-reflection, begins with a journal or brief list and adds reflection on that list in a way analogous to an examination of conscience. One asks oneself questions like, "What did I receive? What did I give? What more could I do?" (Lomas et al. 2014, 7). We can expand this intervention with the practice of contemplating the virtues and vices. In doing this, we seek to understand their nature, how they work, and to appreciate their distinctive value or disvalue. Two examples show how contemplating virtue and vice can both make our examination of conscience richer by allowing clearer perception and deeper insights into our character and enable us to have more effective strategies for improvement.

Let us first take the example of contemplating a vice. In the desert the monks studied the vices the way one at war studies an enemy. Understanding the enemy's strategies, patterns of action, and causes of his actions helps one form an effective plan for battle. Although writing in a different moral framework, Seneca, a Roman Stoic, can provide insight into gratitude and ingratitude for Christians. Aquinas, for example, quotes Seneca often in his treatment of gratitude. In *On Benefits*, Seneca treats the three *benes* in detail, providing a theoretical account of gratitude and a lot of practical advice on the giving and receiving of gifts. Seneca identifies three causes of ingratitude: "Now we must consider what it is that most makes people ungrateful: it is either an excessive regard for oneself—the deeply ingrained human failing of being impressed by oneself and one's accomplishments—or greed or envy. Let us start with the first. Everyone is generous when judging himself, which is why each person thinks that he has earned all that he has, that it is merely repayment of what is owed, and that his real value is not appreciated by others" (2011, book 2, 26.1).

While excessive self-regard causes us to misconstrue gifts as deserved, greed makes us always want more. We cannot properly recognize something as a benefit if every gift is seen as inadequate and enlivens our desire for more. Finally, envy causes ingratitude by encouraging ungenerous comparisons to others and undue regard for our own interests. Seneca helpfully shows how one might intervene to alter the unhealthy construals promoted by envy:

> But envy is a more violent and relentless failing than all of these. It unsettles us by making comparisons. "He gave me this, but he gave this other fellow more, and that fellow got his sooner." Next, it never makes the case for someone else but always puts its own interests ahead of everyone else's. How much more straight-forward and sensible it is to exaggerate the value of a benefit one has been given and to realize that everyone assesses himself more generously than others do. "I should have received more, but it would not have been easy for him to give; his generosity had to be shared among many recipients. . . . Complaining won't make me worthy of greater gifts; it will just make me unworthy of what has been given." (2011, book 2, 28.1–2)

Here we see concretely how the vice promotes one set of construals that, through self-talk, can be counteracted by promoting the construals of a contrary virtue. Understanding the causes of vice can thus help us intervene to promote virtues.

We can learn how to pursue a virtue from understanding why we fail to attain it, but we can also better pursue a virtue by under-standing its nature. Just as understanding the nearby relatives and classifications of a fish can better help the fisherman catch it, so we can better pursue gratitude by understanding how it relates to similar virtues and which cardinal virtue it is classified under. Aquinas's clas-sification of the virtues can help us better see and appreciate gratitude in this way. As he works through the three theological virtues—faith,

hope, and charity—and the cardinal virtues—prudence, justice, cour-
age, and temperance—Aquinas analyzes them according to three types
of parts (1981, ST II–II.48.1). Integral parts are the features someone
must have in order to perform acts of the virtue. For the virtue of
prudence this includes things like memory and foresight (Aquinas
1981, ST II–II.49). Subjective parts of a virtue are species of the virtue.
These have the full character of a virtue but a narrower object. For
example, the subjective parts of temperance, which is moderation in
physical pleasures, have to do with the pleasures of food (abstinence),
drink (sobriety), and sex (chastity).[18] Finally, potential parts have a
likeness to the principal virtue but lack its full character.

Gratitude, Aquinas argues, is a potential part of justice. Justice is
giving a person her due to return to a kind of equality (Aquinas 1981,
ST II–II.58). Returning my sword to me, with proper consideration
of my mental state, brings us back to a kind of equality. Yet in many
cases, only a likeness to equality can be achieved because the debt
can never be repaid (ST II–II.80). We must honor God because of the
excellence of the divine nature, but our acts of worship and honoring can never do justice to who God is. So the virtue of religion,
which concerns such honors, has an imperfect likeness to justice
(ST II–II.81). After treating the virtue of religion, Aquinas turns to
the virtue of piety that concerns what children owe their parents
(ST II–II.101) and the virtue of observance, which concerns what an
authority (ST II–II.102–5), whether it be the government, a military
commander, or a teacher, is owed. These relationships, similar to
our relationships with God, involve both due honor and inequality.
Aquinas then turns to gratitude (ST II–II.106–7). Understanding how
gratitude relates to other virtues can help us better understand our
target. With gifts, justice does not require they are repaid in a way
that returns the beneficiary to equality to the benefactor, but there is
a "debt of gratitude" to use Roberts's language (2007, 136). Giving the
benefactor her due, which can be as little as being willing to repay
the favor (Aquinas 1981, ST II–II.106.6), has a similarity to the demands
of justice, and can help us understand the demands and importance

of gratitude. Thus, contemplating gratitude in itself and in its related virtues and vices can help us grow in gratitude.

Finally, we return to wonder, and Chesterton provides three disciplines that encourage construals of wonder instead of boredom. In *Tremendous Trifles*, Chesterton contrasts his school with others who think we find the extraordinary by traveling to far-off and strange places (I unapologetically quote at length):

> But the object of my school is to show how many extraordinary things even a lazy and ordinary man may see if he can spur himself to the single activity of seeing. For this purpose I have taken the laziest person of my acquaintance, that is myself; and made an idle diary of such odd things as I have fallen over by accident, in walking in a very limited area at a very indolent pace. If anyone says that these are very small affairs talked about in very big language, I can only gracefully compliment him upon seeing the joke. If anyone says that I am making mountains out of molehills, I confess with pride that it is so. I can imagine no more successful and productive form of manufacture than that of making mountains out of molehills. But I would add this not unimportant fact, that molehills are mountains; one has only to become a pigmy like Peter to discover that.
>
> I have my doubts about all this real value in mountaineering, in getting to the top of everything and overlooking everything. Satan was the most celebrated of Alpine guides, when he took Jesus to the top of an exceeding high mountain and showed him all the kingdoms of the earth. But the joy of Satan in standing on a peak is not a joy in largeness, but a joy in beholding smallness, in the fact that all men look like insects at his feet. It is from the valley that things look large; it is from the level that things look high; I am a child of the level and have no need of that celebrated Alpine guide. I will lift up my eyes to the hills, from whence cometh my help; but I will not lift up my carcass to the hills, unless it is absolutely necessary. Everything is in an attitude of mind; and at

this moment I am in a comfortable attitude. I will sit still and let the marvels and the adventures settle on me like flies. There are plenty of them, I assure you. The world will never starve for want of wonders; but only for want of wonder. (1909, 6-7)

The first Chestertonian practice of wonder is the making of mountains out of molehills. If we can become Peters, we will be able to see the adventure in the everyday.

To see the mountain in the molehill, we must be willing to look until we see it. Instead of being entertained by superficially observing people of foreign cultures, we should turn to our neighbor. Chesterton explains, "The school to which I belong suggests that we should stare steadily at the man until we see the man inside the frock coat. If we stare at him long enough he may even be moved to take off his coat to us; and that is a far greater compliment than his taking off his hat. In other words, we may, by fixing our attention almost fiercely on the facts actually before us, force them to turn into adventures; force them to give up their meaning and fulfil their mysterious purpose" (1909, 5).

Chesterton wants us to stare long enough to see things for what they really are, wonderful.[19] Familiarity blinds us to the true magic of things, and we must fight to see it. "We must invoke the most wild and soaring sort of imagination; the imagination that can see what is there" (Chesterton 1987, introduction). One very pleasant way to do this is to read more Chesterton![20]

The next practice provides another route for us to really see things, the "test of fairyland" (Chesterton 1986, 254). To do this we take something constantly conjoined in our experience and see if we can imagine them being disconnected. Separating some things, like 2 + 2 = 4, is unimaginable, but most things in our experience can be imaginatively separated. Consider previous examples and imagine the color of a leaf or the direction water runs. Imaginatively disconnecting features and things—leaf and green, water and downhill—helps us see contingency in the connection. Our familiarity with fantasy and science fiction genres makes it especially easy for us to imagine the possibility of separation. Yet it is not mere contingency in the connection that interests us; separability of two things implies their being put together (Aquinas 1968, chap. 4, para. 6; 1981, ST I.3.4).[21] This practice helps us see the enchantment—the something-having-been-done—within them. To see them as wonderful in this way is pleasant. "It is one thing to describe an interview with a gorgon or a griffin, a creature who does not exist. It is another thing to discover that the rhinoceros does exist and then take pleasure in the fact that he looks as if he didn't" (Chesterton 1986, 158).

The third practice approaches from yet another angle: "It is a good exercise, in empty or ugly hours of the day, to look at anything, the coal-scuttle or the bookcase, and think how happy one could be to have brought it out of the sinking ship onto the solitary island. But it is a better exercise still to remember how all things have had this hair-breadth escape: everything has been saved from a wreck" (Chesterton 1986, 267).

Everything has been saved from the wreck of nonexistence and is a "Great Might-Not-Have-Been" (Chesterton 1986, 267). Chestertonian wonder in the previous practices brought out the contingency of the connection of features within things, but this practice touches the contingency of each thing's existence. Our contingency and the contingency of everything saved from the wreck return us to gratitude. Surely Robinson Crusoe gave thanks for every single thing that washed ashore. Because the contingency Chesterton is concerned with has purpose behind it, revealing an intention in the connection or existence, the gratitude construal has a benefactor.

These practices put us in a place to construe things as they really are; they help us see. Proper vision includes wonder and gratitude, which both fight acedia. They fight it first by starving acedia through preventing the construals it needs to survive. If we see something as wonderful and as a good gift from a benefactor, then we cannot also see it as boring. They also fight acedia by disrupting it. As they produce the virtues of wonder and gratitude in us, they change us from a person with patterns of acedia to someone with grateful and wonderful dispositions structured to think, desire, construe, feel, and act as the person full of gratitude and wonder would. Thus, we can correct acedia through the pursuit of wonder and gratitude.[22]

Notes

1 Such recognition was the surprising experience of Kathleen Norris reading Evagrius, "As I read this I felt a weight lift from my soul, for I had just discovered an accurate description of something that had plagued me for years but that I had never been able to name. As any reader of fairy tales can tell you, not knowing the true name of your enemy, be it a troll, a demon, or an 'issue', puts you at a great disadvantage, and learning the name can help to set you free. 'He's describing half my life,' I thought to myself. To discover an ancient monk's account of acedia that so closely matched an experience I'd had at the age of fifteen did seem a fairy-tale moment. To find my deliverer not a knight in shining armor but a gnarled desert dweller, as stern as they come, only bolstered my conviction that God is a true comedian" (Norris 2014, 4–5).

2 One of the ways recent virtue ethics is responding to the situationist challenge is by developing an account of virtue affected perception. Nancy Snow, building on work in psychology, argues that human agents respond not just to the "objective situation" but to the meaning the features of that situation have for the agent. The same situation would then have different meaning for a person, partially depending on which virtues or vices they have (Snow 2009, chap. 1).

3 Roberts develops this view at length in Roberts (2003), considers the ethical dimensions of emotions in Roberts (2013), and offers a popularized summary in Roberts (2007).

4 See Roberts (2013, 198). Roberts briefly surveys a number of virtues and how emotions relate to them in this section.

5 See Solomon (2015) for a historical survey of depression that includes acedia.

6 See Aquinas (2003, question 11, article 2). See Aquinas's other treatment of acedia in Aquinas (1981, ST II–II.35).

7 See DeYoung (2004, 2011, 2012). See also Nault (2015) for a historical survey of views of acedia with a focus on Aquinas.

8 In terms of lower appetites and reason, flesh and spirit, "So too, the movement of sloth is sometimes in the sensuality alone, by reason of

the opposition of the flesh to the spirit, and then it is a venial sin; whereas sometimes it reaches to the reason, which consents in the dislike, horror and detestation of the Divine good, on account of the flesh utterly prevailing over the spirit" (Aquinas 1981, ST II–II.35.3.f).

9 "Although these eight vices, then, have different origins and varying operations, yet the first six—namely, gluttony, fornication, avarice, anger, sadness, and acedia—are connected among themselves by a certain affinity and, so to speak, interlinking, such that the overflow of the previous one serves as the start of the next one. For from an excess of gluttony there inevitably springs fornication; from fornication, avarice; from avarice, anger; from anger, sadness; and from sadness, acedia. Therefore these must be fought against in a similar way and by the same method, and we must always attack the ones that follow by beginning with those that come before. For a tree whose width and height are harmful will more easily wither up if the roots which support it are exposed and cut beforehand, and pestilential waters will dry up when their rising source and rushing streams have been stopped up with skillful labor" (Cassian 1997, 189 [Fifth Conference, X.1–2]). The concatenation model and other models are helpfully laid out in Wenzel (1968).

10 As quoted by Cassian (2000, IX.II).

11 Roberts's defining proposition helps us see the unity between two types of boredom distinguished by Peter Toohey (2011): situational and existential. Situational boredom "is the result of predictable circumstances that are very hard to escape. Long speeches or long church services or long Christmas dinners are typical examples. This sort of boredom is characterized by lengthy duration, by its predictability, by its inescapability—by its confinement" (4). In contrast, existential boredom can "infect a person's very existence" (5). Toohey thinks the situational boredom gets improperly spiritualized in the capital vices tradition, but his discussion is still helpful to see the various ways boredom is characterized.

12 This is not to say that acedia *only* generates boredom.

13 Philosophers, of course, debate whether laws of nature are necessary, but within a Christian framework where things are created from nothing, laws of nature must be contingent.

14 Pieper (1999, 60): "Accordingly, for St. Thomas, the unknowable can never denote something in itself dark and impenetrable, but only something that has so much light that a particular finite faculty of knowledge cannot absorb it all. It is too rich to be assimilated completely; it

eludes the effort to comprehend it." Aquinas recognizes the limits of our cognitive faculties in *Expositio in Symbolom Apostolorum*, prologue: "But our manner of knowing is so weak that no philosopher could perfectly investigate the nature of even one little fly. We even read that a certain philosopher spent thirty years in solitude in order to know the nature of the bee."

15 See Martin Seligman's two books for a sense of the history and development of positive psychology, *Authentic Happiness* (2002) and *Flourish* (2011). See also the entry on gratitude in Christopher Peterson and Martin E. P. Seligman, *Character Strengths and Virtues: A Handbook and Classification* (2004) in which they identify G. K. Chesterton as a "prototype" for someone who sees gratitude as a cardinal trait (553).

16 "Our results provide weak evidence for the efficacy of gratitude interventions. Gratitude interventions outperformed a measurement-only control with psychological well-being as an outcome (small effect size with only five samples) but not with gratitude as an outcome" (Davis et al. 2016, 26).

17 Again, however, the evidence for these conclusions is mixed. See previous note.

18 See Seneca (2011, II–II.143). For a recent argument that there should also be a species of temperance related to sleep, see Dahm (2020).

19 Applying Chesterton's recommendation for looking until you see connects to the capital vices tradition on acedia in an inverted way to Kierkegaard's aesthetic treatment of acedia in *Either-Or*. Kierkegaard's aesthete assumes that things are really boring and we must learn to look at things until we can find or construct something entertaining about them. Chesterton, on the other hand, thinks we must look to see the wonder that is truly there. For Kierkegaard's aesthetic treatment of acedia, see Brandt et al. (2020).

20 Although, I do not interact with it in this paper, Chesterton's *Manalive* would be a great place to start.

21 Of course, being able to conceive of or imagine separability in some sense is probably not sufficient for actual separability. See Anscombe (1974).

22 Thank you to my students in Foundations of Ethics at Franciscan University of Steubenville for discussing these ideas with me semester after semester. Thank you to Joseph Cherney for inviting me to speak about this at the greatest Chesterton conference that never happened. Thank you to my Deadly Vices course of spring 2020, especially those who read the first draft of this paper (the rest of you can read it now).

Finally, thank you to Hannah Fordice, Caryn Rempe, and the editors of this volume for their feedback.

References

Anscombe, G. E. M. 1974. "'Whatever Has a Beginning of Existence Must Have a Cause': Hume's Argument Exposed." *Analysis* 34:145–51.

Aquinas, Thomas. 1968. *On Being and Essence*. 2nd ed. Translated with an introduction and notes by Armand Maurer. Toronto: Pontifical Institute of Mediaeval Studies.

———. 1981. *The Summa Theologica of St. Thomas Aquinas*. Translated by the Fathers of the English Dominican Province. Grand Rapids, MI: Christian Classics.

———. 2003. *De Malo*. Edited by Brian Davies. Translated by Richard Regan. Oxford: Oxford University Press.

Aristotle. 2000. *Nicomachean Ethics*. Translated and edited by Roger Crisp. Cambridge: Cambridge University Press.

Brandt, Jared, Brandon Dahm, and Derek McAllister. 2020. "A Perspectival Account of Acedia in the Writings of Kierkegaard." *Religions* 11 (80): 1–22.

Cassian, John. 1997. *The Conferences*. Translated and annotated by Bonifice Ramsey. New York: Paulist Press.

———. 2000. *The Institutes*. Translated and annotated by Bonifice Ramsey. New York: Newman Press of the Paulist Press.

Chesterton, Gilbert Keith. 1909. *Tremendous Trifles*. New York: Dodd, Mead.

———. 1986. *Orthodoxy*. In *Collected Works*, vol. 1. San Francisco: Ignatius.

———. 1987. *Everlasting Man*. In *Collected Works*, vol. 2. San Francisco: Ignatius.

Dahm, Brandon. 2020. "The Virtue of Somnience." *American Catholic Philosophical Quarterly* 94:611–37.

Davis, Don E., Elise Choe, Joel Meyers, Nathaniel Wade, Kristen Varjas, Allison Gifford, Amy Quinn, Joshua N. Hook, Daryl R. Van Tongeren, and Brandon J. Griffin. 2016. "Thankful for the Little Things: A Meta-analysis of Gratitude Interventions." *Journal of Counseling Psychology* 63:20–31.

DeYoung, Rebecca Konyndyk. 2004. "Resistance to the Demands of Love: Aquinas on Acedia." *Thomist* 68:173–204.

———. 2009. *Glittering Vices*. Ada: Brazos.

———. 2011. "Aquinas on the Vice of Sloth: Three Interpretive Issues." *Thomist* 75:43–64.

——. 2012. "Sloth: Some Historical Reflections on Laziness, Effort, and Resistance to the Demands of Love." In *Virtues and Their Vices*, edited by Craig Boyd and Kevin Timpe, 177–98. Oxford: Oxford University Press.

Evagrius Ponticus. 1972. *The Praktikos & Chapters on Prayer*. Translated by John Eudes Bamberger. Collegeville, MN: Cistercian.

——. 2003. *Eight Thoughts*. In *Evagrius of Pontus: The Greek Ascetic Corpus*. Translated by Robert E. Sinkewicz. Oxford: Oxford University Press.

Huff, Heather Hughes. 2013. "An Unconditional Surrender: Evelyn Waugh on *Acedia*." *Christian Reflection*: 45–55. Available online: https://www.baylor.edu/content/services/document.php/212242.pdf (accessed on 6 January 2022).

Lomas, Tara, Jeffrey J. Froh, Robert A. Emmons, Anjali Mishra, and Giacomo Bono. 2014. "Gratitude Interventions: A Review and Future Agenda." In *The Wiley Blackwell Handbook of Positive Psychological Interventions*, edited by Acacia C. Parks and Stephen M. Schueller. New York: John Wiley & Sons.

MacIntyre, Alasdair. 1981. *After Virtue*. Notre Dame, IN: University of Notre Dame Press.

McDowell, John. 1979. "Virtue and Reason." *Monist* 62:331–50.

Nault, Jean-Charles. 2015. *The Noonday Devil: Acedia, the Unnamed Evil of Our Times*. Translated by Michael J. Miller. San Francisco: Ignatius.

Norris, Kathleen. 2014. *Acedia & Me: A Marriage, Monks, and a Writer's Life*. New York: Riverhead Books.

Peterson, Christopher, and Martin E. P. Seligman. 2004. *Character Strengths and Virtues: A Handbook and Classification*. Oxford: Oxford University Press.

Pieper, Josef. 1999. *The Silence of St. Thomas*. South Bend, IN: St. Augustine's Press.

Roberts, Robert C. 2003. *Emotions: An Essay in Aid of Moral Psychology*. Cambridge: Cambridge University Press.

——. 2007. *Spiritual Emotions*. Grand Rapids, MI: William B. Eerdmans.

——. 2013. *Emotions in the Moral Life*. Cambridge: Cambridge University Press.

——. 2014. "Cosmic Gratitude." *European Journal for Philosophy of Religion* 6:65–83.

The Roman Missal. 2011. Totowa: Catholic Book Publishing.

Seligman, Martin. 2002. *Authentic Happiness*. New York: Free Press.

——. 2011. *Flourish*. New York: Atria Paperback.

Seneca, Lucius Annaeus. 2011. *Complete Works: On Benefits*. Translated by Miriam Griffin and Brad Inwood. Chicago: University of Chicago Press.

——. 2014. *On the Shortness of Life*. In *Hardship & Happiness*, translated by Gareth D. Williams. Chicago: University of Chicago Press.

Snell, R. J. 2015. *Acedia and Its Discontents: Metaphysical Boredom in an Empire of Desire*. Brooklyn: Angelico.

Snow, Nancy. 2009. *Virtue as Social Intelligence*. London: Routledge.

Solomon, Andrew. 2015. *The Noonday Demon: An Atlas of Depression*. New York: Scribner.

Stewart, Columba. 1998. *Cassian the Monk*. Oxford: Oxford University Press.

St. Gregory the Great. 1844. *Moralia in Job*. Translated by John Henry Parker. Oxford: Oxford University Press.

Toohey, Peter. 2011. *Boredom: A Lively History*. London: Yale University Press.

Waugh, Evelyn. 1962. "Sloth." In *The Seven Deadly Sins*. New York: Quill William Morrow.

Wenzel, Siegfried. 1968. "The Seven Deadly Sins: Some Problems of Research." *Speculum* 43:1–22.

About the Contributors

Francis J. Beckwith is Professor of Philosophy and Church-State Studies at Baylor University, where he also serves as Affiliate Professor of Political Science and Resident Scholar in the Institute for Studies of Religion. He has held appointments also at University of Colorado, Boulder; University of Notre Dame; Princeton University; Trinity International University; Whittier College; and the University of Nevada, Las Vegas. His most recent books include *Never Doubt Thomas* (2019); *Taking Rights Seriously* (2014); *A Second Look at First Things* (with Robert P. George and Susan McWilliams); *Politics for Christians* (2010); *Return to Rome* (2009); *Defending Life* (2007); *To Every One an Answer* (2004, with William Lane Craig and J. P. Moreland); *Law, Darwinism, and Public Education* (2003).

Christopher Tollefsen is College of Arts and Sciences Distinguished Professor of Philosophy and Chair of the Department of Philosophy at the University of South Carolina. He serves on the State Department Commission on Unalienable Human Rights and has held visiting appointments at Princeton University, Wake Forest University, and Spiritan Institute of Philosophy (Ghana). He is author or editor of several books, including: *The Way of Medicine* (2021); *Natural Law Ethics in Theory and Practice* (2019, with John Liptay); *Lying and Christian Ethics* (2014); *Bioethics with Liberty and Justice* (2011); *Biomedical Research and Beyond* (2008); *Embryo: A Defense of Human Life* (2008, with Robert P. George); *Artificial Nutrition and Hydration* (2008); and *John Paul II's Contribution to Catholic Bioethics* (2004).

J. Caleb Clanton is University Research Professor and Professor of Philosophy at Lipscomb University. He has held appointments at

Pepperdine University and Vanderbilt University. His books include *Nature and Command: On the Metaphysical Foundations of Morality* (2022, with Kraig Martin); *Great Ideas in History, Politics, and Philosophy* (2021, with Richard Goode); *Restoration and Philosophy* (2019); *Philosophy of Religion in the Classical American Tradition* (2016); *The Philosophy of Religion of Alexander Campbell* (2013); *The Classical American Pragmatists & Religion* (2011); *The Ethics of Citizenship* (2009); and *Religion & Democratic Citizenship* (2008). He is currently completing a book project on metaethics (with Kraig Martin) entitled *Nature and Command: On the Metaphysical Foundations of Morality*.

Kraig Martin is Associate Professor of Philosophy at Harding University. His research focuses on questions in epistemology, metaethics, and philosophy of religion. His published work has appeared in such journals as *Logos & Episteme*, *Erkenntnis*, *Studies in Christian Ethics*, *American Catholic Philosophical Quarterly*, *Journal of Faith and the Academy*, and *Religions*. He is author (with J. Caleb Clanton) of *Nature and Command: On the Metaphysical Foundations of Morality* (2022).

Janine Marie Idziak is Professor of Philosophy Emerita at Loras College, where she has served as the Director of the Bioethics Center and Consultant for Health Care Ethics for the Archdiocese of Dubuque. Her books include *Ethical Dilemmas in Allied Health* (2009); *Organizational Ethics in Senior Health Care Services* (2008); *Questions on an Ethics of Divine Commands* (1997); and *Divine Command Morality* (1979).

C. Stephen Evans is University Professor of Philosophy and Humanities at Baylor University, where he also directs the Center for Christian Philosophy and is a Senior Fellow for the Institute for Studies of Religion. He serves as Professorial Fellow at the Logos Institute for Exegetical and Analytic Theology at the University of St. Andrews. He has held appointments at Regent College, Western Kentucky University, Trinity College, Wheaton College, St. Olaf College, and Calvin College. His many books include, most recently: *Kierkegaard and Spirituality*

(2019); *A History of Western Philosophy* (2017); *Why Christian Faith Still Make Sense; God and Moral Obligation* (2013); *Natural Signs and Knowledge of God* (2010); and *Kierkegaard: An Introduction* (2009).

Daniel Bonevac is Professor of Philosophy at the University of Texas at Austin. His books include *An Introduction to World Philosophy* (2009); *Today's Moral Issues* (2009); *Deduction* (2002); *Worldly Wisdom* (2001); *Simple Logic* (1999); *Understanding Non-Western Philosophy* (1993); *Beyond the Western Tradition* (1992); *The Art and Science of Logic* (1990); and *Reduction in the Abstract Sciences* (1982).

Blake McAllister is Assistant Professor of Philosophy at Hillsdale College. His research centers on epistemology, early modern philosophy, and philosophy of religion, and his work has appeared in such journals as *Synthese, Faith and Philosophy, Australasian Philosophical Review, Theoria, Religious Studies, American Catholic Philosophical Quarterly*, and *History of Philosophy Quarterly*.

Michael Beaty is Professor of Philosophy and the former Chair of the Department of Philosophy at Baylor University. He is the author of numerous articles and the editor of *Christian Theism and Moral Philosophy* (1998) and *Christian Theism and the Problems of Philosophy* (1990).

Mac S. Sandlin is Associate Professor in the College of Bible and Ministry at Harding University. His areas of expertise include theological ethics, theology and culture, and pneumatology.

J. Aaron Simmons is Professor of Philosophy at Furman University. He also held appointments at Hendrix College, the University of the South, and Vanderbilt University. He has published widely on nineteenth- and twentieth-century European philosophy and philosophy of religion. Some of his most recent works include *Christian Philosophy* (2019); *Kierkegaard's God and the Good Life* (2017); *Contemporary Debates in Negative Theology and Philosophy* (2017); *Phenomenology* *for the Twenty-First Century* (2016); *The New Phenomenology* (2013); *Reexamining Deconstruction and Determinate Religion* (2012); *God and the Other* (2011); and *Kierkegaard and Levinas* (2008).

Brandon Dahm is Assistant Professor of Philosophy and the Director of the MA Program in Philosophy at Franciscan University of Steubenville. His published works have appeared in such journals as *American Catholic Philosophical Quarterly*, *Journal of Analytic Theology*, *Faith and Philosophy*, *International Journal for Philosophy of Religion*, *Religions*, and *Quaestiones Disputatae*, among others.

Credits

C. Stephen Evans, "Does Darwall's Morality of Accountability Require Moral Realism? (And Would It Be Strengthened by Adding God to the Story?)," reprinted in full with only minor modifications from C. Stephen Evans, "Does Darwall's Morality of Accountability Require Moral Realism? (And Would It Be Strengthened by Adding God to the Story?)," *Religions* 12, no. 3, art. 187 (2021): 1–8. Available at https://doi.org/10.3390/rel12030187.

Daniel Bonevac, "John Calvin's Multiplicity Thesis," reprinted in full with only minor modifications from Daniel Bonevac, "John Calvin's Multiplicity Thesis," *Religions* 12, no. 6, art. 399 (2021): 1–16. Available at https://doi.org/10 .3390/rel12060399.

Blake McAllister, "Understanding Moral Disagreement: A Christian Perspectivalist Approach," reprinted in full with only minor modifications from Blake McAllister, "Understanding Moral Disagreement: A Christian Perspectivalist Approach," *Religions* 12, no. 5, art. 318 (2021): 1–14. Available at https:// doi.org/10.3390/rel12050318.

Michael Beaty, "Epistemological Crisis in the Free Church Tradition," used by permission of the author.

Mac S. Sandlin, "Love and Do What You Want: Augustine's Pneumatological Love Ethics," reprinted in full with only minor modifications from Mac S. Sandlin, "Love and Do What You Want: Augustine's Pneumatological Love Ethics," *Religions* 12, no. 8, art. 585 (2021): 1–11. Available at